PRAISE FOR BREAKTHROUGH CREATIVITY

"*Breakthrough Creativity* provides a rare and novel approach to the issues of creative style and ability by crossing the boundaries between creativity and personality differences. This book is recommended reading for practicing managers and for coaches and consultants involved in developing people and in building creatively productive teams."

> David M. Horth, Senior Program Associate, Center for Creative Leadership; coauthor of *Leading Creatively*

"*Breakthrough Creativity* illuminates an essential skill for the new economy and provides practical advice, methods, and tools for optimizing creativity in the workplace. I especially like its emphasis on playing to one's strengths and creating teams with complementary talents for creativity."

> Frances C. Engoron, U.S. Leader, Learning and Education, PricewaterhouseCoopers

"Lynne Levesque's book can certainly make a significant contribution to help better assess the various creative talents that can exist in an organization. This in turn should help find a better fit for individuals in a business, leading to higher exploitation of creativity."

> Jorge P. Montoya, President, Global Food & Beverage and Latin America, Proctor & Gamble

"For present and future leaders, this book reflects a refreshing new direction for facing today's challenging workforce issues. As Lynne Levesque demonstrates, creativity should be part of every executive's thought process, especially those in the financial services industry."

> Nicki Brown, President and CEO, The Wilton Bank

"*Breakthrough Creativity* has a very clear message: everybody can be creative! This book offers new insight and practical guidance for implementing the challenge of identifying and developing the many untapped creative talents in an organization. An important book for all leaders of the 21st century in any country around the globe."

> Kurt Brandenberger, Head of Corporate Transformation, Von Roll Group, Switzerland

"*Breakthrough Creativity* gets us further down the path of uncovering what we didn't lose—our natural creativity. Recognizing and heralding problem-solving capabilities, innovations, and our own imagination will help all of us live our creativity out loud. If we unleash this vital force within us all, we will bring new structures, coordinations, and systems into our hands and into our visions."

> Ron Cretaro, Executive Director, Connecticut Association of Nonprofits

"*Breakthrough Creativity* offers a fresh and exciting look at psychological type and creativity. Filled with insights about how each individual can access creativity, this book is a must read for those serious about taking type to a level of useful application in organizations."

> Roger Pearman, President, Leadership Performance Systems, Inc.; author of *Hardwired Leadership* and coauthor of *I'm Not Crazy, I'm Just Not You*

BREAKTHROUGH
CREATIVITY

BREAKTHROUGH
CREATIVITY

ACHIEVING

TOP PERFORMANCE

USING THE EIGHT

CREATIVE TALENTS

LYNNE C. LEVESQUE

Davies-Black Publishing
Palo Alto, California

To the next generation:
Cyrus, Maron, Max, Raina, Riley, and Zoe
May your creativity forever continue to shine

✳

Published by Davies-Black Publishing, an imprint of Consulting Psychologists Press, Inc., 3803 East Bayshore Road, Palo Alto, CA 94303; 800-624-1765.

Special discounts on bulk quantities of Davies-Black books are available to corporations, professional associations, and other organizations. For details, contact the Director of Book Sales at Davies-Black Publishing, an imprint of Consulting Psychologists Press, Inc., 3803 East Bayshore Road, Palo Alto, CA 94303; 650-691-9123; fax 650-623-9271.

Visit the Davies-Black Publishing web site at www.daviesblack.com.

05 04 03 02 01   10 9 8 7 6 5 4 3 2 1

Printed in the United States of America

Library of Congress Cataloging-in-Publication Data

Levesque, Lynne C.
  Breakthrough creativity : achieving top performance using the eight creative talents / Lynne C. Levesque.—1st ed.
      p. cm.
  Includes bibliographical references (p.) and index.
  ISBN 0-89106-153-3
  1. Creative talent. 2. Creative thinking. 3. Myers-Briggs Type Indicator.
  4. Success in business. I. Title.

  BF408 .L595 2001
  153.3'5—dc21

                                                              00-065970

FIRST EDITION
First printing 2001

Have you ever been at sea in a dense fog, when it seemed as if a tangible white darkness shut you in, and the great ship, tense and anxious, groped her way toward the shore with plummet and sounding-line, and you waited with beating heart for something to happen? I was like that ship before my education began, only I was without compass or sounding-line, and had no way of knowing how near the harbour was.

—HELEN KELLER, *The Story of My Life*

CONTENTS

Organizations in the 21st century are confronting sweeping technological, societal, economic, and political changes that are challenging their abilities to serve their constituents and fulfill their missions. This radical transformation of contemporary life is unintentionally conferring a competitive advantage on individuals and institutions that embrace change, encourage innovation, and exhibit flexibility. Increasingly, organizations with creative leadership are emerging as successful survivors in this new world of rapid and discontinuous shifts in industry and society. And while it is dangerously speculative to try to distill to one or a few factors what differentiates success from failure in this turbulent environment, there is increasing evidence that the intangible stuff we label "creativity" may be one of the most potent ingredients of the "secret sauce" of organizational and individual success. Lynne Levesque's comprehensive and pragmatic treatment of the subject of creativity could not have come at a more opportune time, and it represents a creative triumph for the author, who has devoted much of her distinguished career to discovering what this thing called creativity is all about.

Levesque carefully constructs a research-based model of creative personalities that is rooted in the pioneering work of Carl Jung and tied to the *Myers-Briggs Type Indicator®* personality inventory, an assessment that is widely used in organization development applications in the private, public, and independent sectors. Creatively extracting data from original research and superimposing it on these solid foundations, she identifies the eight "talent" types or orientations that individuals possess, and suggests that everyone has both dominant and auxiliary talents that, if logically revealed through self-assessment, can provide a road map to greater professional and personal effectiveness and life satisfaction. Her typology consists of an appealing nomenclature that divides the world into Adventurers, Navigators, Explorers, Visionaries, Pilots, Inventors, Harmonizers, and Poets. Charting a course that builds on strengths rather than dwelling on deficiencies, Captain Levesque takes us on an internal exploration of the self that is both revelatory and very plausible. We discover attributes, characteristics, and skills that we were largely unaware of until she defined them, and we are treated to a smorgasbord of tools and techniques made accessible and pragmatic through self-study and experimentation.

Underlying this entire book is an unshakeable belief that we all are creative but unaware of how to master the creativity within. Creativity is not limited to artists, musicians, and marketing people, explains the author; it is a tangible and abundant wellspring that anyone can tap into. Leading groups, solving problems, dealing with people, and discovering new opportunities are offered as examples of ways to deploy our creative selves. Levesque's contention is that organizations that recognize creative potential everywhere and can develop an environment and culture that harness it will significantly outperform those that do not, and that individuals who discover and develop their creativity will outdistance their peers by a wide margin. This optimistic view of organizations and people is infectious, and inspires readers to navigate the abundant information, rich detail, and extensive exercises.

This is not light reading since it requires reflection and thought, but it is a potential gold mine for professionals and executives alike, with the caveat that staying the course without expending the necessary time and effort may be difficult if not dangerous. Nevertheless, *Breakthrough Creativity* may be the most comprehensive and useful volume ever written on this fascinating subject, and I commend it to anyone with the curiosity to explore the uncharted waters of the creative inner self. It might just unlock the possibilities that Buckminster Fuller once suggested would result in a world of four billion billionaires!

Lynne Levesque is uniquely qualified to lead us through these unfamiliar straits, having been a student of creativity for most of her adult life. Her doctoral research examined creativity in senior business executives, and she has been a practitioner of creative leadership in her years in management at the Bank of America and Shawmut Bank. Her MBA from UC Berkeley and doctorate in creativity from UMass give her an unusual breadth of academic grounding and pragmatic experience that enables her to appeal to those of us who do real work in companies, governments, and volunteer organizations; it should resonate equally well with educators and researchers who value the rigorous methodology Levesque brings to the party. As the chief human resources executive of AOL Time Warner, a leading Internet-age company that lists Creativity as one of its seven core values, I am especially excited about the potential of using this breakthrough book to help operationalize this essential value in our enterprise of 80,000 associates worldwide, and I am convinced that other HR and management development professionals and consultants will find it very beneficial. Business and public-sector leaders will profit from its no nonsense treatment of how creativity affects organizational results. In our efforts to build respected organizations that attract top talent, *Breakthrough Creativity* is a remarkable guide to success.

Andrew J. Kaslow, Ph.D.
Senior Vice President, People Development
AOL Time Warner

PREFACE

Writing a book like this involves a lot of experiences, research, and the help of so many different people. It's like one of my grandmother's patchwork quilts, sewn together from the various pieces of my life.

In the midst of a business career that spanned seventeen years in management and administration at two very large financial institutions, somehow I fell into the study of this fascinating topic of creativity. I can't remember how it started exactly, but at some point, maybe a decade ago, my friend Sally Shaver heard of my initial forays into creativity. She suggested that I talk with her pal Jim Adams, at Stanford University. Jim was well established in the creativity field and had written *Conceptual Blockbusting* in 1974. I was very pleased when he agreed to meet with me. He invited me to his home for lunch in Palo Alto, California, one sunny day. I remember Jim fixing lunch and advising me to move beyond banking if I really wanted to do anything with my interests in creativity.

At about the same time, I believe, I received a flyer about a conference on humor and creativity. I'm not sure how I got on that mailing list, but I was intrigued. I went and had a wonderful time. At that conference, I learned about a doctoral program in creativity, offered at the University of Massachusetts, Amherst, not far from my home in Hartford, Connecticut. I found out that I could attend the program while I continued to work. I applied and was accepted.

This chain of events significantly altered the course of my life over the next eight years. My interest in the subject of creativity, which began as a bit of a lark, grew into a personal discovery adventure. It continued to evolve through academic study and research, further enriched by summers at the Creative Problem Solving Institute in Buffalo, New York. It grew into my life's work as a result of my experiences consulting with individuals and organizations. My passion for this topic has caused me to leave the safety and security of a professional career and set sail on the rough, uncertain seas of independent consulting.

The intent of my initial research in creativity was to investigate what factors influenced the creativity levels in top executives during their climb to and tenure in office. I interviewed chief executive officers, presidents, and owners of many different companies across a variety of industries and types of organizations. This research has expanded to include the results and observations of my consulting practice, the workshops and classes I have facilitated, and conversations and interviews with many more individuals from all over the world. It has been fortified by extensive study of and practice with the work of Carl Jung, Katharine Briggs, and Briggs's daughter, Isabel Myers.

Several years ago, well before my interest in creativity was ignited, I was introduced to the *Myers-Briggs Type Indicator*® (MBTI®) personality inventory, in a career management workshop. Around that same time, I discovered Jung through several dream analysis courses and study groups. Over the last few years, since becoming qualified to administer the MBTI instrument, I have further explored the original Jungian theory upon which this assessment is based. I am intrigued by the insights that Jungian theory and the MBTI instrument bring to human behavior, especially creativity. The decision to write this book to help individuals make creativity happen in their own lives and in their organizations is thus a wonderful synthesis of my years in management, my study and research, my interest in Jungian theory and the MBTI instrument, my consulting and training experiences, and a lot of serendipitous events along the way.

Writing this book has not been easy. It is one thing to research, write about, and talk about creativity. It is a very different experience, however, trying to be creative! This experience has given me an even greater understanding of the creative process and has tested my perseverance, patience, commitment, and beliefs. It has also given me a much greater sense of gratitude for the many people in my life who have formally and informally been a part of this book. Their stories, formal interviews, and the conversations that occurred as I explored this subject in greater depth are a very significant part of the book. More important, the support of these individuals—both emotionally and intellectually—has been invaluable. Therefore, my deepest thanks and appreciation go out to

- My biological family, for their inspiration, support, and guidance, and especially to my sisters Laurie and Carla, who believed in this project perhaps more than I did.

- My family of friends, for their advice and support, particularly Kathy Albertini, Ann Auburn, Dave Barry and the rest of the Barry family, Susan Roberts Boyle, Natalie Camper, Lou Chagnon, John Clark, Leonel Figueredo, Chris Graber, Don and Roberta Guerette, Marion Holbrook, Lorraine Holden, Carol Lundquist, Debra Woog McGinty, John Mussey, Patricia Prince, Donn Randall, Jay Roston, Sheilah Rostow, Arthur Stout, Anne White, Nicola Williams, and my supporters at the First Baptist Church in Newton, Massachusetts.

- My professors Robert Marx, Paula Nowick, and Doris Shallcross, who all told me that real learning actually occurred *after* the degree is completed. They were right!

- Now-retired professor James Adams, at Stanford University, for his sage advice, and to Sally Shaver for setting up that momentous meeting.

- Marci Segal, who first helped me see the connection between creativity and type.

- The many participants in my research, classes, and workshops who have given me their time and support in the form of informal conversations and formal interviews

- My colleagues from the type and creativity communities, for their knowledge and encouragement, including Teresa Amabile, John Beebe, Alex Hiam, Bryan Mattimore, Mary McCaulley, and my colleagues in the Australian and New Zealand Associations for Psychological Type.

- Bob Johnston and the folks at IdeaScope Associates, Inc., in Boston and San Francisco.

- Theodora Noble and Peter Bartos at Forge Connexions Pty Ltd in Sydney, Australia, whose work, particularly *Positioning Yourself for Career Success,* consciously and unconsciously influenced my direction.

- Vivian Sheldon Epstein, for her last-minute help.

- Jill Anderson-Wilson, Lee Langhammer-Law, Alan Shrader, and Laura Simonds at Davies-Black Publishing, for all their support and encouragement.

- Melinda Adams Merino, who started out as editor and ended up as guardian angel.

To all of you, my deepest thanks, for nurturing my thinking, tolerating my ramblings, supporting my obsessions with creativity and innovation, and helping me through my struggles in writing this book. I could never, ever have completed this project without you.

ABOUT THE AUTHOR

Lynne Levesque, Ed.D., brings more than twenty years of experience in business and training to her consulting and research practice. Prior to starting her practice, she spent seventeen years in management with Bank of America in San Francisco and Shawmut Bank (now FleetBoston) in Hartford, Connecticut. Her areas of responsibility have included strategic planning, information technology administration, organization development and training, and policy management.

Levesque has extensively researched and written about creativity and innovation. Since receiving a doctorate for her studies of creativity in senior business leaders, she has authored "Factors Influencing Creativity in Top Executives" and "Unleashing Creativity Begins with Leadership," edited *The Idea Edge* for GOAL/QPC, and coauthored *The Personal Creativity Assessment* for HRD Press.

Now, combining her business experience with academic research in creativity and innovation, Levesque works with a variety of for-profit and nonprofit clients to support their efforts to implement strategy, manage change, and build more agile, innovative organizations. Her services include facilitation, consulting, and training workshops in the areas of team building, project management, and strategy formulation and implementation.

A graduate of Mount Holyoke College, Levesque holds an M.A. degree in modern European history from Rutgers, the State University, an MBA degree from the University of California at Berkeley (the Haas School of Business) and an Ed.D. degree in creativity from the University of Massachusetts at Amherst. She has studied at the Creative Problem Solving Institute in Buffalo, New York. Certified to administer the Center for Creative Leadership's KEYS: Assessing the Climate for Creativity Survey, she is also qualified to provide *Myers-Briggs Type Indicator* programs. She is a member of the Academy of Management, the Association for Psychological Type, the NorthEast Human Resources Association, and the Charlestown Business Association. Levesque also serves as president of the New England Chapter of the Haas Alumni Network and as treasurer of the First Baptist Church in Newton, Massachusetts.

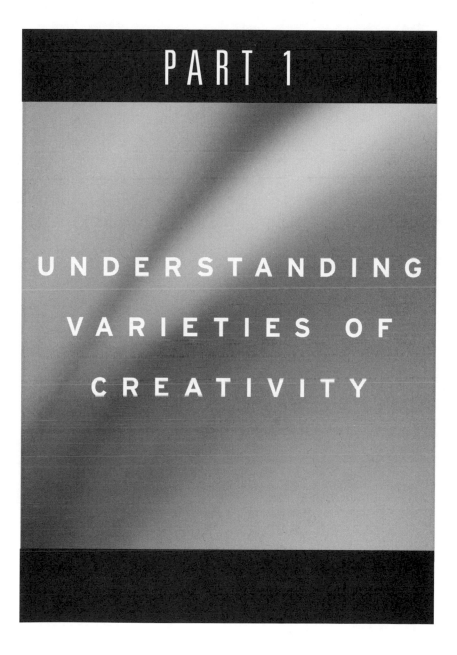

PART 1

UNDERSTANDING VARIETIES OF CREATIVITY

CHAPTER ONE

HOW ARE YOU CREATIVE?

**[Humans have] the distinctive power of creating something new in
the real sense of the word, just as nature, in the course of long
periods of time, succeeds in creating new forms.**
−Carl G. Jung[1]

About four years ago, I was talking
with a very successful senior executive about creativity. In his career to
date, he had successfully turned around a major financial institution and
had led a large law firm to new heights. He was now a key member of the
top management team of a Fortune 50 organization, yet he told me, "I am
not creative." When I probed further, he explained:

> Creativity is not necessarily my strong suit. I have a "people personality" as
> my gift. I don't have new thoughts. . . . I would say drawing on the big can-
> vas of what creativity is all about, my creative impulse or creative ability lies
> in the area of broadly defined interpersonal skills.[2]

After thinking about this issue a bit more, he went on to add:

> I could make the argument that interpersonal skills are the most important
> skills you can have, at least at this level. People don't understand that yet.
> It's really amazing to me. Although they're beginning to see that the ability
> to work with people and have people understand, making people feel

valued—that's a lot more important than understanding their actual business. I could make the argument that it's a skill-set where creativity can manifest itself, but that's not what people normally think about.

That conversation was to a certain extent responsible for this book. It came about as part of my research on creativity that began over eight years ago. The theme of "No, I'm not creative" showed up many times in interviews. It led to one of the study's conclusions: that people don't really understand creativity. It keeps coming up in classes, workshops, and conversations. I continue to hear the same theme: "I'm not creative because I can't sing or play a musical instrument"; "I'm not creative. I'm not an artist like Michelangelo or Beethoven"; "No, I'm not creative because I'm not strategic or brilliant"; "No, I'm not a genius like Einstein."

If these responses reflect what people believe about creativity, the situation is very disconcerting. And it poses a major dilemma. Everyone is being asked to be more creative, to think and do things differently. Creative responses are expected in our organizations, whether in product design, strategy development, or problem solving, because old ways don't work anymore and ready-made solutions often don't solve the problem anyway. We need to be creative to break down worn-out mind-sets and paradigms, search for new responses, and brave new business landscapes.

Creativity helps everyone achieve extraordinary results for their organizations and for themselves. Although the focus at work tends to be on the outcomes that creativity can help achieve, you may also gain much personal benefit from being creative. Developing your creativity strengthens the capacity to be more open, flexible, and resilient and to see different opportunities and possibilities—all important skills for dealing with unstructured, ill-defined challenges and with the uncertainties and complexities of a changing world. Being creative also builds self-esteem. When you're being creative, you feel good about yourself. It's energizing. You derive a great deal of personal satisfaction from being creative. In turn, you reach higher and produce more creative solutions.[3] As you practice, you keep building your confidence about being creative and, in the process, become even more creative. Seeing yourself as creative is thus essential for personal and organizational survival and prosperity.

Too many people, however, either don't see themselves as creative, don't know how to be effectively creative, or don't know what to do to keep their creative edge. The reason for this confusion may be the notion that there is only one way to be creative. It's difficult to believe you are creative if you measure yourself against geniuses like Einstein, Edison, and Michelangelo or if you feel that creativity only involves coming up with "out of the box" ideas or creating something original.

You may think that only certain people, such as artists or musicians, are creative, or that only certain parts of an organization, such as advertising and new product development, need creativity. You may find it hard to apply the concept of being creative to accounting, human resources, or management. You may even believe that creativity can waste a lot of time, money, and resources because you don't understand that a vital component for successful creative efforts is disciplined processes that channel creativity and keep it focused to achieve results. Perhaps you see yourself as creative but don't know how to direct your own creative activities so that you can make the maximum contribution to the organization. Or maybe you have lost your creative edge and don't feel as creative as you used to.

This book is intended to bridge the gap between your knowledge of yourself as creative and those workplace demands and expectations to produce new and different results. It will help you travel from the land of confusion to a continent of clarification and the security of knowing how you are creative and what you must do if you are to produce even more creative results. The basis of the book is the belief that *everyone* is creative. Everyone is not alike in his or her creativity because *there is no one best way to be creative.* You may not have developed your creativity to the same degree as others, but it's there. Everyone has the potential to be creative at work.

I define creativity as *the ability to consistently produce different and valuable results.* This definition is the synthesis of extensive research on creativity, particularly from the psychological perspective, with the study of the lives of artists and others recognized as creative, experience in the business world, and countless informal conversations and more formal interviews. By this definition, creativity is an ability that can be improved; it does not belong to one particular group of individuals, born with a certain, special set of traits.

This approach to creativity combines the generation of new and useful ideas, or what is often called, in the United States at least, "creativity," with the adoption of new and useful ideas by people in organizations, or what is often called "innovation."[4] The goal of the book is to help readers become more creative and be bigger and better contributors at work. It is therefore not necessary to make the distinction here between *creativity* and *innovation,* since it doesn't matter if results are novel ideas, the turning of the idea into a marketable product or service, or the implementation of a change.

Some key points about the definition of creativity as "consistently producing different and valuable results" are worth noting. Results can take the form of new products, designs, and services that increase profitability, quality, productivity, and efficiency and that solve a customer's or manager's tough problems. Results can be novel inventions or minor fixes. They can be new ways of organizing work or organizations. Results can be finding new niches for products or discovering new personal or professional opportunities for yourself. Or they can be coming up with a new way to raise money, to get the attention of a foundation for a grant, or to penetrate a venture capital group's office to get a business plan read. Creative results may come from asking the tough questions that cause people to see a problem differently. They can be new connections, new arrangements of existing or past data, or novel responses to a challenge. They can be big ideas and breakthroughs, or they can be small steps that build on past experience to generate better solutions.

In this definition, creativity is more than a process for solving problems. Although you can use your creativity to solve problems, you can also be creative in the way you manage to bring together different people who might not have meshed before and figure out how to get them to work synergistically. You can also be creative in resolving conflict, working on a team, or motivating others to grow and develop. Or you may be creative at building the right climate where everyone respects, encourages, and challenges each other to achieve his or her personal best.

You can tap into your creativity and find different and effective ways of understanding your colleagues, of listening to clients and customers, and of imagining the impact a new plan will have on the people in and outside the organization. Maybe you're creative in the way you get your message across so that it inspires action or produces the outcomes you need. Maybe you're creative in the way you manage change, create a new life for yourself after planned or unplanned changes, or figure out how to manage your time, balancing parenting with long hours at work.

There are also differences in the contributions individuals make in the successful resolution of a problem or challenge. For example, you may be very good at identifying a hidden opportunity, redefining a challenge from new and different perspectives, or clarifying direction, goals, and objectives in the early stages of a project or work effort. You may excel at leading the project to successful conclusion. Others may be terrific at generating fresh ideas and possible solutions. Or they may be skilled at narrowing down the alternatives and selecting the best one. Other individuals may be great at determining how to implement these solutions, how to package and sell the product or the change initiative, or how to make the new plan work. Perhaps they are more detail oriented or more adept at planning and organizing a change effort and seeing the obstacles that can get in the way of the smooth, successful implementation of some great new product.

Although the definition of creativity as consistently producing different and valuable results recognizes wide varieties of creative contributions, it does assume that to be creative you have to contribute something different from what you've done before. Your results need not be original to the world; few results truly meet that criterion. In fact, most results are built on the work of others. The results of your creative efforts don't have to change the course of business or science. Of course, for some who exhibit what could be called *transformational* or *genius-level creativity,* they do. For most people, those different and valuable results are a bit more down to earth—and still incredibly important.

Just being different doesn't make the grade, however. To be considered creative at work, your results must also be valuable. Eventually, the results have to work, to solve the problem or challenge or satisfy the needs of the situation. Your solutions may not always work right the first time. Being creative often involves learning from mistakes, building on them, and, through trial and error, coming up with the answer that really resolves the challenge. Frequently, it's in the making of mistakes that you learn. It's in the trying of something else that you are led to different connections, unusual solutions, and new discoveries.

Finally, the definition of creativity used in this book assumes that you can be consistent and intentional in the application of your creativity. To be consistent and intentional, you need to be conscious of how you are creative. In other words, creativity at work is not just about having a flash of brilliance or many wild ideas. A lot of hard work is involved in taking ideas and making them happen. You need patience and persistence to develop staying power. You need self-awareness, focus, purpose, goals, and organization to *consistently* produce these different and valuable results.

What's clear from this definition is that *there is no one right or best way to be creative.* Creativity takes many forms and manifests itself in many different ways. If you're going to bridge the gap between the need to be more creative and your perceptions of your own creative abilities, you may need help in defining your creative talents. By identifying your talents, you can then figure out how to be more consistent, purposeful, and effective in producing your creative results.

One method for discovering how you are creative is to determine how you recognize information, define problems and challenges, and then go about producing creative responses and solutions. As you look around, you've probably noticed that there are many different ways to observe what's happening in the world and a variety of approaches for coming up with creative alternatives. For example, two individuals, when asked to come up with a marketing strategy for a children's game, might look at the challenge from very different perspectives. One individual might first carefully examine the details of the game or research what's been done with similar games. He or she might want to know how to play the game, see what it looks like, and find other specific facts about it. Another individual might start out ignoring all that information. Instead, he or she might prefer to experiment with many possibilities, look at trends and patterns in the industry, and be excited about the future potential from this game and other possible spinoffs.

Not only might two people see the challenge from different points of view, but they might also have different responses to it. When facing a decision between possible strategies, one person might first analyze the pros and cons of each strategy and the logical consequences of the different approaches. He or she might relate the different strategies to what has worked in the past. Another individual might first talk with people about the game, have them play it, hold focus groups to find out how they feel about the game, and let those reactions drive the choice of strategy.

These different approaches to looking at challenges, collecting data and information, and generating responses have an impact on your creativity. They can color what data you see, how you define the challenge in the first place, and what you decide to do with all this information. At the same time, the many different ways you take in and make sense of information can result in perceptive filters and biases and decision-making blinders that can keep you from finding the best and most innovative resolution to a situation or challenge.

Defining these different approaches and determining what you need to do to be more creative get easier if you use a model developed almost eighty years ago by the Swiss psychologist Carl G. Jung (1875–1961).

Jung's research and experiences led him to develop a theory about personal differences. While recognizing individual differences, Jung saw stable patterns in behavior across individuals. He traced these patterns to preferences for recognizing, paying attention to, and remembering people, ideas, and things and then for making decisions or judgments about them. These preferences explain some of the reasons for the differences in creative results; they can affect the way you lead, the way you work in teams, the way you communicate, the processes you use, and the environments you need to be more creative.

Jung defined eight different patterns for perceiving information and making decisions. He believed that each of the eight patterns of differences is equally valuable and equally creative. According to Jung, the creative instinct exists in everyone.[5] You just need to identify, understand, and refine your pattern preferences, or creative talents, to be more effective, productive, and creative.

Jung believed that you can discover your creative talents (he actually called them *types*) through analysis and therapy. To make his model more accessible and to help define these preferences, Katharine Briggs and Isabel Myers developed the *Myers-Briggs Type Indicator®* (MBTI®) personality inventory. The more you learn about this instrument and Jung's theory behind it, the more you'll see its applicability to an understanding of creativity. This approach has received very positive responses among students and workshop participants. It is truly a delight to see eyes light up when students and participants change their minds about whether they are creative and find out just how they are creative. Other instruments can be used to address personal creativity styles, such as the *Kirton Adaption-Innovation Inventory* (KAI) and the *Hermann Brain Dominance Instrument* (HBDI), but the MBTI instrument has many advantages.

The MBTI instrument is a validated, tested, and easily accessible personality inventory and has been widely used throughout organizations for many years. Many individuals are thus already aware of the understanding it brings. Numerous books and other materials apply its insight to leadership development, change management, and team building. The study around application of the MBTI instrument has led to a better understanding of how to help individuals build on their strengths, overcome certain blocks and barriers that result from their personality preferences, and thus become more effective. Learning about creativity, identifying your talent, and working to further develop it, therefore, do not require a new instrument.

This book uses Jung's theory and the MBTI personality inventory to define eight creative talents—eight equally important but different ways for you to produce creative results. It provides a structured method for you to find your own favorite creative talents among these eight and then to put together a plan to further develop them. You can use this approach to break through worn-out belief systems, to develop and grow, and to be more productive and creative. By taking full advantage of your strengths, you can make more contributions. By identifying your strengths, you can figure out how to compensate for areas where you may not be as strong. By learning to appreciate how your strengths can get in your way, you can avoid problem areas. Digging deeper into these differences in creative talents is thus a powerful way to develop flexibility in your reactions to the challenges you face, expand your repertoire of responses, and improve your creative results. You can also benefit from this approach if you want to learn how to channel your creativity to be more effective in the workplace.

Whether you're a solo practitioner, involved in running your own business, or employed by an organization, you can benefit from this approach. Since much creative work is done in teams or various groups, understanding individual differences in creative talents can also enhance collaboration with others. You will thus find the descriptions of the talents useful in working with clients, colleagues, and team members.

Once you understand your preferences for certain talents and determine what you need to do to build on those strengths and be more effectively creative, you can then move on to applying that knowledge to produce greater results for your team or for your organization. The organization where creativity flourishes will be around for the next century. According to Robert Reich, former U.S. Secretary of Labor, the fundamental qualities of the company of the twenty-first century are flexibility, resiliency, speed, and creativity.[6] Organizations derive a great deal of benefit from encouraging creativity in their employees, for the following reasons:

- Lack of innovation is a key problem in business today. To successfully address this challenge involves recognizing that it's the *creativity in people and their ideas that produces innovation.*[7]

- An organization that is open to new ideas and new ways of doing things taps into the 40 to 50 percent of employee power that is regularly lost. Such employee power, through higher employee morale and satisfaction, can be channeled into delighting customers, developing new products, and improving business processes.[8]

- An organization that integrates creative approaches and different creative strengths into its normal business processes will have more productive teams, more flexibility, higher employee-retention rates, and better ways of benefiting from diversity and creative collaboration.[9]

- An organization in which managers recognize the different talents of individuals and play to their strengths can win the war for talent by attracting, developing, and retaining outstanding performers.

To achieve the book's objectives of helping you find your creative talents and apply them to your work life and to synthesize a great deal of material about creativity, management, Jungian theory, and the MBTI instrument, the book is divided into three parts. Part 1 lays the foundation for the rest of the book. It includes this introductory chapter on creativity and Chapter 2, which provides a description of the eight different talents and guides you through selecting your most favorite talents. Both chapters are based on extensive research on creativity, Jungian theory, and the MBTI instrument. Even if you are familiar with Jung's psychological types or the MBTI instrument, you should review this chapter for its perspectives on creativity.

In Part 2, you will develop a better understanding of each of the eight creative talents. Each of the next eight chapters (Chapters 3 through 10) describes one of the creative talents in much greater detail. Each chapter explores the typical creative contributions at work of individuals with that talent and looks at how the talent can create certain blocks and barriers that need to be overcome to maximize effectiveness. It then provides tools and techniques to use to further develop the talent's ability to produce the best, most creative resolution to any challenge or situation. The tools can also help keep that talent's creative advantage and retain the "magic" of being creative. For team leaders and others who might be working with this talent, each chapter also has a section on how to optimize the talent's creative contributions. The substance for these chapters comes from interviews; research; knowledge of creativity, team building, leadership, change management, communication, and conflict; and my best guesses about the talents of historical and prominent individuals for illustration.

Part 3 puts the material of Chapters 3 through 10 together, first at the team level and then at the individual level. Chapter 11 focuses on applying the material from earlier chapters to build synergy on a team. If you are working on a team—whether as a team member, team leader, or consultant working with a client—and want to ensure that the team achieves optimum creativity and productivity, then read this chapter. It gives information on how to help the team realize the benefits of the different creative talents through building the right environment and using structured processes to channel and focus creative efforts. This chapter draws upon research and consulting in team building, project management, organization development, and innovation. Chapter 12 provides a summary and recommends some next steps for you to take so that you can make the most of your strengths and further maximize your creative talent.

Finally, at the back of the book are a resources section that lists organizations to contact, and a bibliography.

So, let's begin the voyage to explore and discover how to build your creativity. By the end of this voyage, you will have a much better idea of how to develop your talents and be more effective, productive, and creative. Before moving on, however, you might want to spend a moment reflecting: What does your creativity look like? What are your creative results?

❋

"I find the great thing in this world is not so much where we stand as in what direction we are moving. To reach the port of heaven, we must sail sometimes with the wind and sometimes against it— but we must sail, and not drift, nor lie at anchor."

–Oliver Wendell Holmes

CHAPTER TWO

DISCOVERING YOUR CREATIVE TALENTS

We don't see things as they are, we see things as we are.

–Anaïs Nin

To discover your creative talents, you first need a brief introduction to the framework on which they are built. Carl Jung developed this framework not to label people, or, as he said, not to put them in drawers,[1] but to help them be more effective. This model is like a compass that will guide you through making sense of your creative talents.

According to Jung's model, five important points explain the different creative talents:

1. There are two attitudes, or orientations, to the world: extraverted and introverted.

2. There are four mental functions for taking in and processing data and information: sensation, intuition, thinking, and feeling.

3. Each function can operate in the extraverted and introverted worlds. The combinations of functions and attitudes result in eight creative talents.

4. You develop preferences for using the talents in a certain order, with the first being called your dominant creative talent and the second being called your auxiliary creative talent.

5. The interactions among your creative talents can influence your perspectives, assumptions, and approaches to creative solutions and the kind of creative results you produce.

THE EXTRAVERTED AND INTROVERTED ATTITUDES

When Jung first started studying family, friends, and clients, he concluded that the major differences in individuals' behavior were rooted in their attitudes or orientations toward the world. He defined two different attitudes: "extraverted" and "introverted."

When you operate with an *extraverted attitude* toward the world, you give top priority to the objects and people around you. You tend to focus interest and attention on what is happening in the world, who is doing or saying what, and what is going on. The objective world around you is reality. When operating in an extraverted way, you tend to respond immediately to these external stimuli. You try to influence outcomes, be proactive, and make things happen. You want to be involved. Your creativity is built around interacting with others. You are in turn influenced by events and people. External events, people, things, images, and ideas have an almost inexhaustible fascination for you. You find it easy to share experiences with others, and you readily volunteer your thoughts. You shape your thoughts and opinions as you talk with others.

On the other hand, when you operate with an *introverted attitude* toward the world, you find reality only after external objects have been internally matched up to your thoughts, images, ideas, and feelings. The external world is food for thought, a rich source of stimulation for deliberation and consideration. You rely on your subjective standards and your own past experiences or memories to form your opinions and to shape your impressions and actions. While you're processing information and reflecting, you prefer being alone with your thoughts, feelings, and experiences. Evaluation and resolution take place inside, so they are not visible to observers. You need time to form your opinions before discussing them, although you are willing to share what you are thinking and feeling, if asked. Your creative results tend to be more independent and uniquely yours since you have spent time shaping and forming them internally.

To find out which of these two orientations to the world you prefer, check the choice in each pair below that best describes you:

ORIENTATION TOWARD THE WORLD	
If you operate best in the extraverted world, you tend to	**If you operate best in the introverted world, you tend to**
☐ Focus attention outward: on people, things, and action	☐ Focus attention inward: on concepts, ideas, and feelings
☐ Value external sharing and relationships	☐ Value internal interpretation and understanding
☐ Develop creative ideas with others, externally	☐ Develop creative ideas independently, internally
☐ Have a breadth and variety of interests	☐ Have a depth and focus to interests
☐ Prefer interaction, interruptions, and meetings	☐ Prefer concentration, pauses, and solitude
☐ Be public and out loud	☐ Be private and intense
☐ Communicate by talking	☐ Communicate by writing
☐ Value action	☐ Value reflection
☐ Speak rapidly; volunteer information	☐ Provide information as needed
☐ Have an interest in external events	☐ Have an interest in internal reactions
☐ Plunge in	☐ Pause and consider
☐ Ask questions to clarify expectations	☐ Ask questions for understanding
☐ Accept standards of others	☐ Set your own standards

In which world do you prefer to spend your time? Circle the attitude with the most checks: extraverted or introverted. Then fill in the first blank in the box on page 30.

THE FOUR MENTAL FUNCTIONS: SENSATION, INTUITION, THINKING AND FEELING

After careful study, Jung recognized that people are in fact not extraverted or introverted. Instead, it is the functions they use to take in, organize, and then make sense of the data and information in the world around them that are extraverted or introverted. Jung identified two pairs of functions, or consistent forms of preferred behavior: a pair of perceiving, or data-collecting, functions and a pair of judging, or decision-making, functions. These functions play a role in shaping the information you take in, the challenges you see, and how you produce creative ideas and results. The two pairs of functions are the following:

- The perceiving, or data-collecting, pair of *sensation* and *intuition*. The perceiving functions cause you to take in and register data or information, without any attempt to categorize, evaluate, or analyze it.

- The judging, or decision-making, pair of *thinking* and *feeling*. The judging functions allow you to make sense of, evaluate, and prioritize what you take in through your perceiving function.

The Perceiving Functions: Sensation and Intuition

The perceiving functions allow you to recognize data and information about people, things, events, ideas, and objects and to register and remember that information. At this point, you don't try to figure out how to organize, evaluate, label, discriminate among, order, or judge the information. You just take it in. Each perceiving function takes in qualitatively different, or opposite, forms of information; specifics and details from *sensation* versus general patterns or images from *intuition*. Therefore, they cannot both operate within you at the same time, although you can alternate your use of them.

Sensation

If you prefer the sensation function, you tend to pay attention to and collect facts and details. You gather these facts primarily through the senses of touch, smell, sight, sound, and taste or through experiencing them in your body. You see shapes, textures, sizes, and colors. The data you see first tend to be practical, factual, commonsense, and grounded. With the sensation function you know how you know something because you have experienced it and stored it in your memory. You tend to take in data sequentially, in a linear, step-by-step manner. With the sensation function, you want to see and understand the evidence before you are comfortable making generalizations. You prefer testing out new information against your experiences. You're observant and curious about life's details.

The stories from those who prefer the sensation function are very descriptive and real because of all the details. The imagination of such individuals is full of pictures with specific colors, shapes, smells, textures, and sounds. People who prefer the sensation function might express their creativity by building on the work of others or on the results of many experiments, or by depicting the world they see through the lenses of details and reality. Examples of individuals who might have preferred the sensation function would be the photographers Ansel Adams and Margaret Bourke-White, the Impressionist painters Claude Monet and Mary Cassatt, the film director Alfred Hitchcock, the inventor Thomas Edison, and the naturalist Charles Darwin.[2]

Intuition

If you prefer to gather information through a sixth sense that goes beyond the five senses, you prefer the intuition function. As defined by Jung, intuition involves knowing without knowing how you know. (Intuition as a perceiving or data-collecting function is different from "gut feelings" or "woman's intuition," both of which are actually used for decision making.) With intuition, you often can't explain or discover how you get data. You're observant and curious about trends and patterns. You focus on the future, and you tend to see things from a different perspective of connections and possibilities. You are comfortable making generalizations from relatively limited data.

Descriptions from people who prefer intuition will be interpretative and loaded with big ideas, options, alternatives, and generalities. These individuals focus on future trends and opportunities. Their imagination is full of unusual associations, connections, vague images, and streams of consciousness. People who prefer intuition are those individuals who often have "off-the-wall" ideas and far-reaching visions. They are the ones who are typically labeled "creative" at work. Examples of individuals who might have preferred intuition as their perceiving function are Walt Disney, the anthropologist Margaret Mead, and the physicist Albert Einstein. Current examples of individuals exhibiting this talent are artist Judy Chicago, advertising executive Jay Chiat, Virgin Group's CEO and founder Richard Branson, and Microsoft founder Bill Gates.

To find out which of these two perceiving functions you prefer, check the choice in each pair on the next page that best describes you.

PERCEIVING FUNCTIONS

If you prefer sensation, you tend to	If you prefer intuition, you tend to
☐ Use your body and your senses to know	☐ Know without knowing how you know
☐ Have realistic pictures of what is happening	☐ Develop visions of what could happen
☐ Look at specific parts and pieces, facts, and details	☐ Look at patterns, relationships, and possibilities
☐ Prefer clearly defined expectations and specific instructions, plans, and guidelines	☐ Prefer an overall rationale and a general purpose and direction with plenty of options to explore
☐ Focus on the here and now or on connections to the past	☐ Focus on the future, the unknown, and the unseen
☐ Be seen as pragmatic, concrete, and down to earth	☐ Be seen as abstract, theoretical, and having your head in the clouds
☐ Provide precise descriptions and definitions	☐ Provide general terms, meanings, and interpretations
☐ Learn and work sequentially and methodically	☐ Learn and work rapidly and randomly
☐ Value hard work	☐ Value inspiration
☐ Rely on tangible experience to solve problems	☐ Rely on intangible ingenuity to solve problems
☐ Like to make things work	☐ Like to understand
☐ Build on what has already been done	☐ Prefer to do things differently
☐ Ask "What?" and "How?"	☐ Ask "Why not?" and "In what ways might I?"
☐ Imagine pictures with specific colors, shapes, smells, textures	☐ Imagine unusual images and connections

Which of the perceiving functions do you prefer most often or most consistently? Circle the function you checked most frequently: sensation or intuition. Fill in the second blank in the box on page 30.

The Judging Functions: Thinking and Feeling

The judging, or decision-making, functions of *thinking and feeling* influence the way you sort, organize, and prioritize the information you take in through your perceiving function and how you evaluate and decide what to do with it. Like the perceiving functions, the decision-making functions are also opposites. You can use either the function of logical analysis called *thinking* to make decisions, or the function that involves personal values and concern for harmony and relationships called *feeling*. You can shift quickly between the functions, but you can't use both simultaneously.

Thinking

With the thinking function, you come to conclusions using logic and objective reasoning. You use the thinking function when you make distinctions and definitions and arrange events and ideas into logical groupings, to define, categorize, and name them. The thinking function allows people to analyze and critically process the information or situation, using cause-and-effect reasoning or "if this, then that" logic to draw conclusions. People who prefer thinking as a decision-making function usually come to conclusions quickly because they believe that clear-cut rules and principles can guide their decision making. They tend to see few options; it is either "this or that" or "true or false" or "right or wrong." Their language tends to be crisp and concise.

With thinking as your decision-making function, you ask many questions. You are inclined to build models or systems to structure, organize, and then resolve the situation. Sometimes the decision can almost be given away to someone else because of the objective analysis or rules and procedures that you apply to the situation.[3] You're good at defining problems; determining goals, strategies, roles, and responsibilities; and organizing the project to achieve creative results or to accomplish change initiatives. Examples of individuals who might have preferred the thinking function are the scientists Isaac Newton and Marie Curie and the inventor, engineer, and philosopher Buckminster Fuller. Margaret Thatcher (former prime minister of Great Britain), Alfred P. Sloan, Jr. (one-time president and reorganizer of General Motors), Mary Baker Eddy (founder of the Christian Science church), and the architect Frank Lloyd Wright are other possible examples.

Feeling

People who prefer the feeling function rationally and consciously sort and organize ideas and perceptions and make judgments about them, just as those who prefer the thinking function do. (As defined by Jung, feeling is not about "feelings," "caring," and "emotions." Everyone is capable of strong emotions and intense caring for others. Feeling as a decision-making function is also different from sensations such as cold or hot, smooth or rough.[4] The decisions from both functions can actually be the same, but the basis for the decision and the process for arriving at it will be different.

When using the feeling function to evaluate and decide, you balance personal and societal values, compare tone and qualities, and weigh importance. The feeling function appreciates the needs of the people involved and the values inherent in the situation. Context is critical. People who prefer the feeling function may need more time to reach conclusions because they are taking organizational, cultural, and personal values into account in their decision making. They are considering the appropriateness and timing of the response or action to be taken. They discriminate among shades of differences and subtleties in emphasis. Because it may be difficult for them to articulate their process, people who prefer the feeling function may want to use pictures, diagrams, or other visual aids in making decisions.

If you prefer feeling as your decision-making function, you tend to be socially adept. Your organizational skills are focused on getting people to work together to achieve creative results. You tend to consider people issues in change initiatives. You are likely to be good at communication and tend to be more expressive in your language. Examples of individuals who might have preferred the feeling function are the social reformers Eleanor Roosevelt, Mahatma Gandhi, and Martin Luther King, Jr. Additional examples might be Clara Barton (founder of the American Red Cross), the poets Maya Angelou and Emily Dickinson, and the playwright William Shakespeare.[5]

To find out which of these two judging functions you prefer, check the choice in each pair in the chart on the following page that best describes you.

JUDGING FUNCTIONS	
If you prefer thinking, you tend to	**If you prefer feeling, you tend to**
☐ Base decisions on objective, impersonal principles and facts	☐ Base decisions on subjective, personal, cultural, and organizational values
☐ Appreciate justice, fairness, and equity	☐ Appreciate mercy, empathy, and loyalty
☐ Categorize; think "either-or"	☐ Harmonize; consider "both-and"
☐ Question, analyze, and problem solve	☐ Sympathize, relate, and share
☐ Weigh the evidence	☐ Determine the worth and importance
☐ Use logic, "if this, then that"; focus on consequences	☐ Consider the impact on people, politics, and relationships
☐ Anticipate and plan for obstacles	☐ Anticipate people's needs and reactions
☐ Make classifications	☐ Make connections
☐ Be concise when speaking and writing	☐ Be expressive when speaking and writing
☐ Prefer clarity in decision making and planning	☐ Prefer involvement in planning and implementation
☐ Focus on goals, objectives, and structure	☐ Focus on how personal needs will be met
☐ Create strategies and designs	☐ Create nurturing environments
☐ Ask "Why?"	☐ Ask "Who?"

Which of the judging functions do you prefer? Circle the function with the most checks as elsewhere: thinking or feeling. Then fill in the third blank in the box on page 30.

THE EIGHT COMBINATIONS, OR EIGHT CREATIVE TALENTS

Jung believed that each of the four functions of sensation, intuition, thinking, and feeling has an extraverted or introverted orientation. There are differences within each of the functions, depending on whether the

DATA-COLLECTING TALENTS

EXTERNAL WORLD	INTERNAL WORLD
The Adventurer: Skilled Improvisation	**The Navigator: Thoughtful Adaptation**

FACTS AND DETAILS

The Adventurer: Skilled Improvisation

- Tends to be spontaneous, flexible, fun loving
- Enjoys the aesthetic, sensory experience of life
- Finds self-expression natural and easy
- Quickly assesses status and takes action
- Notices details, shapes, and textures
- Wants the specifics of any given situation; facts about what is happening and what's working
- Believes that any problem can be solved
- Experiments with the group, pushing it to find new solutions that work
- Eases tense situations through humor
- Provides prompt, practical, and ingenious responses to crises and emergencies
- Supplies clever and satisfying solutions to customer and operational problems
- Finds skillful ways to get around obstacles
- Brings an imagination full of specific details how things look, smell, taste, sound, and feel

The Navigator: Thoughtful Adaptation

- Tends to be an astute observer and recorder of concrete, specific facts; wants evidence
- Is careful, thoughtful, and private
- Believes in being thorough, conscientious, and doing it right the first time
- Understands what's been tried in the past: what worked and what didn't
- Applies research and experience to problems
- Asks practical questions to find useful solutions
- Keeps the group or project focused and on track
- Adapts, fine-tunes, and builds on what others have done
- Helps people use new products and services
- Understands possible resistance to new initiatives and can help plan for it
- Provides stability during and after change
- Is able to fix things to make them work
- Brings an imagination full of specific details, with an impressionistic, surreal perspective

TRENDS AND PATTERNS

The Explorer: Pulsating Possibilities

- Enjoys generating many opportunities, possibilities, and alternatives with others
- Is drawn to many different experiences in the external world
- Finds sharing ideas natural and easy
- Focuses on external patterns, trends, ideas, and relationships
- Works in a stream of consciousness
- Sees behind the scenes things not seen by the five senses
- Finds greatest value in the tireless generation and promotion of new enterprises, business ventures, and ideas
- Provides high-energy team leadership
- Inspires ingenuity and discovery in others
- Helps others push past what is accepted and expected
- Pursues possibility thinking to envision the future
- Serves as a catalyst for change
- Brings an imagination full of connections and associations

The Visionary: Far-Reaching Insights

- Has an uncanny sense of the future, often ahead of the times
- Privately sees far-reaching visions
- Keeps a broad, long-range perspective
- Finds the essence of complex situations
- Independently searches for new angles on life
- Needs time to reflect; shares thoughts when well developed
- Has a high tolerance for ambiguity
- Challenges the group to find big solutions and asks provocative questions to find profound answers
- "Incasts" (vs. forecasts)—works back from the future to develop plans
- Develops new designs and solutions through unusual connections
- Provides multidimensional perspectives and penetrating, far-reaching insights into future trends
- Brings an imagination full of hard-to-describe images and futuristic possibilities

DECISION-MAKING TALENTS

EXTERNAL WORLD

INTERNAL WORLD

LOGICAL AND OBJECTIVE

The Pilot: Analytical Strategy

- Provides high energy to the group
- Enjoys organizing people and projects to achieve goals and makes things happen
- Makes tough decisions through logical critique
- Develops and clarifies objectives, plans, roles, and processes
- Wants to solve problems, discover, and classify
- Bases decisions on external standards and objective principles of truth, justice, accuracy, logic, productivity, and efficiency
- Shares ideas freely and concisely
- Provides new and different strategies and programs
- Develops innovative organizational designs and structures
- Supplies a system wide perspective to challenges
- Focuses on progress, improvement, efficiency, productivity, and results in change initiatives
- Is adept at systematic planning and implementation
- Asks thoughtful questions and challenges conventional thinking

The Inventor: Paradigm Shifting

- Tends to be an objective, detached, and curious observer
- Provides tough, unrelenting critique to get to the highest levels of accuracy and objectivity
- Likes to privately analyze and order ideas and information
- Focuses on making sense of the external world by a private, impartial decision-making process
- Thinks matters through carefully before sharing
- Classifies, clarifies, categorizes, and makes precise
- Provides thoughtful solutions to problems
- Has an internal model/blueprint, which may be very different from the mainstream conception of how things work
- Yields insight through systematic questions that challenge the group to shift thinking
- Drives efficient organization of work during innovation initiatives
- Provides conceptual frameworks and models for synthesis of ideas and concepts
- Has quick understanding and intellectual curiosity

SUBJECTIVE AND PEOPLE FOCUSED

The Harmonizer: Human Solutions

- Provides high energy to the group
- Enjoys organizing people to achieve common goals
- Expresses self easily and shares self with others
- Structures environment to support human values and to meet people's needs
- Bases decisions on societal, community, and personal values, importance, and worth
- Focuses on who is involved
- Wants consensus, to ensure that everyone is heard and accommodated
- Appreciates context and circumstances
- Designs new programs and services to help customers, employees, or community
- Applies skills to create different communication strategies
- Deals diplomatically with political problems that can impede change and innovation
- Provides caring leadership, building trust and common understanding for change

The Poet: Values-Based Solutions

- Tends to be naturally curious, flexible, and tolerant of contradictory points of view
- Quietly supports and nurtures
- Is usually sensitive and loyal to people and efforts that matter
- Focuses on values and ideals as a basis for reacting to people and situations
- Concentrates on making sense of what's going on through an internal, private decision-making process based on personal values
- Takes time to process and make decisions
- Appreciates context and circumstances
- Builds a safe place for testing out new ideas and behaviors
- Ensures time for reflection and incubation
- Demonstrates aesthetic appreciation for grace and elegance in solutions
- Deals well with political issues
- Applies communication skills, especially writing, to change initiatives

function is extraverted or introverted. Thus, eight combinations, or creative talents, can impact our creative results and contributions. These eight creative talents will be explored in much more detail in Chapters 3 through 10.

Four of these creative talents are used to perceive or collect data and information:

- The Adventurer (extraverted sensation)

- The Navigator (introverted sensation)

- The Explorer (extraverted intuition)

- The Visionary (introverted intuition)

The other four creative talents help evaluate data and information and make decisions:

- The Pilot (extraverted thinking)

- The Inventor (introverted thinking)

- The Harmonizer (extraverted feeling)

- The Poet (introverted feeling)

These eight talents are described on pages 22 and 23. While reading through the brief synopsis of the eight talents, you might want to check which ones you are most likely to use. Later in this chapter, you will have a chance to determine your favorite talents more systematically.

DOMINANT AND AUXILIARY CREATIVE TALENTS

Each of the eight creative talents has equal value. No one talent is better than another; they just work differently. All talents can produce creative results—just different ones. With each of the talents, you have equal access to imagination and to your unconscious, the source of much creative inspiration.[6] Your imagination, like your creative contributions, just plays out differently. Your talent may or may not follow one of the patterns in large part since it is uniquely your own and not exactly like anyone else's. Each talent is colored by family background, circumstances, education, experience, age, ethnic origin, and gender. It will also be shaped by how well you have developed it and how consciously you use it.

You have access to each of the eight talents all the time. In the best of all possible worlds, in your creative processing you would use the Adventurer's and the Navigator's talents to find the facts in your problem definition, to research and establish what is actually present, what actually exists, and what has happened in the past. You would use the talents of the Explorer and the Visionary to point out the hidden possibilities in the situation, see trends, and generate ideas and options about the future.

You would use the decision-making functions of the Pilot, Inventor, Harmonizer, and Poet to help you select the right solution and then plan and implement it. You would use the Pilot's and the Inventor's talents to logically organize, analyze, judge, and categorize the situation. You would use the talents of the Harmonizer and the Poet to tell you the context of the situation, how people are affected, and the value and importance of the challenge and its resolution.

Dominant Talent

Although you have access to all eight talents, you tend to develop over time a preference for one talent over the others. When reading over the descriptions of the eight talents, many people recognize one that stands out as their most favorite talent. This talent, your *dominant talent*, is the way you habitually react to and experience the world. You trust it more, rely on it more, and are more comfortable using it. It becomes better developed than the other talents. Through this dominant talent, as an expression of your particular strengths, you tend to become known, particularly if you restrict yourself primarily to the use of just this one talent. When you were reading the descriptions of the talents, did you find one you tend to use most often?

For example, if your dominant talent is the Adventurer or the Navigator, you tend to focus on concrete reality or the past when looking at problems or challenges. You are not likely to easily consider the possibilities hidden in a situation or alternatives and options to challenges. You are likely to prefer to continue to research, gather as much data as possible, and generate as many ideas as you can. It might take you some time before you feel a need to come to conclusions about the data.

Individuals who have the Explorer or the Visionary as their dominant talent are likely to concern themselves most often with possibilities when looking at challenges. They may be less likely to want to deal with the reality of the situation. They tend to prefer to generate possibilities or look for hidden trends and meanings. Evaluating or making decisions about the information is usually not a top priority.

Individuals who have the Pilot or the Inventor as their dominant talent tend to focus on what they rationally and intellectually understand about the challenge or the situation. They want to look at goals, strategies, and models to get to a solution. They tend to jump to conclusions and make assumptions without paying attention to facts or possibilities or the context of the situation until later. Nor do they tend to look naturally at the people side of the situation.

Finally, those whose dominant talent is that of the Harmonizer or the Poet are guided in almost everything they do by relationships, values, the context of the situation, or the circumstances surrounding the challenge. They want to organize people to solve the problem. They may also jump to conclusions and make assumptions without paying attention to facts or possibilities. They may need to be reminded to use logical analysis or to look at advantages, disadvantages, and consequences for additional perspectives on the decision or solution.

Auxiliary Talent

In addition to a dominant talent, Jung believed that you also develop a preference for an *auxiliary talent,* available to balance and support your dominant talent. For Jung, balance of at least two talents is vital. You need to collect data and information *and* evaluate and judge it. You also need to operate in both the external *and* internal worlds. You need to be attuned to what is going on in the world around you, yet you also need time to reflect and discover for yourself what is really happening. Balance also significantly enhances your creative contribution. Being effectively creative and productive requires an interaction between collecting information *and* making decisions about it, as well as between acting *and* reflecting.

Your auxiliary talent provides that balance for your creativity. As a support to your dominant talent, the auxiliary talent provides you with the ability to operate in both the outer and the inner world and to manage those worlds from both a perceiving and a decision-making perspective. Your auxiliary talent tends to be one that operates in the world opposite from the world of your dominant talent (extraverted or introverted) and is from the other functional group from your dominant talent (data collecting/perceiving or decision making/judging). For example, suppose your dominant talent is one of the four decision-making talents, such as the extraverted thinking Pilot talent. To come up with a truly creative solution, you need an introverted perceiving talent as your auxiliary talent to draw in information and consider it internally for meaning and impact. So, your Pilot talent would be teamed up with either the Navigator or the Visionary talent (the two introverted perceiving functions).

Likewise, suppose your dominant talent is the introverted sensation Navigator talent (a perceiving function). You need an auxiliary talent for managing in the external world and for making decisions in that world so that you don't just continue to collect data and look at variations. Thus, your dominant talent would be teamed up with either the Pilot or the Harmonizer as an auxiliary talent (the two extraverted decision-making talents).

This balance is like having two hands to catch a ball or type a paper. You have a preferred hand and a nonpreferred hand. You normally write with only your preferred hand, but you tend to need both to fully function. However, one is usually stronger and more adept than the other. This balance is also similar to the role that the keel and the sail have on a ship. A sailing ship needs both if it's going to maneuver and make headway through the water. Some ships will have bigger sails than keels, for speed; others will have larger keels than sails, for stability.[7]

Your dominant and auxiliary talents are not evenly balanced. They don't have equal weight since your dominant talent will normally be in charge. But without the help of the auxiliary talent, you would become extremely one-sided in the world in which you best operate. You might, for example, spend too much energy collecting data and not bother to make any sense of it or to evaluate it. You might move from idea to idea, project to project, never completing anything or drawing any conclusions. You would be the perennial dilettante and not be very effective in producing creative results. On the other hand, you might spend your time drawing assumptions, jumping to conclusions, and making decisions about your thoughts and feelings without taking in enough information. You might become so locked into your judgments that you refuse to see anything that doesn't fit with your preconceived notions. You might be seen as an obstinate, closed-minded, and not very creative individual.

If you don't have a balance to your external orientation to the world, you might never take time to ponder how you really think or feel about an issue. Creative solutions might be a series of responses to what's happening or to other people's ideas. You might not stop to ponder the meaning of what's happening or what you really believe. Conversely, you might spend too much time in your internal, private world, processing what's happening. You might never be able to function in the external world if your dominant talent is internally focused and overdeveloped. The world might not ever benefit from your creative contribution. As a balance to your dominant talent, the auxiliary talent thus adds new perspectives and flexibility to your creative ability.

Determining Your Dominant and Auxiliary Talents

There are many ways to determine your dominant and auxiliary talents. Going through the descriptions on pages 22 and 23 and picking out the one from each group that feels most comfortable to you is one way. However, without a more systematic approach, you can often have blinders on about your natural preferences. You can also have developed ways to work around your preferences or to augment them, either because of positive or negative feedback in your environment or because of training and application through experience. Sometimes asking those close to you or those with whom you work can help you define your dominant and auxiliary talents.

Another way to define your talents is by using the *Myers-Briggs Type Indicator* (MBTI) instrument, developed by Katharine Briggs and Isabel Myers. One of the key contributions Briggs and Myers made was determining how to identify dominant and auxiliary talents. To do this, they added to Jungian theory by defining a dimension that describes the function that you show to others. It identifies the behavior that helps you manage your *external* world. (This function—your extraverted function—may or may not be your dominant function.)

If you prefer an external world that is orderly and planned and if you enjoy a deliberate, punctual external life, then you prefer your judging, or decision-making, function of either extraverted thinking or feeling. With a decision-making function as your extraverted function, you tend to see life as a plan to be worked. Change is something you need to manage. You tend to be proactive about getting things done and organized, persistent, and focused in your drive to accomplish creative results.

If you prefer your external world to be more spontaneous and open ended, your extraverted function will be one of the perceiving, or data-

FUNCTION USED TO MANAGE EXTERNAL WORLD

If you prefer judging/decision making, you tend to	If you prefer perceiving/data collecting, you tend to
☐ Want to know what's going to happen in order to prepare	☐ Want to be more spontaneous
☐ Prefer closure	☐ Keep options open
☐ Limit options to get them off your mind	☐ Never feel you have enough information
☐ Enjoy the product	☐ Enjoy the process
☐ Plan ahead and follow schedules	☐ Adapt as you go
☐ Prefer decisions to be settled and completed	☐ Prefer decisions to be open, pending, and emergent
☐ Be seen as deliberate, purposeful, and decisive	☐ Be seen as flexible, adaptable, and curious
☐ Build a hypothesis first and then collect data	☐ Collect data and then build the model or hypothesis
☐ Want to manage	☐ Want to understand
☐ Believe in project plans and timetables	☐ Believe in explorations
☐ Prefer few surprises	☐ Be ready for anything
☐ Be viewed as self-disciplined and organized	☐ Welcome new light on situations or challenges
☐ Control events	☐ Respond to the moment

collecting, functions of either extraverted sensation or intuition. In this case, you enjoy the process, adapt as you go, and lead a more "emergent" life. You tend to enjoy handling situations as they arise. Life is to be lived. Change is something to be enjoyed. You tend to be flexible and more divergent in collecting data and generating ideas.

To find out which of the functions you use in the external world (your judging or perceiving function), check the choice that best describes you in the chart above. Which function do you use in the external world? Circle the function with the most checks: perceiving/data collecting or judging/decision making. Fill in the fourth blank in the box on page 30.

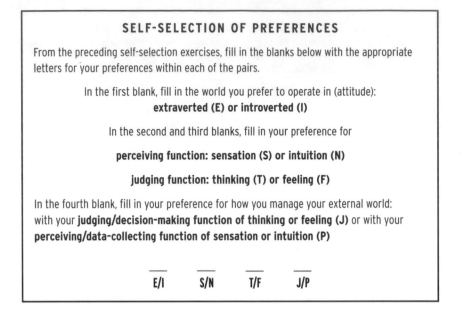

This self-selection exercise results in a four-letter code, or your MBTI code. Using the four-letter code, you can now find your dominant and auxiliary talents in the table on page 31. (Although completing the preceding exercises can lead to a reasonable guess at your four-letter MBTI code, a completed MBTI instrument will validate your self-selection. The MBTI instrument is available through individuals who have been qualified to use it. See the appendix for a list of contact organizations.)

Now that you have your dominant and auxiliary creative talents, go back and see if they match your notes on the eight creative talents described on pages 22 and 23. If they don't agree, you will find more information in Chapters 3 through 10 to help you make final choices about your talents.

THE INTERACTIONS OF YOUR DOMINANT
AND AUXILIARY CREATIVE TALENTS

The more you learn about yourself and explore your creative talents, the more you will be able to consciously access them and use them to produce creative results. To look at situations, challenges, and problems more creatively, you need to move back and forth between your dominant

DEFINING YOUR DOMINANT AND AUXILIARY CREATIVE TALENTS

MBTI® CODE	DOMINANT TALENT	AUXILIARY TALENT
ESTP	The Adventurer	The Inventor
ESFP	The Adventurer	The Poet
ISTJ	The Navigator	The Pilot
ISFJ	The Navigator	The Harmonizer
ENTP	The Explorer	The Inventor
ENFP	The Explorer	The Poet
INTJ	The Visionary	The Pilot
INFJ	The Visionary	The Harmonizer
ESTJ	The Pilot	The Navigator
ENTJ	The Pilot	The Visionary
ISTP	The Inventor	The Adventurer
INTP	The Inventor	The Explorer
ESFJ	The Harmonizer	The Navigator
ENFJ	The Harmonizer	The Visionary
ISFP	The Poet	The Adventurer
INFP	The Poet	The Explorer

and auxiliary talents to be sure that you are taking in enough information before coming to conclusions. According to one consultant, "I need to get in touch with what's important to me. To figure out what to work on. It's like being on a team, with everyone playing a role. My dominant and my auxiliary [talents] have to work together and be integrated. Otherwise, the result will come back to haunt me."

At the same time, the interactions between your dominant and auxiliary talents can serve as filters for the information you take in and can affect your ability to produce the most creative results. They can cause blind spots and biases to the way you see problems and make assumptions about challenges. They can limit your perception and decision making and keep you from coming up with the best, most creative solutions to a problem.

For example, the decision-making talent that is either your dominant or auxiliary talent influences the *type* of data you take in or pay attention to. If your decision-making talent is that of the Pilot or the Inventor, you are likely to focus on quantifiable information, ideas, or impersonal objects. On the other hand, if your decision-making talent is the Harmonizer or the Poet, you may be inclined to take in more personal, relationship-oriented data and information. You may focus on the people issues and other more qualitative data. If you are not careful to consider the bias from your decision-making talent and take steps to compensate for it, you may not get the full array of information that comprehensively describes the situation. Your perspectives on a challenge could be limited so that the alternatives you come up with might not produce the most creative solution.

Your perceiving talent also impacts the creativity of your solutions. It influences the *shape,* or *form,* of information you take in to make evaluations and find meaning. It can impact what you see and what you remember. It also affects what your imagination looks like. If your perceiving talent is the Explorer or the Visionary, you may primarily see patterns, trends, and possibilities, without the specifics and facts to back them up. If your perceiving talent is the Adventurer or the Navigator, you may tend to pick up details and specifics of the immediate situation, and you may be blind to patterns, trends, and possibilities. Such limitations from either perspective can affect your creative approaches to a challenge.

Another factor in the quality of your creative contribution is the attitude of your dominant talent. If your dominant talent is extraverted, you may be very focused on the external world. You like to communicate your thoughts and share your ideas. However, you may not spend enough time processing the information internally. If your dominant talent is introverted, you may not be so willing to share the results of your reflection. And you may tend to spend a long time in introspection and internal analysis, without ever taking action. Both orientations are important to your creativity.

Finally, your dominant talent influences your approach to finding creative solutions. If it's a perceiving talent, you may be very open to data and information. You may enjoy collecting data, conducting research, being divergent, and generating alternatives. You may not relish the process of having to come to any conclusions. If, on the other hand, your dominant talent is a decision-making talent, you may want to move quickly to find a solution. You may be ready to organize, make progress, and conclude the activity before all the necessary data have been collected. Since both perceiving and decision making are critical to your creative contribution, you need to be careful to use both processes, alternating as solutions emerge.

SELF-DEVELOPMENT AND GROWTH

Understanding your dominant and auxiliary talents, the worlds in which they operate, and the balance they provide can help you evaluate your approaches to the activities involved in being creative. Your talents can have an impact on where you make your most creative contribution—in the definition of the challenge statement, through generation of alternatives, to solution implementation and reflection. They can influence what problems and challenges you see and the type of results you produce.

Becoming aware of your talents is a first step in nurturing your creativity and enhancing your creative contributions at work. After becoming comfortable with the strengths of your dominant talent, you can then become more familiar with your auxiliary talent and use it consciously to balance your dominant talent. Fully appreciating the strengths of your own talents can then help you understand what other talents have to offer to provide diversity of perspective, balance, and flexibility. You can start to see what you need to do to be most effective and creative in any situation. Becoming consciously aware of your gifts and talents can make it possible for you to assess your attitudes and behavior in any given situation and then adjust them accordingly. It can help you both compensate for your personal disposition and be tolerant of someone who does not function as you do—someone who has, perhaps, a strength or facility you may lack. From this point of view, the important question is not whether you are extraverted or introverted, or which function is dominant or auxiliary, but, more pragmatically, In *this* situation or with *that* person, how did you function? With what effect? Did your actions and the way you expressed yourself truly reflect your judgments (thinking and feeling) and perceptions (sensation and intuition)? And if not, why not? What were the outcomes? What does this say about your preferences? What can you do about it? What do you *want* to do about it?[8]

Becoming clearer about your creative talents can help you see where you need to pay attention to stretch and grow. It can also lead you to your unconscious, a great inspiration for your imagination. The unconscious provides you with an inner collection of deep instincts and connections and supplies an inexhaustible capacity to create. This is where the mystery of creativity often comes in. The unconscious can be a fascinating source of new ideas and solutions. This inner collection is full of images, myths, symbols, remnants of real happenings, lost memories, and forgotten experiences and knowledge. It's the unconscious that accounts for those flashes of inspiration that seemingly come from nowhere. A variety of strategies will be addressed in Chapters 3 through 10 to help you access this source for your imagination and your creativity.

SUMMARY

In this chapter, you have learned about the different talents that can affect the way you see the world and color your creativity. In the next eight chapters, you will find detailed information on the eight creative talents and explore how these talents produce different contributions to an organization and how they result in different needs for support from the environment in which you live and work. You will come to understand how different processes and tools work to bring out the highest level of creativity. You will also explore what you need to do to be more fully creative, to overcome blocks and barriers, to capitalize on your strengths, and to develop skills and abilities to bolster the areas in which you might need help.

As you read through Chapters 3 through 10, you should select the material that applies to you and your particular situation. Just as there is no one pure psychological type, there is no one description of a creative talent that will fit you exactly. You first want to find the dominant talent that is the best match. Then find an auxiliary that is a good fit. Use the information on those two talents to figure out what might be keeping you from being as creative as you might be. Choose three or four suggestions to work on first—to build your strengths further and to minimize what's getting in the way.

PART 2

THE EIGHT
CREATIVE
TALENTS

CHAPTER THREE

THE ADVENTURER

ESTP: AUXILIARY CREATIVE TALENT—INVENTOR

ESFP: AUXILIARY CREATIVE TALENT—POET

Adventurers are like the daredevils who go to sea for the experience and fun of it all. They enjoy experimenting with clever improvisations and skillful adaptations to solve challenges.

The creativity of Adventurers comes through their pragmatism, flexibility, openness, good humor, and high energy. Because they tend to concentrate on the present reality of what is happening around them, they keep themselves and their colleagues focused on the problem at hand. They make sure that their colleagues see the relevance of what they are trying to achieve. They have a great capacity to find the facts about a problem. Using firsthand knowledge of hard evidence, Adventurers can quickly cut to the heart of the problem and come up with a variety of solutions.

With their down-to-earth practicality and because their creativity is not "off the wall," Adventurers often don't see themselves as creative.[1] One executive director of a nonprofit organization defined her creativity as resourcefulness, or the ability to think on her feet, assess the situation, and quickly respond. When she finds herself in a crisis, she'll come up with twenty different solutions that have an immediate impact. A consultant reflecting the Adventurer's talent had this to say about her creativity:

ADVENTURER	Results and Contributions

- Clever and satisfying solutions to customer and operational problems
- Practical applications that recognize shape, line, color, and texture, which can be handled and taken apart
- Adding fun, curiosity, adaptability, flexibility, and positive energy to the team
- Imagination full of specific details: how things look, smell, taste, sound, and feel
- Prompt, practical, and ingenious responses to crises and emergencies
- Experimentation with the group, pushing it to find new solutions that work

What creativity? Actually, I just jump in and think quickly how to get out. When a client presents me with something that I don't really have any experience with or know how to do, I say yes, then scramble to figure out how to do it. I just figure that if I'm really in the soup, I will have to come up with something, like learning how to swim really fast if you're suddenly thrown overboard. So far, this technique has usually worked. . . . I just try to figure out the most sensible way to do something, then bull my way through it.

Adventurers are great at going with the flow, managing the details, responding to the twists and turns of everyday life, picking up the pieces, and making the best of the situation. The executive director of the non-profit organization described one position she took on after the previous administrator had been fired:

The job immediately blew up on me. The agency was losing money. There were resignations, unionizing activity, and employee suits. But I plunged in, pulled together the staff who had been there for a while, used available resources, and, within a year and a half, found a solution through a merger. When you're in the muck, you just work your way through it!

Adventurers tend to have broad interests and usually have a wide network of contacts and friends. They love adventures and new experiences. They are positive about life. They learn best through on-the-job experience and like to experiment with new approaches for doing things, particularly if they involve handling and taking the pieces apart.

They can be playful and divergent. Like the Navigator, they do best dealing with situations that are variations of what they or others have done before. They like to experiment with new ways of dealing with situations that build on past practices. They like to copy, change, and come up with their own renditions. "I can always improve on my own or someone else's prior work," said one Adventurer. "There is no end to my ability to embellish it."

The results they are likely to produce when they are being creative come from their flexibility, curiosity, and daring approach to life. Some examples of well-known individuals who may have had this talent are the writer Ernest Hemingway, the photographers Ansel Adams and Margaret Bourke-White, the singer Elvis Presley, pioneers such as the aviatrix Amelia Earhart, and some of the great jazz musicians such as Duke Ellington and Charlie Bird. Leonardo da Vinci also showed many of the characteristics of the Adventurer in his interests in a wide variety of subjects, his curiosity, and his attention to detail. His genius came from the "combination of his open, questioning mind, his reliance on actual experience, and his uncanny visual acuity."[2]

Adventurers' ability to observe and remember an immense number of facts and details and then to make use of them is most helpful to a group's problem-solving process. At work they can usually be counted on to relate who was in a meeting, what was said, and all the other important details about the session. Their photographic impression of factual reality and specific essentials helps a team stay grounded and see a situation as it really is. When listening to Adventurers, people often believe they are talking with a reporter. Adventurers use a wide variety of detailed descriptions, stories, and anecdotes to illustrate the points they are making. Appreciating the beauty of the world, they see many different forms, shapes, textures, colors, and tones. They notice fine points that others fail to see. Their imagination is focused on specific details: how things look, smell, taste, sound, and feel.

On a project, Adventurers use their practical realism and keen powers of observation to pay attention to details and focus on getting clarity about facts and circumstances. Adventurers trust actual experiences and tangible, concrete data, although the data may not be spoken; because of their acute sense of observation, they are very capable of absorbing nonverbal information from people and circumstances. Their originality finds expression in a more open and less prejudiced view of the facts than others hold.[3] They thus have much to contribute during the problem-definition and fact-finding phases. They look at cold, hard facts about people and situations and accept them at their face value. Questions Adventurers tend to ask include the following:[4]

- What do we know about the problem?

- What is it and what isn't it?

- What is happening, when, where, and how?

- How will the solution work?

- How will it fit into what we are doing now?

- Will it solve our current problems?

- Who else has this problem? How are they fixing it?

- How will it affect the organization and the bottom line?

- What do we need to do?

The creative talent of Adventurers is influenced by their introverted decision-making auxiliary talent of either the Inventor or the Poet. If their auxiliary talent is that of the Inventor, they tend to focus on facts about ideas, things, and objects. Such facts are specific, data driven, and practical. These Adventurers take in those external details, analyze the situation using internal logic and models, and come up with realistic evaluations of reasonable solutions. The decisions they make are based on objective criteria and underlying principles. Adventurers with this combination may be inclined to use the best practices of others as matched up against the specific circumstances of the immediate situation, as long as they have had a chance to observe those practices firsthand. Their judgment is accurate and reliable in straightforward matters. Their creative resolutions to challenges and problems tend to be made from looking at the logical consequences of an act or decision, as opposed to considering how other people might react to the situation.

If the auxiliary creative talent of Adventurers is that of the Poet, their facts tend to be related to people, as opposed to objects and things; they center their interest and attention on people. These Adventurers use great tact to easily handle people problems and human relationships. They see the social and political environment realistically and look at practical options for negotiating and resolving people-related problems.

These Adventurers can empathize; they would thus be quite good at dealing with people and at looking at a situation's impact on external relationships. They can use their creative talent to find different ways to motivate people during times of change and crisis.

With either auxiliary talent, Adventurers are inventive in building on or embellishing what others have done and finding new ways to solve problems. They see creative problem solving as tweaking, adjusting, and changing things to make them better, more relevant. They throw ideas out, get feedback, and then twist and adjust.

Adventurers are spontaneous and have a hands-on approach to getting things done. Making something work—no matter what it takes—is their main goal in life. They often find that standard operating procedures get in the way, but they seldom let such rules or set procedures interfere with getting things done.

Adventurers tend to be curious about anything new, particularly if it has to do with their senses. They tend to enjoy the good things in life. They love to try new food, activities, and gadgets. They like to play with ideas and build on them. They are interested in meeting new people. They enjoy using their bodies to achieve creative results; many Adventurers are skilled artisans, athletes, dancers, performers, carpenters, woodworkers, and sculptors, all of whom take great pleasure in using their hands and bodies to craft beautiful objects and movements.

Adventurers have a lot of fun at work, and people enjoy working with them. They are usually a source of great, positive energy. Their playful spirit and zest for experience of all kinds frequently lead to the generation of many interesting ideas and alternatives. They are usually outgoing, tolerant, and action oriented. Their spontaneity and enthusiasm for life bring a sense of liveliness and joy to their work and to any group. Their optimism that a solution will always appear if the facts are pursued adds a positive tone. They trust their ability to find resources and the wherewithal to succeed, and their efforts usually result in a very practical solution.

Because of their easy-going attitude and tolerance, Adventurers are also good at pulling conflicting factions together to find a workable, creative solution. They are skilled at putting a team together and ensuring successful teamwork and cooperation. As leaders, they prefer the more unstructured environment that can promote creativity and innovation. They support diversity, risk taking, and practical innovation. Adventurers appreciate and promote flexibility in job and work design and encourage the flow of information across the organization.

Adventurers are inclined to immediately resolve problems and challenges, usually without a detailed plan. Their flexibility helps them plunge straight into a problem, rapidly assess the status of the situation, seize on immediate options, take action, and get the problem fixed. They will try many different solutions, experiment with variations, and be open to iterations. Their willingness to experiment in a free-form fashion increases their ability to improvise solutions to operational and customer problems and get them immediately resolved.

Here is what a city planner said about his approach when faced with designing a new program:

> I gather lots of actual information—find out what's happening, what's the situation, and what's causing it. I will spend a lot of time figuring out who's involved, what are the politics in this thing. I might do this on my own first, then I will get input from others. I will do a draft and rework it many times. If I get stuck, I try to look at it from a different angle or talk with friends who can play devil's advocate.

When the team is planning the implementation of a solution, Adventurers add the perspective of how changes and innovations will look, sound, and feel—important considerations for a successful effort. They can often look at implementations as "gigs," or performances, and will ensure that the lights, ambiance, and setting all contribute to the enjoyment and triumph of the effort. Adventurers are skilled at negotiating and can help ensure that the chosen alternative will work. They can also help plan for and manage contingencies and emergency situations.

Adventurers tend to respond reflexively to their surroundings. They can often handle a crisis situation almost instinctively. They are great at thinking on their feet, juggling multiple tasks, and pulling "a rabbit out of a hat" at the last moment. They can thus add significant value in leading a group through the unexpected crises that often develop in executing plans. Like jazz musicians, dancers, and great athletes, particularly basketball players, Adventurers can play off mistakes and choreograph to successful solutions. They enjoy taking some risk, although they don't see situations as risky because they trust their abilities to adapt and improvise. Adventurers push the group to try new approaches and to stretch, if only for the fun of it all. Their preference for "do it now" keeps the team from inaction and overanalysis. They push for learning by doing and making mistakes over planning, analysis, and too much talk.

At the same time, they bring grounding to the effort. Adventurers add value in terms of keeping the team relatively focused on a realistic evaluation of what can be done. They can also give substance to a vision by focusing on the practical impacts of different alternatives. They tend to question the use of any information and want to know why it is important for the team to make a decision or to solve this problem. They want to know what practical benefits will come from change initiatives. Adventurers keep the team from making change just for the sake of change. They can also help maintain stability through times of change by building temporary structures that will keep the organization functioning as it moves into the future.[5]

OBSTACLES

As with all the creative talents, several blocks can get in the way of the Adventurer's creativity. These blocks have to do with their orientation to the immediate, external world, where they may not get encouragement and support; their focus on the specifics of the here and now, and their spontaneity, love of freedom, and openness. After reviewing some of the key blocks, you will find strategies for overcoming them in the next sections

ADVENTURER	Blocks to Optimal Creativity

- Focus on the external world in the short term
- Obsession with the process and the joy of the moment
- Impatience with inaction
- Unwillingness to get into the deeper issues behind the situation or the conflict
- Tendencies to be easily distracted and quickly discouraged
- Failure to see the value of new ideas, theories, and possibilities
- Lack of direction or appreciation for structure and deadlines
- Biases of their auxiliary talent to certain types of data
- Fear of the unknown and the unconscious

Adventurers can be very focused on the external world of people, objects, and things. They are extremely tuned in to what is going on around them and open to sharing information about what is happening. If what is happening and the people involved do not support or encourage their inventiveness, they may get easily discouraged.

Because of their focus on the external world, they may get obsessed with facts and sometimes be too accepting of them. Adventurers may also get impatient with inaction, preferring to jump in, gather data, and put off analysis and evaluation. They frequently get so caught up in the moment that they don't take time to process the information, make sense of it, give it meaning, or pursue it for understanding. They sometimes fail to see that some of the work of life happens inside through inner reflection. Adventurers may also end up solving the symptom, not the underlying problem or root cause. In their rush to solve a problem, they may not spend the time needed to explore in depth the possible causes or differences of opinion. Quickly implemented solutions may work for now, but not necessarily for the long term.

Adventurers can easily get distracted and find more fun in moving on to something new. They sometimes avoid taking responsibility and making commitments. They may find it hard to stay focused on a strategic vision or goals and objectives. Like Leonardo da Vinci, they may find themselves starting projects and rarely finishing them.

Adventurers prefer dealing with specifics and details. They may not give intuition—either their own or that of others—the credibility it deserves. Adventurers also may not always see possibilities, trends, and patterns, nor do they seek out the hidden implications, meanings, and past traditions of the situation. They often don't have much patience for theories and abstract ideas. Their trust is in the reality that can be grasped through the senses; they have little faith in the mysterious. Adventurers are inclined to reduce unusual inner reactions and dreams to objective causes, such as the weather or something they ate or some movie they saw.[6]

Although Adventurers generally are quick to adapt to new circumstances, a new idea is never wholly liked or trusted until it has been mastered and fixed firmly in a framework of solid facts.[7] They can thus be a bit hesitant to consider change unless convinced of the advantage in it. Adventurers sometimes find it hard to see the reason for the change or innovation unless it is explained in terms of practical needs and concrete terms. They may prefer tweaking the situation instead of making major changes.

Adventurers are usually not deadline focused. They can get annoyed at those who want to set specific dates for a plan, especially at the beginning of an effort. They know full well that the effort will evolve over time and that plans and dates will change. They hardly ever share the concern that others have for written procedures and a documented, structured project-management process or systematic decision-making methodology. They prefer the freedom in adjusting the needs of the moment to the particular situation. "I can put all my energies into having fun. Sometimes the process is all that matters," said one Adventurer. Project schedules, timetables, and deadlines are likely to suffer. Their "plunge in and just do it" approach can work, but often the lack of planning causes costly mistakes and rework.

Their auxiliary creative talent may also get them into trouble. Those Adventurers with the Inventor as their auxiliary talent may not see all the people and political issues involved. They may be too quick to make tough choices, without looking for the impact on people. Those Adventurers with the Poet as their auxiliary talent may be too lenient in dealing with people. They may not take a hard look at the situation and spend time at analysis. They may put aside tough choices in order to maintain good relations.

If Adventurers are overusing their dominant talent without balancing it with their auxiliary talent or if they are spending time with people who are extremely focused or structured, they may start to have negative fantasies, frightening thoughts, and foolish suspicions. They may have anxiety attacks brought on by fears about wild possibilities and unnatural premonitions. These reactions may also occur if Adventurers are asked to deal with the future too much, if there is too much structure, or if their options get closed off.[8] These responses can significantly interfere with their creative contribution.

BOOSTERS

Depending on the particular situation, there are several steps Adventurers can take to gain maximum benefit from their creative talent and improve the effectiveness of their creativity:

1. Trust your strengths. Make sure that the team recognizes the need to play with ideas, to build on them, and to experiment and improvise. Continue to push for flexibility and fun. The team also needs to allow you to apply your practicality and give grounding to their ideas.

ADVENTURER   **Enhancing Your Creative Talent**

- Trust your strengths
- Develop greater self-awareness
- Find the right creativity tools and techniques
- Develop your abilities to organize and structure project efforts
- Find an approach to time management that works for you
- Learn to reflect on what you are taking in
- Slow your listening and reacting down
- Access your auxiliary talent for its decision-making abilities
- Recognize and practice your own creative process
- Team with others who take a broader view of the situation

---

2. Develop greater self-awareness. Making a candid assessment of your strengths and any areas where you need to focus attention as a creative individual is a critical step toward greater self-awareness and creativity. Be honest with yourself about blocks and barriers from your experiences, knowledge, and creative talents. Ask for and listen carefully to feedback from colleagues, friends, and family about your talents and what might be getting in the way. Be clear about what might be keeping you from being your creative best and making your greatest contributions.

3. Find the right creativity tools and techniques. Experiment with some creativity tools and techniques that suit your talent. If you are going to turn the mere recording of facts into creative, imaginative solutions, you need to twist your perspectives. Adventurers appreciate tools designed to promote more creative ideas and alternatives, particularly those that are fun and practical. However, they need to be real. Adventurers may prefer creativity tools such as the following:

- The Morphological, or Idea, Box, which allows you to work incrementally, building variations and scenarios, as opposed to trying to grab new ideas from nowhere. Such an approach helped one team come up with the idea for a granola bar; they played around with alternatives for the time of day people eat (e.g., breakfast, brunch, snacks) and where they can be found eating (at home, traveling, eating out, at the office, or at vending machines).[9]

- Playing with ideas, bringing the five senses of sight, sound, taste, touch, and smell to bear on the problem, a technique known as Sensanation. Questions such as "If your problem were edible, what would it taste like?" or "If it were an animal, what would it look like, feel like, sound like?" can elicit interesting new views on the problem.[10]

- Comparisons to what you know or what has worked in the past. Looking at similar situations, asking, "What's this problem like?" and "How did I solve this problem before?," can bring insight and revelations.

4. Develop your abilities to organize and structure project efforts. Although Adventurers offer the alternative of informed experimentation to project efforts, increased use of some organizational and planning disciplines may be appropriate. Get some training in project-planning tools to help you stay focused on what needs to be done. Identifying the tasks to complete the project and in what sequence doesn't have to be seen as tying you down or reining in your freedom to act. Instead, this process can ensure that you have a list of what needs to be done so that nothing falls through the cracks. Plans also help you avoid costly mistakes and waste of resources.

Such planning can help you sort through the priorities of all the many things to which you need to be paying attention. Recognize the value of routines: They allow you to get the mundane tasks done more quickly so that you can move on to more fun things.[11] Explore project management books and courses.[12] Consider using a standard but flexible creative problem-solving process (see Chapter 11) to ensure that you are making the most of valuable resources.

5. Find an approach to time management that works for you. Perhaps a day planner is not the best tool for your talent. However, find a time-management system that allows you to schedule, set priorities, and avoid the tyranny of urgency but still gives you flexibility with your time. Another approach is to learn to plan backward: Figure out when something has to be done, and then work out how much time you will need to complete each task in order to meet the deadline.[13] Set a deliverable for the very near future and get started on it right now. Put limits on the time you allow yourself to explore ideas and then move on.

6. Learn to reflect on what you are taking in. Go for a drive, listen to music, or find other techniques, such as writing in a journal or meditation, to help you find time for reflection and introspection.[14] Access your auxiliary decision-making talent to help you analyze how the data fit into your own set of personal values or your own internal framework of understanding. If you spend time reflecting, then you will be able to digest and interpret your rich experiences and observations. Reflecting on and evaluating internally what really matters can help you develop your independence and give you greater determination to see something through to completion, no matter what the opposition. Said one Adventurer, "I get fresh air or do something totally off the subject to relax. I get centered first, even do breathing exercises. Then when I come back, I write down all that I have to do, organize my work space, clear my surroundings, and dig into the problem."

7. Slow your listening and reacting down. Adventurers live in such a whirlwind of activity that they may sometimes fail to hear what others are saying. Not everyone works at the same speed as you. Learn to take the time to listen and really hear. Count to 10 and then think things through *before* you speak or act. Curb your impulses to plunge right in. Be sure to take the time to explore differences of opinion behind conflict. Your tendency to want to quickly solve problems can interfere with finding the real reasons for conflict and with finding a truly creative solution to the problem.

8. Access your auxiliary talent for its decision-making abilities. Use your auxiliary talent more deliberately to balance your externally focused perceiving strengths with your internally focused decision-making talent. Ask yourself what all your sense impressions add up to.[15] What do they mean? Is there a pattern? Ask yourself, "What can I make of these data?" and "What do I need to do with all these facts?" Use your auxiliary decision-making talent to stand back and evaluate a situation and gauge the consequences of your actions. Then set priorities and make contingency plans. Your auxiliary talent can help you stay focused, complete tasks, and get things done. Refer to the chapter on the Inventor (Chapter 8) or the Poet (Chapter 10) for more details.

9. Recognize and practice your own creative process. Although Adventurers bring a flexible, open-ended approach to problem solving, they can still benefit from becoming more conscious of how they come up with creative answers. Find out what works for you and what doesn't.

Review the approach defined by the city planner (page 42) and see if that would work for you, or review the creative problem-solving process in Chapter 11. Identify what would be an appropriate process for you. Experiment with writing down your reactions and how you solved a problem. Practice keeping notebooks, as Leonardo da Vinci, Thomas Edison, and the poet Walt Whitman did.[16] Make sure that you include time in your process to gather all sorts of data, to reflect on what they could mean, to come to conclusions about what to do with the data, *and* to make plans for implementation.

10. Team with others who take a broader view of the situation, seeing it within the system in which it resides. It is difficult sometimes for Adventurers to see systemwide linkages on their own. Your auxiliary creative talent can help you get a sense of how your actions reach beyond your own world and affect the rest of society.[17] Such awareness can help you develop a sense of responsibility and commitment to make a creative contribution to that larger world. Learn to appreciate the strengths that other team members bring to the project. Reach out to individuals with different creative talents to get their perspective on the problem or situation. Recognize the value of new ideas and the contributions of the talents of other team members. Be careful to avoid shooting down ideas that seem crazy or irrelevant to you. Practice using the *PPC method*: What are the *pluses* and *potentials* of the idea? What are the *concerns you might have*?[18]

To stretch and grow your creative results and contributions even further, here are some additional strategies for Adventurers:

1. Balance the possible biases of your auxiliary talent. Be careful to balance hard facts, people issues, logic, and values in making decisions. Check out the blocks and barriers described in the chapters on the Inventor (Chapter 8) and the Poet (Chapter 10) for more information and action steps.

2. Work to become more integrative and expansive in your thinking. Look beyond the specifics of the here and now to see patterns and trends. Experiment with a wider variety of creativity tools and techniques, such as those described in the chapters on the Explorer (Chapter 5) and the Visionary (Chapter 6). Build your appreciation for the future, for off-the-wall ideas, and for the abstract and the conceptual. Imagine yourself in someone else's shoes, especially someone with a broader view, to bring a new perspective. Find role models who can help you think more systematically and systemically.[19]

3. Open up to possibilities for the future. Investigate the Creative Problem-Solving Institute, held in Buffalo, New York, every June.[20] Or perhaps there is a local creativity group you can join. Check out magazines, such as *Fast Company*, especially the sections "Report from the Future" and "How to Be Your Own Futurist."[21] Take a workshop in strategic thinking. Attend a World Futures Society conference.[22] Learn about the Future Search process or Open Space Technology, open-ended group processes that help participants define the problems for which they want to find solutions.[23] Listen to tapes about trends for the future. Explore techniques, courses, and books to get in touch with your intuition.[24] Check out some of the tools and techniques recommended for Explorers and Visionaries (Chapters 5 and 6).

4. Suspend consciousness, explore the unknown, and tap into your hidden knowledge. When under stress, Adventurers sometimes find it helpful to talk with others about their concerns and fears in order to return to their normal, positive self. Or they may decide to engage in solitary activities, such as gardening.[25] Often it helps to purposely access your auxiliary decision-making talent to remember what's important to you and to regain your grounded perspective. Or experiment with some of the abilities of the other talents, especially those of the Visionary, to find new and different perspectives.

Experiences of negative fantasies, frightening thoughts, and foolish suspicions can bring significant benefits. They may help you begin to value the mysteries of intuition and become more comfortable with hidden possibilities. Playing with possibilities may also help you access the treasure of your unconscious.[26] This moving into the unknown is often scary at first, but you can become more secure in the process and see the value and insights it brings to your creative contribution.

HOW YOU CAN HELP AN ADVENTURER

If you work with Adventurers, there are several steps you can take to maximize their creative contributions to the organization:

1. Provide an environment that brings out an Adventurer's strengths. Adventurers enjoy a variety of tasks and a job with a fast

ADVENTURER	Maximizing Their Contributions

- Provide an environment that brings out their strengths
- Allow for fun and celebration
- Give them mutually agreed-on goals and schedules
- Help them organize their writing and their presentations
- Challenge their processes
- Build a diverse team
- Work on a development plan
- Recognize the signs of stress

pace. They prefer a great deal of independence and freedom in their work, and they cherish that autonomy. Help bring out their creativity by structuring their job with these preferences in mind. Provide them with opportunities to juggle multiple projects or activities, especially those that use their aesthetic taste and sense of design.[27] Adventurers need to be appreciated for their contributions and their approaches to problems and challenges. Recognize that they need to play with ideas and variations, let them have fun, and be flexible about rules and restrictions.

2. Allow for fun and celebration. Time pressures and work requirements often don't encourage playfulness and celebration, yet these are key contributors to creativity and higher morale. Let Adventurers be in charge of such events so that they have a chance to contribute from their strengths.

3. Give an Adventurer mutually agreed-on goals and schedules. When you work out goals and schedules with Adventurers, avoid telling them how to do something. Adventurers need the freedom to improvise and produce their own solutions within mutually agreed-on goals. Give them the problem, let them know when you need a solution, and provide any major criteria that they need to consider. Agree to limits on the amount of time that they will spend on exploring ideas. Then let them go after a solution. Set up review meetings to be sure that they are headed in the right direction and aren't floundering in collecting data or setting priorities. Discuss their work priorities to be sure that there is appropriate time to complete the assignments they have taken on. Remember that their results may be different from the way you might have tackled the challenge, but the important consideration is whether the solution works.

4. Help them organize their writing and their presentations. Encourage Adventurers to write out an executive summary of any presentation or report on which they might be working so that they capture the critical points.[28] You can work with them on drafts and iterations. Suggest that they rehearse their presentations with a few trusted colleagues, for feedback on clarity.

5. Challenge their processes. To help Adventurers see from a broader perspective, ask them questions about patterns, trends, and meanings. Encourage them to slow down their listening and reacting. Ask them questions to elicit what they think or feel about a recent development or what happened in a meeting. Challenge them to see the wider implications of actions and decisions and to play with possibilities. Help them develop more integrative thinking; several exercises in the *Fifth Discipline Fieldbook* can promote systems thinking.[29] Recommend reading about future trends. Suggest that they attend a World Futures Society meeting.

6. Build a diverse team. Wherever possible, team an Adventurer with individuals with different talents so that they can learn from and support one another. Make sure that they have the tools and techniques necessary to benefit from one another's strengths and contributions.

7. Work on a development plan. Discuss their strengths and limitations with Adventurers. If appropriate, recommend development of the time-management, project-planning, and strategic skills that they may need to be even more effectively creative. Build such courses, workshops, on-the-job training, and self-study into their performance plan.

8. Recognize the signs of stress. When Adventurers appear to be excessively anxious and losing touch with reality, make sure that they take time for a break. Help them develop contingency plans and set priorities to ensure that they return to their inventive, clever selves.[30]

SUMMARY

The Adventurer talent helps the team see the external world in terms of concrete sensations, facts, and events that are happening now. People with this talent are creative in the way they quickly and responsively improvise to solve immediate problems. Their natural strengths are in the investigation of the situation and the facts surrounding it and in improvising resolutions. They keep the project team grounded on the practical, in the here and now. They promote playful ways of dealing with the situation and add curiosity, flexibility, and adaptability to any project effort. If a team doesn't have an Adventurer as one of its members, team members may miss out on the fun of finding creative, practical solutions through the realistic assessment of facts, flexible and emergent approaches to the challenge at hand, and truly successful and enjoyable implementations. By developing their implementation focus, slowing down to examine all sides to an issue, and opening up to possibilities, Adventurers can make even more contributions to the creativity of the organization.

SELF-ASSESSMENT

How does this talent impact my life as a dominant or auxiliary talent?

_____

_____

_____

If this is not my dominant or auxiliary talent, how do I demonstrate the use of this talent?

_____

_____

_____

How could I have used this talent in the past?

_____

_____

_____

How can I use this talent in the future?

_____

_____

_____

What do I need to do to better manage an Adventurer team member?

_____

_____

_____

CHAPTER FOUR

THE NAVIGATOR

ISTJ: AUXILIARY CREATIVE TALENT–PILOT
ISFJ: AUXILIARY CREATIVE TALENT–HARMONIZER

**By keeping the logs and charts, planning out the voyage,
and building on past knowledge, Navigators enable discoveries
and practical adaptations of what others have already done.**

Navigators may have trouble getting their hands around creativity. They see what they do as making sure things work right. Comments one Navigator, "I don't spend much time thinking about creativity. I know I need to know my stuff. If you don't know how to think in the box, how can you ever think out of it?"[1] Another adds, "Necessity is the mother of invention. If it's necessary or needed, I will come up with something." One Navigator who feels comfortable with his creativity says, "I can be very creative if there's a need, but it definitely has to be applied to something." Another Navigator, a nutritionist, defined her creativity as her ability to uniquely interpret facts.

One individual with this talent notes that he can "envision what is possible in concrete terms." Some Navigators compare this process to a "stained-glass artist who carefully contemplates each unique piece of colored glass to see where it fits into the overall design."[2] Navigators can be creative in how they form an idea into a workable final project. They turn visions into reality.[3] One individual with the Navigator talent describes his creativity this way:

NAVIGATOR	Results and Contributions

- Practical adaptation, fine-tuning, and building on what others have done
- Ability to fix things to make them work
- Skill in helping people understand new products and services
- New rites, rituals, and systems to make the change work
- Imagination full of specific details, with an impressionistic, surrealistic perspective
- Keeping the group or project grounded, focused, and on track
- Understanding of and planning for possible resistance to new initiatives

> Mine is not off-the-wall creativity. Mine is on-the-ground creativity. I like making things and ideas useful. I'm good at designing programs that get to the issues. I design things creatively to show what the facts are telling me. I expand the facts. . . . I [use] all five of my senses to gather everything that is going on . . . , every bit of light, every small detail of furniture, every shade of color that's out there. . . . It's a deep, rich, experience, not just a basic count.[4]

Navigators bring their grounded experience to creative solutions. Their creativity comes from building on this experience in a "line extension" approach.[5] Thomas Edison, in his Menlo Park, New Jersey, laboratory, used "old ideas, materials, or objects in new ways" to produce an incredible number of inventions.[6] One very successful entrepreneur, winner of retailing awards for innovation, reflected the Navigator talent by pointing out that "innovation very rarely means coming up with something completely new. . . . Rather, it's finding a new application for something that's already been done." In his case it's combining color schemes from one national coffee chain, the merchandising talent of another retailer, and checkout counters that resemble those of a third.[7] A banking executive exhibiting the Navigator talent said,

> I borrow ideas from other people. . . . I then look at what other people are doing and put a different spin on it. How does it fit our organization? How does it really make a difference for us? I'm sure a lot of my own programs are bits and pieces of what other people have done and done successfully.

Explained another Navigator,

> Creativity is doing something in a different way. . . . It's like 3M where they figure out about a million ways to use sandpaper or those Post-it® Notes. It's that adaptive creativity I'm good at. I need reality. I need a fact. Then that will spark me and I'll take it and run with it.[8]

The Navigators' talent is focused on data collection; they like to take in many details and facts. In this respect they operate much as Adventurers do. Both are astute observers and recorders of what is happening right now. Both are very grounded in the reality of the physical world of facts and details; they want to feel, touch, smell, taste, and see what the world has to offer.

Unlike the Adventurer, however, the Navigator is internally focused. After picking up external data, Navigators take it inside and reflect on it. What they store away is not just the facts but the background to the facts, the details, and their impressions of the situation. They might, for example, remember not only what someone did or said on a particular day but also how he or she appeared, how his or her voice sounded, and what kind of a day it was. This storehouse of facts and rich impressions gives Navigators an incredible amount of information that can be useful in coming up with new directions. Their imagination is full of specific details, with an impressionistic, surreal perspective.

Navigators can get others to focus on pertinent facts, making sure that a team faces the realities of the current situation as they pursue new ideas and possible alternatives. They apply their knowledge and their experience to help the team determine practical solutions. Their decisions are generally based on past experiences and what they know they can and cannot do. They can recall what happened in the past, as well as what worked and what didn't. They have penetrating insight when they can use their database of experience and knowledge.

Navigators have a well-developed sense of space, function, and color and great artistic judgment. Their memory and sensitivity to facts in Dickensian detail can bring a scene to life and capture a deep experience in the presentation of ordinary, everyday life. They share this ability with artists such as Claude Monet, Mary Cassatt, Paul Cezanne, and others.[9] The stories of people who prefer the Navigator creative talent will be research based, with many corroborative facts. They will be down to earth and practical since Navigators tend to write about what they know.

When describing an organization, they explain the history of the organization, its heroes, and all its stories and rituals.

Navigators ask for specifics to get clear on the problem. They test new ideas to see if the facts support them and to be sure that they are consistent with what they already know. In evaluating people or circumstances, they marshal numerous incidents and details from the past to support a conclusion. Their questions can introduce new directions for defining a problem and gathering data to support the search for solutions. Their questions also help in solution selection and in planning for implementation. They will ask questions like the following:[10]

- Where is the evidence that there is a problem?

- What's the history of the problem?

- Can we do it incrementally? Would minor changes fix the problem?

- What will happen if we don't make changes?

- How will the solution work?

- How will it impact operations?

- Will it solve our current problems?

- Where has this solution been tried before, and what was the impact?

- Is it practical? Cost-effective? Efficient?

- What's the impact on people? Will the workforce have the necessary skills?

- How will it impact the organization and the bottom line?

- How will we maintain production or service while we change to the new system?

Their auxiliary extraverted decision-making creative talent will influence the type of data Navigators pay attention to and the questions they ask. If Navigators have the support of the Pilot talent, they are logical, analytical, and decisive in their approach to creatively studying and solving a problem. The facts and data they encounter will be objective ideas, things, and events. With this auxiliary talent, they frequently are asked to look at possible solutions and plans to see if they make sense. These Navigators first establish rules and criteria on how to go about their analysis and review. Then they make sure that every aspect of the change and the plan is addressed. They are very good at catching omissions and mistakes. Their database and their stories are full of objective facts and details, memories, and impressions of things, events, and objects.

If, instead, the Harmonizer is their auxiliary creative talent, Navigators are more focused on people and interpersonal issues and problems. Their database is usually full of memories and anecdotes of experiences with people: their facial expressions, other visual images, and the tones of their voices. They focus on what people want and need. They make sure that established procedures are in place to get these needs met. They tend to focus on helping people, as opposed to just seeing that the task is accomplished. They are most concerned for the interests of their customers, any subordinates, and colleagues as they build creative solutions.

With either auxiliary talent, Navigators are terrific at organizing and planning what needs to be done to implement the chosen solution, by whom and by when. Although Navigators often undervalue the creativity of their contributions, their attention to detail and their incredible memory are extremely valuable in the creative process. They approach a problem in a careful, deliberate, methodical, step-by-step way that shows an accurate grasp of the immediate and practical aspects of the issue at hand.[11] They can help identify the tasks involved in moving toward implementation. They come up with details and tasks that others might have forgotten, and their patient and methodical adherence to the process and appreciation for structure ensure that no stone is left unturned.

One Navigator described how she goes about finding creative solutions, both at work and at home:

> Often, I "research" before acting. I gather information and adapt the best of the data I have accumulated to the specific situation I am addressing. In decorating, I will spend many hours looking for just the right material, the right colors. I will try many different combinations to see which one works best. . . . I will seek opinions from others, but I am not afraid to make decisions and move on. At work, the process is much the same. While I may not have as much time to devote to a specific activity, I will still try to look for examples of material that I am producing and adapt them to the situation.

Navigators take obligations and responsibilities very seriously. They make sure that things get done on time and that everything meets specifications. They make sure that other people and the project stay on track.

Their willingness to systematically research and track down facts is extremely important in the data-collection stage of creative problem solving. During implementation, they are diligent in the planning and preparation for change. Once Navigators understand a change and the reasons behind it, they doggedly pursue implementation of all essential components for its success. Navigators who determine what needs to be done are hard to distract. Said one, "If I am in the middle of a project, I will keep at it until completion, no matter how much time it takes."

Navigators can help establish policies and standardize procedures to promote consistency and to make the change or innovation work. They may be very good at writing and producing any manuals that are needed to ensure that the solution operates correctly. They can also work to create the temporary structures that are needed to standardize and stabilize the situation after any required change.[12]

Another area where Navigators can make important contributions is in their ability to understand the resistance that many people have to change. Their own resistance can be helpful if it is put to productive use. They can use their own normal reactions to help others understand the impact of the proposed change and what could go wrong. One Navigator, a financial planning consultant, uses his creativity to "help people get unstuck, to get past their anguish and move through obstacles."

Because they are so attuned to reality and their subjective impressions of that reality, they are often able to read between the lines and find the hidden meaning in what someone is saying and how they are reacting. Navigators are very observant, seeing things others don't notice. They can then help the team or their colleagues figure out how to communicate with those who might not appreciate change. They can also help communicate the vision in ways that are understandable to a large group of people.

Navigators can be creative in putting together deals and transactions that take advantage of tax laws and still meet all legal and accounting requirements. They can be creative in developing new accounting systems that meet standards but also take into consideration new factors such as the accumulation of knowledge and the "balanced scorecard" approach to looking at organizational results.

The scientist and naturalist Charles Darwin could have been using the Navigator's creative talent when he conducted his systematic inquiry into the origin of the species. He is quoted as saying, "I think I am superior to the common run of men in noticing things, which easily escape attention, and in observing them carefully. My industry has been nearly as great as it could have been in the observation and collection of facts."[13] George Washington Carver, with his incredible number of uses for the peanut, is another example of the Navigator talent, as is Florence Nightingale, who reframed the practice of nursing in the nineteenth century. Another individual who displayed many of the characteristics of a Navigator is Thomas Edison. It took many attempts (and failures) for Edison to develop his inventions; he is reported to have said, "Genius is 1 percent imagination and 99 percent perspiration."[14]

OBSTACLES

As with the other creative talents, several forces work against a Navigator's creativity. These blocks include a preference for the status quo, time needed to process and understand change, and lack of comfort with unknown or ambiguous situations. After reviewing some of the key blocks, you will find strategies for overcoming them in the next sections.

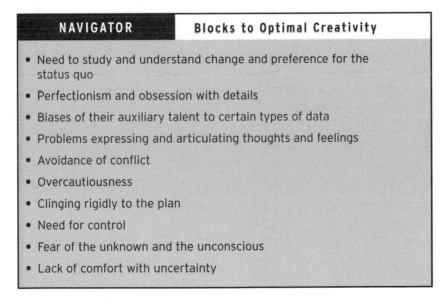

NAVIGATOR	Blocks to Optimal Creativity

- Need to study and understand change and preference for the status quo
- Perfectionism and obsession with details
- Biases of their auxiliary talent to certain types of data
- Problems expressing and articulating thoughts and feelings
- Avoidance of conflict
- Overcautiousness
- Clinging rigidly to the plan
- Need for control
- Fear of the unknown and the unconscious
- Lack of comfort with uncertainty

Navigators are often seen as change resisters. In fact, they can be slow to accept change and see the value of something new. When Navigators face a new situation, they want to know the details of how things will work, what their role will be, what time frame is planned, and who will be doing what. Often the fact that answers are not yet available for these questions can be very disconcerting.

These concerns about change can cause other blocks. Navigators tend to want to use tried-and-true ways and well-worn models to process information and make decisions. They tend to evaluate situations in light of their relevant experience. Situations in which they have no experience can seem threatening. Navigators can be overly cautious about treading too far beyond expectations.

Their need for understanding and control can cause Navigators to cling rigidly to a plan or to the ways things have always been done in the past. They usually need plenty of time to use their carefully developed expertise to deal with the new situation.[15] Giving them the time they need to digest and process information can be very difficult in today's world of constantly changing rules.

When faced with new information, Navigators tend to spend a great deal of time studying it so that they can clearly understand how it fits into their database of experiences and memories.[16] Their endless pursuit of facts can get in the way of deadlines and deliverables and keep them from producing creative results. Too much new information can be overwhelming and can confuse Navigators; sometimes they are so focused on details that they miss important patterns and trends. At times, if they can't find a place for the new data, the facts are ignored. Said one individual with the Navigator talent, "If it's important to me, I'll remember facts and details. I'm like those wacky wall-walkers, those things you throw on the wall. Sometimes they stick, sometimes they won't. If I'm not interested in a fact, it just won't stick."[17] In addition, their auxiliary decision-making talent can cause them problems by filtering the data they see. The Pilot auxiliary talent can cause Navigators to miss people and political issues, while the Harmonizer auxiliary talent can bias them against a more objective, quantitative point of view.

Navigators are by nature private and reticent. They may appear to be somewhat eccentric, since they tend to see things other people do not notice. Therefore, they may be uncomfortable sharing what is going on inside themselves. Navigators may also have a hard time expressing their thoughts; converting their inner impressions into verbal or visual form often isn't easy.

Their private nature and reticence can also affect their ability to deal with conflict. Navigators, especially those with a Harmonizer auxiliary talent, will normally retreat in the face of disagreement. Their reluctance to deal with conflict is not helped by their usual suspiciousness toward change. When they do express their opinions, these often come out as negative comments. They may compare the change to present or past experiences and have a hard time seeing any positive opportunities.

Since "it's what we think we know already that often prevents us from learning,"[18] Navigators' need for data and their focus on the past may get in the way of their seeing the positives about change and innovation. Their comfort with the status quo and the way things have always been done may get in the way of their envisioning the future. It also may be difficult for them to speculate on possibilities. They tend to distrust the unknown world and the contributions that intuition can bring. They are generally not comfortable with their unconscious or the possibilities of an unknown world.

When Navigators are rushed or when they can't devote the necessary attention and time to the task, they may get stressed. When too many ideas and possibilities surround them, they may get overwhelmed and start generating all sorts of unpleasant and sinister possibilities for the future of the world around them. They may call up dark prophetic fantasies of what might happen to society or to their family. They may become obsessed with worry or get rigid and critical and may not trust anyone to do the job right. They tend to imagine the worst for the world. In this state, they may then decide that the only way out is to continue to do what has worked before. They may doggedly hold on to the past to feel safe.[19] All these behaviors will seriously impede their willingness to take risks and make creative contributions.

BOOSTERS

Depending on their particular situation, there are several steps Navigators can take to gain maximum benefit from their creative talent and improve the effectiveness of their creativity:

1. Play to your strengths. Insist that the team spend time on data collection, research, study, and examination of the facts. Everyone should recognize the value of building on the past and of thoughtful consideration of data. Acknowledge the fact that although your thoughts and reactions may be viewed as absurd, irreverent, and idiosyncratic, they are important perspectives for the team to understand. Be willing to share them.

2. Develop greater self-awareness. Making a candid assessment of your strengths and areas where you need to focus your attention as a creative individual is a critical step toward greater self-awareness and creativity. Be honest with yourself about blocks and barriers from your experiences, knowledge, and creative talents. Ask for and listen carefully to feedback from colleagues, friends, and family about your talents and what might be getting in the way. Be clear about what might be keeping you from being your creative best and making your greatest contributions.

3. Find the right creativity tools and techniques. Tools and techniques that facilitate building on work that has been done before may appeal to individuals with the Navigator talent. These include

- Idea, or Morphological, Boxes, in which the team takes the components of the problem, considers options and variations on those components, and builds different and unusual combinations from them. Such an approach helped one team come up with the idea for a granola bar; they played around with alternatives for the time of day people eat (e.g., breakfast, brunch, and snacks) and where they can be found eating (at home, traveling, eating out, at the office, or at vending machines).[20]

- Brainwriting, in which team members write down their ideas for solving a problem, share them on a written form, and develop their ideas in silence, thus giving Navigators time to think through and build on the work of others.

- Looking to nature for interesting connections. Leonardo da Vinci suggested that inspiration can be found by looking at stains on walls, ashes of a fire, the shape of clouds, and patterns in the mud, for different shapes, objects, and figures.[21]

- Investigating and building on what's been done before. Explore how you could create something different by making it larger or smaller; by eliminating a part or all of it; or by rearranging it, reversing it, combining it, or replacing part of it with other objects or problems.[22]

- Using Sensanation, a technique that brings the five senses of sight, sound, taste, touch, and smell to bear on the problem. Questions such as "If your problem were edible, what would it taste like?" or "If it were an animal, what would it look like, feel like, sound like?" can elicit interesting new views on the problem.[23]

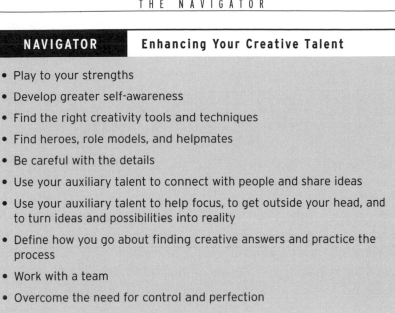

NAVIGATOR | **Enhancing Your Creative Talent**

- Play to your strengths
- Develop greater self-awareness
- Find the right creativity tools and techniques
- Find heroes, role models, and helpmates
- Be careful with the details
- Use your auxiliary talent to connect with people and share ideas
- Use your auxiliary talent to help focus, to get outside your head, and to turn ideas and possibilities into reality
- Define how you go about finding creative answers and practice the process
- Work with a team
- Overcome the need for control and perfection

4. Find heroes, role models, and helpmates. Study the lives of great inventors or some of your heroes to see what they did to be creative. Learn from their experiences and apply their techniques to your problems and challenges. Imagine how they would see the challenge you are facing. Find creativity buddies or helpmates who can support your moving "outside the lines." As one Navigator put it, "I find that when I move toward wanting to be precise and perfect, it helps a lot to have others who can encourage me to be a little less precise and perfect and just see what happens. My creativity is bolstered by having others support it, and my fear of the unknown is lessened."

5. Be careful with the details. Navigators need to be sure that they don't frame their creative problem solving too narrowly. Define the problem broadly enough so that you don't unnecessarily cut off options. Stay open and suspend judgment for a while. Premature closing off of alternatives can get in the way of finding an ideal solution. Look beyond the concrete facts that are available to you. Recognize alternatives beyond the status quo. Step back and ask what the facts are telling you or what's behind those facts. Be careful to avoid becoming a prisoner of facts or listening too closely to experts whom you have come to trust. Don't give too much weight to data that come easily to mind.

Remember that just because something has worked in the past doesn't always mean it will work now. Rules are changing, and fast. Building more flexibility into your responses will help you deal with what's happening in the world today. Look for new information. Go to bookstores, as one Navigator does. She browses the appropriate section to see how others have approached the subject: "The Internet also falls in the category of research. That pursuit doesn't necessarily give me the answer, but it generally opens up other avenues of thought that might get me to a more creative approach."

6. Use your auxiliary talent to connect with people and share ideas. By nature, Navigators are quiet and private. Their reactions and answers to questions are usually well considered, and they often have a hard time articulating their thoughts and ideas. While you may prefer, as a Navigator, to share your rich collection of facts only with people you know well, try opening up with others to avoid wasting all your incredible knowledge. Your extraverted auxiliary talent of the Harmonizer or the Pilot can help you explain your ideas and how you came to your conclusions. Practice brainstorming ideas with others, or find allies who will support your efforts and work with you to promote your ideas. You might also consider joining a professional, business, or trade association to build your self-confidence.[24]

7. Use your auxiliary talent to help focus, to get outside your head, and to turn ideas and possibilities into reality. Navigators need to access their extraverted auxiliary decision-making talent of either the Pilot or the Harmonizer to help them expand their decision-making abilities. Like many individuals who prefer operating in the introverted world, you have probably had to develop your auxiliary talent in order to function in the world outside yourself. By accessing your extraverted auxiliary talent, you can balance your search for data with a need to move on. You can avoid spending too much time living in the past, enjoying all the memories and stories you have accumulated. Ask yourself, "How can I organize this information?" "What conclusions can I draw from this data?" Use your auxiliary talent to focus on the world around you, to organize and evaluate the facts and data you have acquired, and to move toward a decision, sometimes without all the information you would like to have. Review the chapter on either the Pilot (Chapter 7) or the Harmonizer (Chapter 9) to learn more about effectively using this talent.

8. Define how you go about finding creative answers and practice the process. At times, pressure from the outside world or from an overdeveloped auxiliary talent can emphasize moving to closure and making decisions. Balance the conflicting need to gather data with the desire to come to a conclusion. Identify what steps to take to find creative answers and solutions and practice using them regularly. Try out the creative problem-solving process described in Chapter 11 and then modify it for your needs and preferences. Be willing to take small actions and experiment with unconventional methods in order to go beyond your comfort zone.

9. Work with a team. Recognize the value of new ideas and the contributions of the talents of other team members or colleagues. Be open to their points of view. Be careful to avoid shooting down new ideas. Practice using the PPC method: What are the pluses and potentials of the idea? What are the concerns you might have?[25] Learn to appreciate those who circumvent rules in their eagerness to get things done.

10. Overcome the need for control and perfection. With an overwhelming drive to have every *i* dotted and *t* crossed, you may get waylaid. Be sure to clarify what is expected of you. Define what you really need to do to get the job done so that you are not expending more effort than necessary. Set limits on your search for information. Move out a little from the safe shore by risking a little and speaking up a bit sooner than you are normally comfortable doing. Otherwise, the world or the team might not benefit from your contribution. Push yourself to take some risks even if it means making a mistake. Spend time at the end of each week reviewing all you've done that's new and different. Treat yourself to celebrations for small achievements.

To stretch and grow your creative results and contributions even further, here are some additional strategies for Navigators:

1. Get and stay centered. Navigators need space to deal with emotions and feelings of imperfection. They need to be centered to be creative. Strategies that can help are submerging yourself in peaceful, quiet, natural surroundings; getting into nature; lightening your schedule; and taking time out. One Navigator regularly swims eighteen laps in a swimming pool. "It's like meditation for me. I feel renewed."

2. Consider the biases of your auxiliary talent. Your auxiliary talent could also lead to some possible blocks to your creative contribution. With the Pilot's talent, you may overlook the impact of the change initiative on the people involved. You may not see that individuals involved could have legitimate reasons to object. You may not take the time to praise or connect with the individuals affected. Instead, you could be focusing on competence, achievement, and creating something that works.

With the Harmonizer as your auxiliary talent, you may also run into trouble. This combination could cause you to worry so much about harmony and cooperation that you lose sight of what needs to be done. You may end up generating unduly positive, confirming alternatives, or you may generate alternatives that you think people want. Paying attention to and compensating for these biases will enhance your creative contribution. Review the chapter on the Pilot (Chapter 7) or the Harmonizer (Chapter 9) for more information on blocks, barriers, and strategies for further developing your auxiliary talent.

3. Experiment with creative ways to manage conflict. Finding creative solutions often involves exploring differences in perspective and opinion. Examine the way you deal with such disagreements. Do you tend to avoid conflict or to procrastinate on decisions because you know they might put you in a position of conflict? One suggestion would be to take a course in mediation. Another possible way to overcome a natural reluctance to confront such differences is to view the conflict as a problem to be solved. Look at the goal and overall objectives, find the facts, explore alternatives, and figure out how to resolve the situation. (See Chapter 11 for more details on this approach.)

4. Open up to possibilities. Open yourself up to other ways of doing and seeing things. Looking for possibilities and opportunities in a new situation can help you overcome some of your natural resistance to change. Investigate the Creative Problem Solving Institute, held in Buffalo, New York, every June.[26] Or perhaps there is a local creativity group you can join. To pick up new ideas, check out magazines, such as *Fast Company*. *Fast Company* also has local groups that meet to exchange ideas.[27]

Change your routines. Go to work a new way. Wear a color or a tie you would never have thought of wearing. Take an unusual or unexpected vacation. Take up a hobby you haven't tried before. Try reading a book or a magazine outside your typical reading list. Take a class in a subject you know nothing about. Take a workshop in strategic thinking.

Attend a World Futures Society conference.[28] Listen to tapes about trends for the future. Explore techniques to get in touch with your intuition.[29] Check out some of the tools and techniques recommended for the Explorer (Chapter 5) and Visionary (Chapter 6) talents. Recognize that although there can't always be structure and stability, you can still thrive. Learning to see new possibilities can also help you access your unconscious.[30]

5. Consider finding a place to store your memories so you can make room for new ideas. At times you may need to get rid of some of the physical and emotional baggage you, like everyone else, have accumulated over the years. Go through your files and storage boxes and figure out what you could get rid of or store somewhere else to make room for new experiences. It's easy to fall in love with the things that seem true. You can treasure those truths even though they become old and shabby and lose their utility. They are comfortable, but they can clutter your mind up. You don't need to discard this stuff, but you need to create a mental attic and store away those old, best-loved treasures.[31]

6. Recognize the power of your unconscious. Learn to trust your hidden resources. One Navigator, a lawyer, has learned to go home from the office and sleep on a tough problem before making a decision. Another Navigator, a medical researcher, has recently started having incredible dreams and is now interested in exploring the meaning of them. This unconscious pool of ideas and inspiration needs to be investigated for its power in helping you be more creative.

HOW YOU CAN HELP A NAVIGATOR

If you work with Navigators, there are several steps you can take to maximize their creative contributions to the organization:

1. Structure the right environment. One strategy for bringing out the best in Navigators is to ensure that they are working in an environment that supports them. Give them enough structure for a sense of stability. Make guidelines and expectations clear.

2. Provide focus and limits. Limit the time for research and analysis. Suggest that they first write an executive summary or a statement of scope on the subject before doing research and then determine what

NAVIGATOR	Maximizing Their Contributions

- Structure the right environment
- Provide focus and limits
- Provide space and time
- Show appreciation
- Provide the information they need to process a change
- Encourage an attitude of positive possibilities
- Teach conflict management
- Build a development plan
- Watch for symptoms of stress and suggest time-outs

holes they need to fill in with more investigation.[32] Since Navigators can at times go off in unproductive directions, be sure that they are working on the right problems.

3. Provide space and time. Find ways for Navigators to have private time and space for working most effectively. If this is not possible in the work space, then explore ways to help them find the reflective time they need (e.g., working out of the home, providing white noise, or wearing earphones). Give them time to process information.

4. Show appreciation. Navigators tend to work in the background. Their work can often go unnoticed and unappreciated. Show them how much you value their knowledge of and memory for organizational history and traditions. Use their storehouse of data and experience to provide historical perspective, background information, and an understanding of the culture and to help the team design new rites and rituals to institutionalize changes and innovations. Appreciate their role as a rock, an anchor, and the keeper of the organization's culture, memory, and values. Use their concerns about the future to proactively build contingency plans for worst-case scenarios. Encourage their attempts at being creative. Suggest that they take small steps, using tools and techniques that build on what they know.

5. Provide the information they need to process a change. Make sure that Navigators (as well as other team members) have the answers to their questions regarding an innovation or change. Be prepared to answer such questions as "What's the time frame, and what will the change look like?" "Who's in charge and what role am I to play?" "Where can I get more information and training so that I can responsibly fulfill my role?" Help them see how the present relates to the past.[33] Be honest if you can't answer all their questions, but assure them that you will give them the information when you have it.

You also need to provide realistic pictures of the future that make the changes real and provide clear guidelines on expectations, roles, and responsibilities. Another possibility is to give Navigators opportunities to design the structure they need. Addressing their concerns and answering their questions will likely lead to better, more complete, and less risky change preparations for the rest of the team and the organization.[34] By helping Navigators see change more positively, you will help them avoid missing opportunities to make a creative contribution.

6. Encourage an attitude of positive possibilities. Don't tolerate a culture of negativity or complaining without suggestions about what can be done.[35] Suggest that Navigators not immediately put ideas down. Using the "PPC" response to negative reactions will help, as will asking such questions as "How can we?" and "In what ways may we?" Give them time to sort things out. Suggest that they try generating ideas by themselves or with others for a limited amount of time to see what happens. Encourage their small steps at experimentation. Help them understand that all data do not have to be 100 percent verified before they can be acted on. Talk to them about the value of informed trial and error.

7. Teach conflict management. Help Navigators see that the inevitable clash of ideas that comes with diversity of perspectives is only adding to the quality of the final solution. Encourage them to speak up and share their thoughts and concerns. Make sure that they don't shy away from such clashes, especially Navigators with a Harmonizer auxiliary talent. In dealing with conflict, political challenges, and the fallout from change, Navigators with a Pilot auxiliary talent may also need help to ensure that they are considering people issues.

8. Build a development plan. Review the suggestions about communication, assertiveness, and conflict-management skills development. Incorporate programs, workshops, and self-study courses that are appropriate into their performance plan. Make sure that evaluation criteria address their strengths, as well as areas for development.

9. Watch for symptoms of stress and suggest time-outs. Since the wrong level of stress can negatively impact anyone's creativity levels, be sure that Navigators are dealing with stress appropriately. If you notice Navigators getting bogged down in the facts, becoming obsessed with details, or predicting catastrophes, encourage them to take a break or go for a walk and ask, "In what other ways can we look at this?" Help them work through their concerns. Encourage them to share their issues with a trusted colleague. Help them deal with the details that seem to be overwhelming them.[36]

SUMMARY

Without a Navigator's creative talent, a team could get lost, like a ship without a rudder. The Navigator talent helps a group be astute observers and recorders of what is going on in the world and what has gone on in the past, assuming that their incredible memory bank is put to use in solving problems. Knowledge of facts and events and a sense of history are important in making sense out of new situations and bringing invaluable experience to bear on problems. Navigators can build on what others have done to find new ways of solving the challenge or situation. They will also ensure that a change effort is well planned and carefully implemented. Navigators need to learn to appreciate their own creative contributions and their own creative process. Taking small steps away from safe shores, opening up to the possibilities and opportunities of the future, and sharing perspectives and opinions can help optimize their creative contributions.

SELF-ASSESSMENT

How does this talent impact my life as a dominant or auxiliary talent?

_____

_____

_____

If this is not my dominant or auxiliary talent, how do I demonstrate the use of this talent?

_____

_____

_____

How could I have used this talent in the past?

_____

_____

_____

How can I use this talent in the future?

_____

_____

_____

What do I need to do to better manage a Navigator team member?

_____

_____

_____

CHAPTER FIVE

THE EXPLORER

ENTP: AUXILIARY CREATIVE TALENT–INVENTOR

ENFP: AUXILIARY CREATIVE TALENT–POET

**Explorers journey to find new lands and discover new routes.
Their worlds are full of pulsating possibilities.**

The strengths of the Explorers' creative talent lie in their bold imagination and ability to see patterns, relationships, connections, and trends in what is happening in the external world. They are gifted with tremendous insight and with the power to inspire. Explorers have the advantage of knowing and being recognized in the world of work as creative and original. Their life is often about being creative "almost all the time." Said one Explorer, "I thrive in a creative environment and love to let creative energy flow. Creativity is key!"

Explorers are the quintessential idea generators, brainstormers, and catalysts for change. They use a lot of "what-if" talk and are always looking at the future and emerging possibilities. They are often heard to ask, "In what ways might we . . . ?" or "How else could we see this problem?" They will question and challenge others to reach higher and farther. They will look for "happy collisions" that connect seemingly unrelated ideas, people, or circumstances.

Explorers find self-expression quite natural and easy. They use speculative and imaginative terms to get their ideas across. They can keep the total situation in mind as the creative process develops and can continuously redefine the problem as it unfolds. They can rapidly generate alternatives and quickly consider and discard possible solutions.

EXPLORER	Results and Contributions

- Ability to see external patterns, trends, and relationships
- Tireless generation, promotion, and initiation of new enterprises, new business ventures, and new ideas
- Inspiring ingenuity and discovery in others
- Imagination full of connections and associations
- High-spirited team-building and successful change initiatives because of their enthusiasm, energy, and passion
- Helping others push past what is accepted and expected
- Possibility thinking to envision future

Explorers tend to have a broad range of interests and abilities and a wide array of friends. They get their energy from being with other people. Explorers are usually full of new and different ideas and possibilities, and they love to talk about them. In fact, Explorers often need to talk with others in order to experiment and play and come up with new ideas. Explorers work best in groups, since the majority of their ideas come from interacting with other people. One Explorer, a very successful entrepreneur, admitted that she is usually stymied trying to generate ideas on her own. However, when she adds another person to the mix, ideas start to flow—and most of the ideas are her own. She just needs the stimulus of another person to start the flow.

> I need another person, often just in the room. They may not be able to get a word in edgewise because I may do all the talking. But without that other person in the room, I cannot think of a thing on my own. I hear ideas in others, and I articulate them.

Said another Explorer, who recently became a self-employed consultant,

> I need to work with someone else. I like to explore ideas on my own, but I feel that they are only made real by introducing them to someone else. The greatest challenge of the last six months (since starting my own business) has been to recognize that I need to work with others in development, not only in delivery, and then to develop networks and an approach to planning that support this need.

Explorers relish new projects and new experiences. They usually have plenty of new challenges since one of their biggest fears is being bored. Said one telecommunications entrepreneur with this talent, "I need to be learning and exploring all the time." Individuals with this talent are stimulated by difficulties and can be most ingenious in solving them. The telecommunications entrepreneur, upon being told that his Rotary group couldn't possibly get a BMW automobile as a raffle prize for an upcoming fund-raiser, immediately took up the challenge, went to the local dealer, and got the car! Said one Explorer, another entrepreneur, "I love challenges. . . . Tell me something can't be done and I will find a way to do it. Tell me 'you can't get into that account,' and I'll get into it."

Explorers enjoy collecting information from the world around them and exploring ideas and possible approaches to a situation. They like to figure out how to unlock every door and find fresh outlets for new ideas. Their original minds help Explorers see beyond the boundaries and have different perspectives. They tend to do things differently than other people. Here's one example of an Explorer "thinking out of the box," or actually on top of the box:

> I once worked as a production foreman for a tall and physically intimidating production manager. He was in the habit of using his physical presence to intimidate subordinates in order to "win" arguments. Faced with this approach in a heated discussion, I asked him to wait for a moment while I pulled a packing crate across the floor and left it at his feet. Standing on the packing crate (now towering above him), I asked him to please continue!

Explorers tend to be independent and flexible, divergent and integrative in their approaches, and positive and passionate about their work. They value vision and inspiration above everything else. They will follow their visions confidently into all sorts of opportunities, ventures, explorations, promotions, and projects. They are usually comfortable acting on their hunches. They may also frequently use humor to reframe a problem and to get people to see it differently. The questions they tend to ask during creative problem solving can help reframe the challenge and generate multiple alternative ideas and solutions. These include the following:

- In what ways might we . . . ?

- How else could we see this?

- What would happen if . . . ?

- How could we do this differently?

- What could we do about this if we had all the resources we needed?

- What if we . . . ?

- What's the big picture?

- What would be ideal?

- Can you imagine . . . ?

- How would Superman or Wonder Woman (or other cartoon character) see this problem? What would he or she do about it?

Acting as a catalyst for change, they frequently initiate and promote innovation efforts. Explorers can be very successful, enthusiastic change agents. Their high energy, optimism, and enthusiasm are contagious and can carry the team through tough times. Explorers stimulate the team to consider all options and angles, to look for the positives, and to search for new routes for growth and expansion.

Their visions of the future are most often inspiring and address global concerns. They can process information from many different sources simultaneously. Explorers have the ability to rapidly scan much information for general impressions; they can walk into the middle of a meeting and almost immediately pick up where the group is. Their intuition is usually finely tuned. Their imagination is full of connections, associations, streams of consciousness, and vague images.

Explorers are versatile and flexible. They tend to be intolerant of rules and formulas. Instead, they prefer to stay alert to fresh opportunities and new developments. For this reason, they may be more comfortable working outside of large, more formal organizations. They like to experiment with and test out possibilities. Explorers may just wholeheartedly dive right in, frequently without a detailed plan, because the answer is bound to emerge. Plans aren't needed since they can constrict and limit options. Said one Explorer, "It just happens. The right direction will emerge. We will sift, and sift, and sift, and wow! The right design appears."

Their introverted decision-making auxiliary talent is important in giving Explorers focus and direction. It also affects the types of data they take in and how they go about making sense of them all. If their Explorer talent is supported by the Inventor's talent, they may be independent, analytical, and somewhat impersonal in their relations with people. They are constantly and rapidly scanning the environment for opportunities and taking in data about concepts, ideas, and things. They are concerned with product quality, dependability, flexibility, and innovation. With this combination, Explorers look at challenges from a systemwide point of view. They are more apt to consider how others may affect their projects than how their projects may affect others. They look for experts with whom to explore their futuristic ideas and plans, favoring theoretical, conceptual, and technical possibilities. They provide a clear strategic vision for where the organization needs to go.

If they are supported by the Poet's talent, Explorers are more enthusiastic and concerned with the possibilities and potential of people. They are skilled at handling political and interpersonal issues. They are adept at handling groups and at getting people to work together. Explorers with this combination of talents do not mind the need to bargain and adjust to people's needs. They pay attention to the way people are responding to their suggestions or presentations; they know that important decisions cannot be uncoupled from personal views and desires of powerful people. These Explorers are adept at reconciling different opinions and views and finding common ground. They are likely to take on a missionary zeal to help the world see the power of their visions. Their desire is to promote a flexible organization with long-term goals. Explorers with the Poet auxiliary talent want to bring out the best in others, and they filter their decisions through their set of internal, personal values to come to conclusions that usually take others into consideration.

With either combination of talents, Explorers can make many creative contributions as team leaders. Their enthusiasm brings people out and stimulates their ideas. They have a passion and liveliness that keeps the group creatively energized. Life is a fascinating game for Explorers, and they are one of the key players. They can help the team avoid the rigidity of facts and keep them focused on the potential for change, improvement, and new directions.[1] With their leadership, the team can learn to be more flexible and to explore a broad range of interests.

Explorers are also open to the ideas of others, since they are eager to develop a wide understanding of the problem. They know how to give and receive encouragement and support. They are thus skilled at bringing individuals with different perspectives together to examine the various points of view and then to generate new approaches to the challenge.

They can set a tone of acceptance, which is very important to the creative process. Their passion and optimism can appeal to the group's imagination and curiosity.

Richard Branson, CEO and founder of British Virgin Group, who has developed new ways of challenging the airline and retailing business, is one example of an individual who might have this creative talent. Another is anthropologist Margaret Mead, who broke new ground in a variety of different arenas to study the cultures of the world. Other examples might include Walt Disney, the artist Judy Chicago, advertising giant Jay Chiat, and entrepreneur Ruth Mosko Handler, cofounder of Mattel, Inc.

Explorers are terrific at initiating entrepreneurial ventures. They are full of ideas for new businesses and have the creative impulse to get them going. They are comfortable with the amorphous, fluid, early stages of projects and start-up ventures. They like to figure out how to structure the deal and then bring others in. They are the mavericks who are not afraid to take risks and make mistakes and learn. They are constantly looking for opportunities to explore, expand, and grow. One entrepreneur, in reflecting on his business career, saw the pattern of always looking in every job for the career opportunity that others might have overlooked:

> I always asked myself how could I find some benefit from this situation. Part of this constant questioning comes from my fear of being bored. Part comes from the fact that I need these challenges to keep growing. And, of course, the recognition and advancing of my career didn't hurt either!

Explorers tend to really enjoy the thrill of starting up a new business and the many tasks involved in getting it off the ground. Says one successful business owner,

> This business calls for me to do a hundred things at once. You have to be a juggler because you are dealing with so many different things. I've always been able to juggle a million things at once. . . . You have to always be proactive because if you are not proactive, the train passes you by. . . . And you have to keep on being creative. You can never lose the competitive edge.

OBSTACLES

As with all the talents, several forces can impede the effectiveness of the Explorer's creativity. These blocks include lack of focus, organization, and

EXPLORER	Blocks to Optimal Creativity

- Irresistible pull of the external world
- Unfocused energy and overextension of self
- Tendency to be easily distracted and become impatient
- Failure to address facts and details
- Preference for idea generation over implementation
- Overwhelming or silencing others
- Biases of their auxiliary talent to certain types of data
- Not understanding or appreciating facts, history, or resistance to change
- Burnout and loss of their creative edge

direction; randomness and inconsistency; ignoring details; impatience; and preferring idea generation to implementation. After reviewing some of the key blocks, you will find strategies for overcoming them in the next sections.

Explorers are driven by what is happening in the world around them. They sometimes find themselves at the mercy of external conditions since outside possibilities have an irresistible pull for Explorers. They may get so caught up in talking with others, generating ideas, getting fresh inspirations, and helping solve problems that they fail to keep track of time and get their own work done. They may get easily distracted and appear unpredictable, scattered, disorganized, irresponsible, or impulsive. They may seem to go off on tangents wherever inspiration takes them. They hate to admit that something is impossible since they believe they are the master of possibilities. Explorers may often find themselves overextended and overcommitted and may end up squandering their energies. Their strengths do not necessarily lie in completing projects.

Explorers tend to dislike schedules and routine and may be unrealistic about the time required to make a vision real and to do the work. If their auxiliary talent is not well developed or fails to operate on a given day, Explorers may find themselves ignoring deadlines and commitments. Said one, the president of a consulting company, "Getting ideas is not the challenge. The challenge is implementation." Explorers may prefer to wait until the last moment since that pressure inspires them. They find process or systematic methods tedious and boring. Admitted one Explorer,

> In general, I will say that my response to "challenges" is inconsistent from the point of view that sometimes I simply walk away, sometimes I get mad and create chaos (although less often these days!), sometimes I work through the challenge in a methodical and painstaking way, and sometimes I have an inspired idea and it carries me through on a wave of enthusiasm.

The natural passion and fast pace of the Explorer can overwhelm or exhaust a group. While relishing the new ideas that can come from differences of opinion, they may often find that they squelch conflict, though usually not consciously. Their high energy level and enthusiasm for new ideas may lead others to be afraid to voice differing opinions. Or others may not feel that Explorers want to hear their opinions since they may mistake their enthusiasm for conviction. In addition, Explorers may be guilty of not listening as they get carried away with their own ideas.

Their auxiliary talent may also cause problems. If it's the Inventor's talent, Explorers may find themselves railroading ideas through without concern for the group's feelings. On the other hand, a Poet's talent may dampen an Explorer's passion for change because of a concern for the possible impact of the change on values, relationships, and people.

Explorers may be too focused on the future without really understanding the present situation, its facts, and realities. It may be difficult for them to concentrate and prove to others the viability of their ideas. They can overrate possibilities and then underestimate the time needed to produce results. Overlooking details and specifics can cause problems when changes are initiated. Explorers can have a difficult time understanding reactions to change that differ from their own. They often don't appreciate the reasons that cause people to resist, and they may fail to take those reasons into consideration in the change initiative. Explorers may be too impatient to take the time to carefully convince others of their ideas. Said one entrepreneur with the Explorer talent, "My energy can exhaust other people. . . . I just won't take no for an answer." She went on to add, "I also don't have patience for people with no sense of urgency, who just plod along, who can't keep up with me, or don't even try to keep up with me. That drives me crazy."

In addition, routine details may often get in the way of an Explorer's creativity. Said this same Explorer, in commenting about what gets in her way, "It's the mundane things of running a business that get in the way. You need to be close to the details, but you can't get so close that you get sucked in, bogged down."

In valuing new and fresh approaches to challenges, Explorers often end up reinventing processes over and over again because information gets discarded once it is used, instead of being stored for a similar situation. Explorers may not learn to rely on their experiences or even feel the need to learn from experience.

Explorers may get overwhelmed by having to deal with too many details, bureaucracy, or idea generation. Sometimes they get so involved in possibilities and the future that they fail to pay attention to their own physical and emotional needs. As one Explorer said, "A big problem for me is getting tired out, burned out. That's a real problem for creativity. You need a fresh outlook." A major challenge for them is to keep their competitive edge and innovative spirit.

When they are mentally exhausted or physically tired, Explorers may become defensive or obsessed with details and overvalue the relevancy and use of facts. If others attempt to control them, they may become rebellious and scattered, even critical, and fail to follow through on commitments. Explorers may also become obsessed with their body and concoct all sorts of imaginary pains and illnesses.[2] Obviously, these symptoms can greatly interfere with their creative contribution.

BOOSTERS

Depending on their particular situation, there are several steps Explorers can take to gain maximum benefit from their creative talent and improve the effectiveness of their creativity:

1. Trust your strengths. Make sure that the team recognizes the need to explore new ideas and possibilities. Encourage the team to share these skills and to hold off focusing on the end result until they have examined many different alternatives.

2. Develop greater self-awareness. Making a candid assessment of your strengths and areas where you need to focus your attention as a creative individual is a critical step toward greater self-awareness and creativity. Be honest with yourself about blocks and barriers from your

EXPLORER	Enhancing Your Creative Talent

- Trust your strengths
- Develop greater self-awareness
- Find the right creativity tools and techniques
- Find ways to capture ideas
- Get help in organizing and executing ideas
- Access your auxiliary talent for balance
- Practice good time-management techniques
- Reflect and grow
- Become more conscious of and practice your own creative process
- Learn to communicate with other talents

experiences, your knowledge, and your creative talents. Ask for and listen carefully to feedback from colleagues, friends, and family about your talents and what might be getting in the way. Be clear about what might be keeping you from being your creative best and making your greatest contributions.

3. Find the right creativity tools and techniques. Most tools and techniques to expand options and promote breaking out of mental models are built just for people with the Explorer's talent. You probably enjoy these tools and techniques—particularly brainstorming, analogies, and associations—because they are fun and can have unexpected results. Make sure you are using these tools and techniques appropriately to get the most advantage out of them. For example, one of the reasons that brainstorming sessions often don't produce the results they potentially can is that the team falls into analysis too quickly and does not follow the rules of brainstorming:

- Set some general boundaries around the purpose of the session.

- Generate as many ideas as possible. The more ideas the better; quantity will lead to quality.

- Defer judgment. Hold off criticizing until the session is over and the decision is made to move to analyzing ideas.

- Build on the ideas of others. Combine and improve on the ideas of your teammates.

- Encourage "freewheeling" of ideas. The wilder the idea, the better; it is easier to tame down than to think up.[3]

- Write down every idea to ensure that none get lost.

In addition, make sure that you keep your creative edge and promote its growth. It's easy for Explorers to fall back on past successes and reputation. Several creativity tools and techniques can take your idea-generation skills to an even higher level. These tools include techniques that make the problem strange and using analogies from nature—all of which make the original problem significantly different and cause you to look at it from totally new perspectives. These techniques will help you use your well-developed imagination in new ways.[4]

4. Find ways to capture ideas. Explorers need to have a way to capture their ideas. One Explorer has three tape recorders—one in the car, one by the bed, and one at work—to make sure that she doesn't lose any great idea. Another also uses a tape recorder to get his ideas down; he then has the draft typed so that he can edit it and send it out for feedback. Another Explorer talked about needing plenty of space around her, to be able to write on the walls and see everything. H. H. Richardson, the famous American architect, had walls of cork in his room to which he pinned drawings.[5]

5. Get help in organizing and executing ideas. To balance your natural ability to generate lots of ideas and possibilities, find techniques to help you focus, select the best ideas, make decisions, and get them implemented. If you can't find partners who support your efforts, tools can help. One Explorer, a successful CEO of a training company, credits his knowledge and frequent use of the management and planning tools of the Total Quality Management (TQM) programs with helping him be more effectively creative. Using the tools of Gantt charting, force field analysis, and decision charts, he can better structure and apply the results of idea-generation sessions. The TQM tool known as Affinity Diagrams can be used to group ideas together and to organize the output of an idea-generation session. Nominal Group Technique is another TQM tool that can be used for voting on and then selecting the best options.[6] One Explorer described his use of mind mapping, a visual technique that allows you to represent your thoughts using bubbles of key words and organizing those bubbles in a web of connecting lines in all directions.[7]

I get out some colored pens and start mind mapping. The things that appeal to me about mind mapping are the ways that it facilitates the exploring of many alternatives and allows you to express them on a single page. You can also have fun drawing sketches and cartoons.

6. Access your auxiliary talent for balance. Explorers can bring needed structure to the creative process by using their auxiliary talent of the Inventor or the Poet. A well-developed auxiliary creative talent that helps evaluate, organize, and judge can add stability to your incredible ability to take in all sorts of data. Accessing your auxiliary talent can increase your dependability and help you focus, settle down, and stick with a solution. Ask yourself, "What does all this information mean?" "How do I organize it?" "To what use can I put it?" "How does it fit in with my values?" As one Explorer said,

> My auxiliary talent targets where and what I feel is important. There is so much I could pursue. I need focus. I have a dialogue between my 'king and queen' [his term for his dominant and auxiliary talents] about what to do next. It's not an argument, but it's exploring issues that need to be resolved. They will undermine me if they are not both happy or excited.

Refer to the chapter on the Inventor (Chapter 8) or the Poet (Chapter 10) for strategies for further developing this talent.

7. Practice good time-management techniques. To help ensure implementation of great ideas, learn to plan backward: figure out when something has to be done, and then detemine how much time you will need to complete all tasks in order to meet the deadline. Put limits on the time you allow yourself to explore ideas and then get ready to move on.[8] Another suggestion is to identify what routines might help you be more efficient and avoid wasting time. Such routines can free up time for you to explore and do more of the activities you enjoy doing.[9]

8. Reflect and grow. Reflecting can help Explorers grow their creativity by learning from past experiences and mistakes. Explorers need to find a quiet place for reflection. Schedule time between meetings or planning sessions to process and digest information and to regain your energy. Sometimes writing in a journal or practicing relaxation techniques is also helpful. Learn to take long walks, enjoy nature, and return to your grounded center. Said one Explorer, "I walk in the woods, pray, get away from daily habits, daydream." The time you take reflecting may help you value facts and details and come to appreciate structure and planning. Another Explorer said, "I tend to work in bursts of energy. I need down time to recharge and for ideas to percolate while I'm thinking of other things." One Explorer talked about the need to "step back from the dance floor and get up on the balcony." Another business leader reflecting the Explorer talent indicated that it's always important for her to take time to process experiences:

> There are always problems that you have to resolve. And then usually out of that comes the evaluation process. It takes you through all the other things you could have done to avoid the problem in the first place, what you should do to avoid it the next time, and then from that, what you could do.

9. Become more conscious of and practice your own creative process. Explorers *naturally* bring a divergent approach to problem solving, but they can still benefit from becoming more conscious of how they come up with creative solutions. Experiment with writing down your reactions and how you solved a problem. Practice keeping notebooks as Leonardo da Vinci, Thomas Edison, and the poet Walt Whitman did.[10] One consultant reflecting the Explorer creative talent talked about his technique called "inventive reading":

> I look for conceptual nuggets or building blocks in all kind of books. Then I will look for concepts, frameworks, and patterns. A thought in a book will, for me, light up, and I know it's part of a bigger pattern that I'm in the process of discovering.

Learn to alternate between exploring ideas with others and wrestling with the problem on your own. One Explorer describes her process this way: "I learn about and consider whatever the challenge may be. Next I find a quiet place and generate an action plan. Then I join with the group discussion and remain flexible, using all the ideas to find collaborative, out-of-the-box solutions." Such alternating can help you develop independence and avoid biasing your own thoughts and feelings with those of others.

As part of your process, include a step that causes you to stop to determine if the question, challenge, or situation really calls for your creativity. There are times when you may want to consciously shut it off to avoid wasting your energy. Make sure you also give yourself time away from the problem. Not every problem needs to be addressed immediately. Said one Explorer, "If I'm really stuck, I won't push it. I've learned that the world won't fall apart if I wait two hours to find an answer!"

10. Learn to communicate with other talents. Sometimes more grounded and practical colleagues find an Explorer's stream of consciousness a bit tricky to follow. To your team members, your ideas may seem to come out of nowhere. Your team members may prefer a more step-by-step approach to understanding a situation and can be more focused on today than you are. To be more effectively creative, you might try stating up front in a meeting what you're going to be doing—throwing out ideas or trying to come to a decision so that everyone is clear about purpose and expectations.

Learn to slow down and express yourself more clearly. Take time to listen. Developing better listening skills as well as techniques for speaking the language of those with the Navigator or Adventurer creative talent can help you translate your vision into a reality that others can understand. Count to 10 before you speak. Give others time to talk. Develop patience, appreciation, and respect for the contributions of other creative talents. Having different creative talents on a team will result in different ways of presenting data and articulating thoughts. You may find gaps in plans that you hadn't even considered. Be careful not to belittle others' ideas or dismiss them too quickly, or make erroneous assumptions about their resistance to change. You can squelch exploration of conflicting opinions without even knowing it. Recognize that you can get carried away with ideas and possibilities. You need the assistance of others to be brought down to earth and to help you see details, choose among options, and accept the consequences of your ideas.

To stretch and grow your creative results and contributions even further, here are some additional strategies for Explorers:

1. Bring in partners, preferably those with different creative talents than yours. Many entrepreneurs work with partners who have complementary talents. The different talents can bring stability and structure to any effort, but especially new ventures. Such support will help your team or organization thrive. One Explorer has teamed up with a partner who can scope out in detail what needs to be done to execute his great ideas: "My partner is so skilled at defining and sequencing the tasks, he can do it three to five times faster than I ever could."

2. Get physical. Get in touch with your senses of taste, hearing, smell, touch, and sight to ground yourself. Listen to what your body is telling you. One Explorer finds that running grounds him and gives him the time he needs to reflect and organize his thinking. Another finds that "working with my hands, whether it be building a deck, painting a wall, tiling a kitchen or a bathroom, is when I do my best thinking." Said another Explorer, when asked how he gets in touch with his creativity,

> I read a book or go for a bike ride or a swim—I find these activities relaxing both physically and mentally and find that both reading and sport prompt me to begin to think more creatively, certainly less linearly. As I read, I am noticing the meaning of the text and experimenting with applying the beliefs, actions, models, attitudes, and story lines that appear in the text to real situations in my life . . . new perspectives leading to new meaning. The sport is more about being in touch with myself and clearing my mind from the clutter of external noise.

3. Consider the biases of your auxiliary talent. Your auxiliary talent can lead to some blocks to your creative contribution. With the Inventor's talent, you may overlook political and people issues. You may not see that individuals involved in a change initiative can have legitimate reasons to resist. You may not take the time to praise or connect with the individuals affected. Instead, you may be focusing on competence, achievement, and creating something new. Having the Poet as your auxiliary talent, on the other hand, can cause you to focus on your own values and to be more concerned with harmony and cooperation. You may end up generating positive, confirming alternatives or alternatives that you believe people want. Paying attention to and compensating for these biases will enhance your creative contribution.

Review the chapter on the Inventor (Chapter 8) or the Poet (Chapter 10) for more information on blocks, barriers, and strategies for further developing your auxiliary talent.

4. Learn more about change and how to manage it effectively. Take courses in change-management strategies or read books on the subject.[11] Such study can help you understand the different roles in a change initiative and the steps needed for a change to take hold or for resistance to be overcome. Make sure that you consider such issues as the following:

- What do other team members need to get through this change?

- What does the organization need to implement this change?

- Who is going to take care of business while the change is being implemented?

- How do we bring in stability after the change has been made?

5. Develop an appreciation for the past. Explorers tend at times to discount the past and be impatient with those who cling to it and resist moving on. Yet the past can have incredible value. One possibility for learning to appreciate and value the past is to spend more time in historical hobbies. You may find historical research or collecting fine things restful and restorative. This interest in facts and historical data can help you stay grounded and put your creativity to even greater use.[12]

6. Take time to study and research the details. Because your insights and "aha's" often lack evidence in facts and reality, your creativity can benefit from delving into details. The CEO of the training company, for example, commented on how getting into the detail and doing research triggered new ideas and unexpected ways to significantly save on telephone expenses. Study and research into the facts can help Explorers get to their unconscious, an even richer source of imagination. Said one Explorer, "The nitty-gritty can be a jumping point for more ideation." Take a course in aesthetics to improve your skills at observation of sensory details. Check out the chapters on the Navigator (Chapter 4) and Adventurer (Chapter 3) for more tools and techniques.

HOW YOU CAN HELP AN EXPLORER

If you work with Explorers, there are several steps you can take to maximize their creative contributions to the organization:

1. Make sure that they have the right environment. Explorers need a lot of freedom and variety. Since a bureaucratic structure can seriously impact their creativity, they need to find the right environment. They may have to leave certain workplaces where there are too many constraints or where their contributions are not appreciated.

2. Help them with timing issues. Explorers can contribute a great deal through their sometimes off-the-wall ideas. However, they have to

EXPLORER	Maximizing Their Contributions

- Make sure that they have the right environment
- Help them with timing issues
- Assist them in developing sensitivity to others
- Set goals and objectives
- Explore the facts with them
- Make sure that they take time to reflect before moving on
- Help them find balance between the personal and professional worlds so that they don't burn out too quickly
- Recognize signs of stress

be sensitive to the fact that the culture of the organization may not always appreciate their talent. In organizations where those in charge tend to make most of the decisions, the constant speculation and idea generation of an Explorer team leader can cause confusion on a team. Explorers may be only throwing out ideas, but their colleagues might assume that those ideas are decisions to be acted on. Explorers may want to preface meetings with a disclaimer about their ideas not being decisions, but rather just explorations of possibilities.

3. Assist them in developing sensitivity to others. Encourage the development of their listening skills. Explorers can benefit by refraining from responding, by listening to others, and by letting others take the lead. Doing so can increase the involvement of all team members and can improve the variety of ideas and the creativeness of the solutions.

4. Set goals and objectives. Mutually agreed-on boundaries may be needed for their efforts so that they don't lose sight of what they are working on and don't get carried away. Such boundaries can help channel and conserve their energy and enthusiasm. Agree on priorities and mutually establish regular times for progress checks. Work on a mutually acceptable project-management approach, with appropriate milestones and decision points. Help them think through their plans and estimates for activities. Ask them how they arrived at their estimates. Meet with them regularly to review the plan and progress on deliverables. To avoid having these sessions appear to be control points, structure them as brainstorming sessions around issues and concerns.

5. Explore the facts with them. Encourage Explorers to use specific, concrete facts in reports. Help them with presentations that provide structured, step-by-step discussions of information. Question Explorers to be sure that they have considered the facts. Ask them sensation-type questions such as "What are the facts that support your ideas?" and "What does the research tell us?" Work with their ideas to ground them.

6. Make sure that they take time to reflect before moving on. Encourage Explorers to schedule time between meetings to process what went on in the meeting and to write down notes about the details of the meeting. Ask questions that cause them to process their reactions, such as "What are the implications of the results?" and "How might we do things differently the next time?"

7. Help them find balance between the personal and professional worlds so that they don't burn out too quickly. Teach Explorers how to deal with boundaries. Suggest that they have scripts available to deal with constant interruptions, such as "I am working on a project that requires my full concentration. Can we schedule a time to meet later today?"

8. Recognize signs of stress. When Explorers get stressed, they may get overwhelmed with details and lose their ability to generate possibilities. They may experience physical exhaustion and even start to strangely distort the challenge or problem or turn negative. Suggest that they take a time-out, get some physical exercise, and find an excuse to reflect, to return to their normal creative self.[13]

SUMMARY

Explorers add energy and enthusiasm to any effort. Without an Explorer, the team would miss patterns, trends, and future possibilities. It might have a harder time generating many options and alternatives. Explorers are creative in the way they discover and generate new and different ideas. They have great instincts for new trends and connections. They provide passion, possibility thinking, and inspiration and will test the limits of the team's imagination. They can be wonderful catalysts for change and innovation. By developing their abilities to organize and execute and by teaming with and appreciating others with different talents, Explorers can be even more effectively creative.

SELF-ASSESSMENT

How does this talent impact my life as a dominant or auxiliary talent?

_____

_____

_____

If this is not my dominant or auxiliary talent, how do I demonstrate the use of this talent?

_____

_____

_____

How could I have used this talent in the past?

_____

_____

_____

How can I use this talent in the future?

_____

_____

_____

What do I need to do to better manage an Explorer team member?

_____

_____

_____

CHAPTER SIX

THE VISIONARY

INTJ: AUXILIARY CREATIVE TALENT–PILOT

INFJ: AUXILIARY CREATIVE TALENT–HARMONIZER

**Visionaries have bold, heroic minds and far-reaching imagination.
They are passionate for grand, uncommon ideals.[1]**

Visionaries make many important contributions with their creative talent, from both a personal and a process point of view. They tend to be independent systems thinkers who are curious, flexible, and divergent. They have an unusual way of organizing information to help shift mind-sets. They can rearrange and restructure this information in many different ways. As one said, "I am always looking for connections and interesting insights. I constantly scan the environment and look for context to understand trends and innovations." Visionaries believe that changing frames of mind can change the world.[2]

Visionaries have an uncanny ability to predict the future and can thus provide very unusual, quite futuristic perspectives on a problem. They can pick up subtle clues and nuances before others notice them. This remarkable sense for the future can have an almost mystical quality to it. Visionaries seem to have antennae to detect trends that others cannot see. This is a critical capability for leaders in any size organization or any industry in this rapidly changing world. One Visionary defined this ability as being able to "see around the corner." When asked to describe their ability, Visionaries talk about seeing images that are very hard to describe. As one executive director with the Visionary talent put it, "I can be listening to the radio in the car, to one of the radio hosts who uses quirky quotes and sayings. I've found several of these quotes 'just in time' for a speech I'm giving. It's as if a certain wavelength is open, and I'm receiving just when I need to." Another Visionary said, "I feel comfortable with things that I can't touch, see, or feel." Visionaries have been compared to prophets or seers because of their "uncanny capacity for smelling out the future, the not-yet-manifest possibilities of a situation."[3]

Their introspective nature and independence promote this inner insight and analysis. Visionaries privately see possibilities and notice complex patterns and connections. Their inner resources provide them with ingenious visions of the future that could be. While keeping a long-range perspective, they can imagine multiple possibilities. One Visionary talked about his capability to see things graphically as jigsaw puzzles: "Three-dimensional [imaging] does not upset my stomach or my mind-set. I can work in four dimensions, in five dimensions, in n dimensions. That's how I put processes together."

Because they have broad interests and tend to read a lot from many different fields, they end up with a variety of sources of inspiration and multidisciplinary perspectives. After picking up a piece of information in the external world, Visionaries spend time internally searching out new angles for viewing, interpreting, and understanding the situation. Flashes from their unconscious provide them with unusual and powerful perspectives and inspiration for new solutions and an unhampered view of the possibilities. They often have no idea where these flashes of inspiration come from. As one leader reflecting the Visionary talent put it, "I don't know where I get my ideas. They just come. They get stimulated. . . . An idea that gets input through my eyes and ears bounces around against something in there, and out comes something else . . . sometimes it's blind alleys, sometimes not." One business leader describes her experience with this talent:

> I see relationships among actions, images, and events that are unusual or off-kilter or maybe even eccentric. [When I needed to come up with a design for a costume or for a new quilt] I saw a jester's costume in a *Gray's Anatomy* engraving and abstract quilting patterns in sidewalk cracks. I tend to be able to put together seemingly unrelated comments and events to form an outlook that generally turns out to be accurate. This process is usually very subtle, as are the outcomes.

VISIONARY	Results and Contributions

- Provocative questions that challenge the group to find profound answers and big solutions
- "Incasting" (versus forecasting)—working back from the future to develop plans
- New designs and solutions through unusual connections
- Imagination full of hard-to-describe images and futuristic possibilities
- Multidisciplined perspectives
- Penetrating, far-reaching insights into future trends
- Ability to integrate, synthesize, and move the group forward

Their private, inner sorting through of images, connections, and associations can make Visionaries at times appear to be disconnected from the external world. They are focusing on their own inner knowing, trying to find the meaning behind the words. Internally, they are reframing their perspectives and developing and elaborating theories. As one Visionary described her experience, "When I consider the future, I practice counterintuitive thinking. I look at what the reality is, what the prevailing wisdom is, then I will see if I agree or whether I choose to make it a different world." Because these insights and ideas are often arrived at through internal processing, Visionaries are seen as independent thinkers who have an extraordinary breadth and depth of knowledge.

Visionaries share their thoughts and ideas when they are well developed. Their stories and conversations focus more on possibilities, implications, and the future. There are many hidden meanings, patterns, trends, and connections with data from other times, places, and sources. They cover broad themes, using speculation and symbols. Their language is more general and indirect and may be full of metaphors and unusual terms. Their imagination is usually full of hard-to-describe mental pictures, strange themes, and futuristic connections.

Visionaries have a talent for making the complex simple. They often can see through a situation and provide insightful analyses. They can cut through extraneous data to focus on the essential meaning of complex, confusing situations. A Visionary pays attention to social, technological, economic, ecological, and political trends. Visionaries are great at asking tough questions about the future, questions such as the following:[4]

- How will the industry evolve and change over the next three to seven years? Could these same events happen this year or next?

- What global trends will affect the business?

- With the sky as the limit, what new approaches can we take?

- What can we do that's new and different?

- What business are we really in? What business should we be in?

- Who are our customers, and what do they want?

- How will all the new technologies affect us?

- What might the competition do over the same time frame? What should we do?

- If we were the competition, how would we counter our moves?

- What is our competitive edge? Why?

- Why are we doing what we're doing? Should we rethink that strategy?

The result of these questions for Visionaries is an ability to "incast." Visionaries assume that a major transition has taken place or a goal has been achieved. They can then work backward to deduce the events that might have led to it. Incasting is "different from forecasting, which involves looking at current events and speculating on where they might lead. It's also different from predicting—which is nearly impossible."[5] One CEO described his father, clearly a Visionary, as he incasted:

> To me, people who can look behind the picture and really figure out another angle, to see if there is something else there, are really creative. Most people think clockwise, but my father thought counterclockwise. He'd have solutions that made people say, "Well, that's the craziest thing I ever heard." Then he'd go through and explain the whole thing back to where they were so they could understand.

Because of their focus on the future, Visionaries welcome change. Without it they can easily get bored. They look forward to new assignments, with more challenging and complicated problems to stretch their skills and abilities. A management consultant for nonprofit organizations has taken on many projects outside his work. At various points in his life, he has run a farm that produced exotic fruits and vegetables, raised sheep for wool, and learned to cane chairs in order to keep his life interesting.

Visionaries' auxiliary extraverted decision-making talent of the Pilot or the Harmonizer influences the type of data and information Visionaries take in, the questions they ask, and the process they use to make sense of and to share that information. If their auxiliary talent is that of the Pilot, Visionaries ask more objective questions and focus on ideas and concepts. They relate with others through discussing ideas and theories about how things work. They constantly come up with and test new ideas about reality. They connect knowledge from a variety of different fields. Said one Visionary with the Pilot auxiliary talent, "I have a knack for and have fun doing what I call warehouse-type things. Organizing-type challenges. How do you put these types of things into [something orderly]? How do you clean up your cellar and make it look like it makes sense?" With this combination of talents, Visionaries tend to focus on the tangible benefits of a change initiative in order to move it forward.

If their auxiliary talent is that of the Harmonizer, Visionaries ask questions that focus more on people. Their interests lie in envisioning a world full of potential for all who inhabit it. They have more concerns about rectifying injustices and inequities, and the focus of their attention is on personal growth and finding meaning in the world. These Visionaries use their skills and abilities to help find common ground among different perspectives of the future. They champion a cause, finding roles for everyone.[6] Their focus is on the more intangible benefits of a change initiative, such as heightened employee morale or improved community contribution.

With either auxiliary talent, Visionaries are very interested in new ways of organizing, integrating, and synthesizing knowledge. Given their zeal for new information, they are comfortable adjusting or reworking old theories to accommodate new data.[7] For Visionaries, there are many ways to view a situation. They are capable of dealing with the complexities of the world. These skills can be very valuable to a team trying to make sense out of ambiguous challenges. The consultant to nonprofit organizations talked about his ability to see where the group needs to go. He can then help them wander around a bit to get there.

Possible examples of individuals with this talent are Bill Gates of Microsoft and Mary Baker Eddy, a pioneer in the field of mind–body medicine, leader of a worldwide church, and founder of the *Christian Science Monitor*. Another example might be Mary Lyon, who, in having the vision to establish Mount Holyoke College in 1837, transformed the course of women's education in the United States.

Visionaries can bring much to a group effort. Through their penetrating insights and unusual perspectives, they can challenge the group's imagination to see beyond normal boundaries. From the Visionary's perspective, anything is possible and anything can be improved. They may refuse to abide by established rules. They are always looking for better solutions and are always searching out new angles and associations for insight and understanding. Visionaries like to take especially big leaps. One said, "I don't like doing things that give you ten or fifteen percent return. I like things that take something and cut it by a factor of twenty or thirty." They are willing to pursue giant ideas and opportunities, even if they are unpopular and unconventional.

In addition to sharing their insights, Visionaries also help a team in supporting its creative processes. As a project is initiated, Visionaries help the team create a bold vision and a broad-brush plan to make the vision work. They make sure that the vision is inspiring, clear, and compelling. As the project unfolds, they keep the team challenged in its thinking, making sure that it finds bold solutions and builds off everyone's ideas. They can trust their processes to bring out the collective wisdom of the group. They also draw on people and experiences from outside the industry to solve problems in new ways. They propose outrageous goals to force the team to think unconventionally about the challenge.

They can also help the team achieve its objectives. Their auxiliary talent is usually well developed since they need it to manage in the external world. Visionaries can thus be very goal directed and driven in the world external to them. They will often pursue a goal despite resistance. They rarely take no for an answer. For them, a difficult challenge translates into a wonderful opportunity.[8]

OBSTACLES

As with all of the creative talents, several forces can block Visionaries' creativity. These blocks include their neglect of facts, their private nature,

VISIONARY	Blocks to Optimal Creativity

- Neglect of relevant facts and details about people and things
- Constant pursuit of new ideas
- Perfectionism and need for mastery
- Overly independent and private
- Biases of their auxiliary talent to certain types of data
- Reluctance to share ideas and information
- Making the simple overcomplex
- Possible single-mindedness and tunnel vision
- Stubbornness and rebelliousness
- Not taking care of themselves

and possible stubbornness. After reviewing some of the key blocks, you will find strategies for overcoming them in the next sections.

A Visionary's picture of the future may neglect everyday details and sensibilities. This bias may result in a challenging concept or vision of the future, but it can also lack realism and grounding. In addition, Visionaries may ignore details and facts that don't fit in with their theories. They may draw conclusions based on an appreciation of alternatives that are really just coincidental.

Their dominant creative talent is a perceiving one. If their auxiliary extraverted decision-making talent is not well developed, they may be forever caught up in the search for new ideas and possibilities. Given all the information that is available today, Visionaries may lose focus or get overwhelmed. It may be hard for them to keep their many ideas, images, and thoughts around for long. They may get caught up in feeling that they never have enough information and need to pursue a never-ending supply. Instead of moving toward ideas that can be acted on, they may prefer to build the perfect theory and master it.

Their auxiliary talent can also cause problems in defining the facts and possibilities that they recognize. If it's the Pilot talent, they may pay attention only to quantitative information, ignoring people issues as they drive forward to achieve results. If it's the Harmonizer talent, they may focus too much on people issues and a concern for harmony and consensus over action.

Since they at times find self-expression difficult, Visionaries may appear to be private, fiercely independent, intense, and even mysterious. They identify problems, patterns, and trends; reframe problems; and generate alternatives—all in their head. This privacy and independence can be frustrating to those who expect them to share their thoughts and processes. Often Visionaries don't communicate their ideas and creative insights until they have spent much time on their own, mulling them over. In fact, they may have a hard time brainstorming in a group session or sharing their ideas. They may need to listen and then let the ideas incubate before they can come up with unusual connections or uncommon linkages with other concepts from far-reaching sources. For these reasons, their involvement with the team in developing new ideas may often be limited.

Their new perspectives and visions may be hard for others to understand. One reason for this difficulty is that their ideas are often far ahead of their time. Another reason is that they are so comfortable with complexity that they tend to overwork and overanalyze even simple ideas so that they become more complex than they need to be. A third reason is that they may have a hard time expressing their thoughts. These inner images have to be converted into verbal or visual form. This transition is sometimes hard for Visionaries to make since the images are often vague and indescribable. Explaining where they come from may be even harder.

In addition, a Visionary's process of coming up with the vision and then figuring out how to articulate it can lead to confidence and even single-mindedness about the validity and relevance of that vision. Their perspectives can be so future oriented, and they can form them so quickly and so privately, that they may forget that others need time to move into that future. When they do articulate their carefully worked-out ideas, Visionaries may appear rigid, intractable, or arbitrary in their decisions. Moreover, they may express their views directly and forcefully and appear less willing to work with the group to solve a problem. Another reason for possible rigidity is, according to one Visionary,

> because I make elaborate interconnections and mull them over internally for a long time. If I talk about them and someone questions them, it feels as if the whole structure or model is unraveling. If one element is questioned, the whole conceptualization needs to be reconfigured. Yikes!

Visionaries may also experience emotional blocks that cause problems for their creativity. These blocks occur when Visionaries feel overwhelmed by details, especially unfamiliar ones; if unexpected events interrupt planned activities; or if they spend too much time relating in the external world. Such stressors may cause Visionaries to lose their long-term, global perspective. Their usually broad perspectives may assume a narrow, limited focus. They tend to make little mistakes that take on importance out of proportion to their impact. They may start to live in a more primitively instinctive and intemperate fashion. They may become dependent on sense impressions, perhaps even overindulging in sensual pleasures, such as eating, sleeping, exercising, and watching reruns of old movies.[9]

Such stress may cause them to take on an adversarial attitude toward the outer world. They may become less willing to contribute. The immediate reality of the outer world may start to spell difficulty and danger. They may become negative and begin to look for obstacles and problems. Anticipating the worst can bring anger, distrust, and blame. They may become unreasonable, totally irrational, closed minded, and impatient. They may feel vulnerable. They may withdraw and hide, unable and unwilling to communicate with anyone. They may gloss over missing details and become defensive if they overlook an important fact.[10] All these behaviors will seriously impede a Visionary's creative contribution.

BOOSTERS

Depending on their particular situation, there are several steps Visionaries can take to gain maximum benefit from their creative talent and improve the effectiveness of their creativity:

1. Play to your strengths. Insist that the team spend time on collecting information, generating ideas, taking a big-picture view, and exploring different, unusual alternatives and possibilities. Develop your insight by keeping track of your hunches and what happens to them. Learn to trust that insight, particularly if it has proven to be accurate over the years.

2. Develop greater self-awareness. Making a candid assessment of your strengths and areas that need your attention as a creative individual is a critical step toward greater self-awareness and creativity. Be honest with yourself about blocks and barriers from your experiences, knowledge, and creative talents. Ask for and listen carefully to feedback from colleagues, friends, and family about your talents and what might be

VISIONARY	Enhancing Your Creative Talent

- Play to your strengths
- Develop greater self-awareness
- Find the right creativity tools and techniques
- Be sure to capture your ideas
- Review and reflect on those ideas
- Use your auxiliary talent to help focus, to get outside your head, and to turn ideas and possibilities into reality
- Use your auxiliary talent to connect with people and share ideas
- Know and learn your creative process
- Appreciate the team
- Limit your search for information

getting in the way. Be clear about what might be keeping you from being your creative best and making your greatest contributions.

3. Find the right creativity tools and techniques. Some of the creativity tools and techniques that work especially well with this talent include the following:

- Creative visualization of the ideal final solution

- Guided imagery

- Keeping a dream journal

- Making time to meditate or to take long walks

- Metaphors, associations, and analogies to generate new ideas through connections with seemingly unrelated pictures, randomly selected words, and catalog items

- The reflective brainwriting tool, in which team members write down their ideas, share them, and build on the ideas of others in silence

- The active brainwalking technique,[11] in which ideas are posted on the walls and team members walk around in silence building on the posted ideas

4. Be sure to capture your ideas. As a Visionary, you tend to generate many great ideas at unexpected moments, so you need ways to capture your thoughts. One Visionary said, "I will start thinking about the
problem, maybe scribble a few things on paper, then let my mind wander. Maybe also talk to a few people whose ideas I respect." Another
Visionary describes her process:

> I use a large whiteboard where I can identify the big chunks of the overall
> picture. I draw the chunks in cloudlike forms and see the natural pattern of
> the thoughts. I move them around until the natural order emerges. Then I
> identify the main pieces of each chunk. If necessary I reduce that further
> with more detail. I cannot effectively begin until I see the big picture and
> the main chunks. I sometimes draw a picture of the outcome I want. I find
> that I become very attached to the overall picture and usually transfer the
> big picture to a large piece of paper, date it, and keep it in a file. It is quite
> satisfying to revisit those pictures or maps of my process years later.

One executive reflecting the Visionary talent discussed how thoughts
just pop into her head, without her putting them there. "When I get that
feeling that pushes up to my head, I sometimes get up in the middle of
the night and write a note. Or I'll be driving down the road, and I'll call
my voice mail to put a message on my machine because I'm afraid I'll forget it."

An important source of new ideas for Visionaries is their dreams.
Taking a dream class to be able to analyze your dreams or reading books
on dream interpretation can help you access this very vivid source of
imaginative ideas. Learning to remember them and write them down is
key.[12]

5. Review and reflect on those ideas. The following comment from
a nonprofit organization's executive director incorporates another important strategy for Visionaries: take time to revisit ideas—both your own
and those of others—to generate new perspectives:

> I'm most creative at conferences where I'm just listening and open to new
> ideas. Then miraculously, I'll hear something and all kinds of "aha" and "syn-
> ergies" pop into my head. I've learned I have to write them down in the
> moment or I lose them. After I get back from the conference and reread all
> my ideas, not all are doable, but some trigger longer-term strategies and
> insights that I act on months or years later.

6. Use your auxiliary talent to help focus, to get outside your head, and to turn ideas and possibilities into reality. The auxiliary extraverted decision-making talent for Visionaries helps them function successfully in the external world, so it is usually well developed. However, if it isn't, Visionaries can lose themselves in idea collection and fail to move forward to action. You thus need to use your auxiliary talent to help you define a structure for the project and to plan out progress. Your auxiliary talent can help you organize your thoughts. Decisions about what needs to be done next can be thought through on your own or with other people. Then you can analyze, sort things out, and decide what is really important. Using your auxiliary talent to filter data and focus your attention, while recognizing its possible biases, can be very helpful in the creative process. Project-management tools and idea-selection tools, such as Nominal Group Technique, designed to help the team rank choices, narrow down a list of ideas, and reach consensus about next steps, may also be helpful for Visionaries to be more organized, and thus more effectively creative.[13]

7. Use your auxiliary talent to connect with people and share ideas. You may need to learn to communicate better and to share your thoughts and ideas so that they don't appear arbitrary. One Visionary finds it helpful to tell people, "What I am about to say won't come out fully formed. It will come out rough because I can often 'see' connections better than I can articulate them in the early stages."

Your extraverted auxiliary talent of the Harmonizer or the Pilot may also help you explain how you came to your conclusions and to sell to, collaborate with, and involve others. Your auxiliary talent may help you express your ideas more clearly, connect with people, and build bridges of understanding. Clarity and plain talk are important because they are more likely to lead to action: "You may disagree with a simple plan, but you can't claim confusion as an excuse to ignore it."[14]

If you are to achieve your goals and implement your ideas, temper your tendency to be impatient. Help team members get to a common level of understanding through giving them an opportunity to discuss and process your ideas and solutions. One Visionary, a strategic planner, knows he has to spend time working back from his goal and vision, to slow down and bring others along if he is to reach his objectives.

There are other ways to learn to connect with people. One Visionary got involved in politics because he decided he needed to repackage himself to deal with some of the interpersonal issues with which he had been struggling. Another strategy is to ask for help. Find someone you trust and share your ideas with him or her.[15]

8. Know and learn your creative process. Pressure from the outside world or from an overdeveloped auxiliary talent can encourage moving to closure and making decisions too quickly. If this is an issue for you, stop and gather data and balance the desire to come to conclusions. Learn how your process works and practice consciously accessing it. Include a step for generating all sorts of information, including the details. One Visionary indicated that she asks for time in order to allow her introverted intuition talent to have an opportunity to work. Another Visionary usually has two or three other projects in progress. If he gets stuck on one, he turns his attention to another one, all the while letting his unconscious process the issues of the first one. Another prefers to

> lie in bed thinking about what I'm going to do and make random notes until I run dry. After that I keep the paper with me as I go about my morning chores. Then I get on the computer and type up the notes and add to them. After that, I can really start humming for several hours.

A business leader, using her Visionary talent, has learned to trust her process:

> When I have a problem, or when I have a deadline and I don't know exactly what I'm going to do, I no longer dwell on it or churn on it. It just comes to me. I know it will come to me. I used to get paranoid about meeting deadlines. Now I don't even think about it. I know when the deadline is, and somehow my body just starts doing it and it gets done. So I take a lot of stress off myself. I don't stop working; I just don't worry that I'm going to miss the deadline.

9. Appreciate the team. Visionaries are usually more interested in pioneering a new road than in anything to be found along the beaten path. Consider this bias as you work with a team. Other members don't always share that approach. Additionally, building on current strengths or products can be just as creative as coming up with novel ideas. Collective work can be significantly more creative than independent work, especially when it involves cross-organizational issues. Working with a team means including others in your planning for the future and working on articulating your images in terms others can understand. You may need to be patient and restate your ideas until others understand your vision.[16] Be willing to share your ideas even if they are not fully developed. Be sure that others understand that you really are open to changing your conclusions when you receive contradictory information.

10. Limit your search for information. With an overwhelming drive to seek the perfect piece of information or the perfect way to express a thought, you may get lost. Set limits on your search for information. Be realistic as you set expectations about your performance. Learn to celebrate little accomplishments. Recognize that making mistakes is part of the human condition. Risk sharing your thoughts even if they are not perfectly formulated. Otherwise, the world or the team might not benefit from your contribution.

To stretch and grow your creative results and contributions even further, here are some additional strategies for Visionaries:

1. Get and stay centered. Visionaries need space to deal with emotions and feelings of imperfection and to get out of their head. They need to be centered to be creative. Submerging yourself in peaceful, quiet, natural surroundings; getting into nature; lightening your schedule; and taking time out—all are strategies that can help. You might even take a nap, exercise, or retreat to your garden. As one Visionary said, "I like to go to the seaside, allow 'dreaming time,' go for a walk, be with nature, or brainstorm with others to match my 'inner knowing.'" Another plays the piano or does anything sensual to relax in order to get in touch with her creativity. One said, "I find that my creativity is enhanced by sleeping on and thinking [about] a variety of approaches to a given problem. Extensive conversations with one or two other people occasionally help."

2. Address the details. In their scenario building of the future, Visionaries need to consider the details in the current reality that can impact their plans. Their ideas, although intuitively correct, may need to be tested against reality. Working with people with the Adventurer's or Navigator's talent can help fill in the details. Getting involved with details in the here and now can actually help you get in touch with your unconscious. Collecting data and grounding your visions is extremely powerful.[17] Tools recommended for the Adventurer or the Navigator are also excellent techniques for Visionaries to use to enhance their creative contributions and get in touch with their unconscious. For example, Sensanation, a technique designed to explore each one of the senses, can produce surprising insights.[18]

3. Consider the biases of your auxiliary talent. Your auxiliary talent can also lead to some possible blocks to your creative contribution. With the Pilot's talent, you may overlook the impact on people of a change initiative or innovation. You may not see that individuals involved can have legitimate reasons to object. You may not take the time to praise or connect with the individuals affected. Instead, you may be focusing on competence, achievement, and creating something new.

With the Harmonizer as your auxiliary talent, you may also run into trouble. This combination can cause you to worry so much about harmony and cooperation that you lose sight of what needs to be done. You may end up generating very positive, confirming alternatives or alternatives that you think people want. Paying attention to and compensating for these biases will enhance your creative contribution.

Review the chapter on the Pilot (Chapter 7) or the Harmonizer (Chapter 9) for more information on blocks, barriers, and strategies for further developing your auxiliary talent.

4. Pay attention to your health. Visionaries may not pay too much attention to their physical and emotional health since they spend so much time inside themselves. You thus need to discover how to bring that aspect of your life back into balance as well. One executive director with this talent indicated that she likes to go to a comfy bookstore to read or to play with her four-year-old daughter: "When I'm down at her eye level and see the world from her point of view, I'm amazed at how joyful and creative I feel." Learning to live in the moment, physical exercise, and breathing practices all can help. Taking an "artist's date,"[19] such as going to a museum, visiting a craft store, or taking a class in a new hobby, can also be helpful.

5. Reframe conflict. Visionaries love to explore ideas; such exploration can lead to conflict. Seeing conflict as part of the creative process can help you overcome any reluctance to face unpleasant or tough situations that might cause potentially negative confrontation with others. Learning to manage conflict creatively is particularly helpful for those with the Harmonizer auxiliary talent.

HOW YOU CAN HELP A VISIONARY

If you work with Visionaries, there are several steps you can take to maximize their creative contributions to the organization:

1. Structure the right environment. One strategy to bring out the best in Visionaries is to make sure that they are working in an environment where they are appreciated and that works for them. Said one Visionary working in such an environment, "If you can produce creative things, the system gives you support. People like to see creative output. As long as you produce neat stuff, they like you. They like to use you. They want to use you. It's a self-nurturing thing that brings you further into the goal." Make sure that Visionaries have the right amount of freedom and variety in their work to keep them challenged.

2. Provide focus and limits. At the same time, you may need to provide Visionaries with focus. As one Visionary commented, "I like edges to my sandbox. Then I know I can play within them." Agree on deadlines for data collection and be sure a project-management process is in place. Review progress against the plan to be sure that Visionaries are limiting their search for more data and moving forward on deliverables.

3. Provide space and time. Find ways for Visionaries to have private time and space for working most effectively. If this is not possible in the work space, then explore ways to help them create the reflective time they need (by working out of the home, using white noise, etc.).

4. Work with their ideas to ground them. Question Visionaries to be sure that they have considered the facts. Encourage them to use specific, concrete facts in reports. Help them with presentations that provide step-by-step discussion of information.

5. Help them share their thoughts and ideas. Encourage Visionaries to share what's on their mind and what they are working on. Ask them how they came to their conclusions. Use open-ended questions that get them talking. Promote discussions with team members who have different talents and different perspectives. Encourage them to incorporate others into their process in the early stages. Make sure that they are filling in the steps and pieces necessary to go from current reality to their vision.

VISIONARY	Maximizing Their Contributions

- Structure the right environment
- Provide focus and limits
- Provide space and time
- Work with their ideas to ground them
- Help them share their thoughts and ideas
- Help them with managing conflict
- Encourage the use of their decision-making talent
- Work on development plans
- Encourage time-outs and play

6. Help them with managing conflict. Help Visionaries see the inevitable clash of ideas that comes with diversity of perspectives as only adding to the quality of the final solution. Make sure that they don't shy away from such clashes. Encourage them to share their ideas early on in the problem-solving process to minimize surprises. In dealing with conflict, political challenges, and the fallout from change, Visionaries with a Pilot auxiliary talent may also need help to ensure that they are considering people issues.

7. Encourage the use of their decision-making talent. Work with them to carefully plan out the steps needed to reach their visions. Help them sort through the issues that can get in the way of success and mutually figure out strategies for dealing with those issues.

8. Work on development plans. Mutually agree on courses, workshops, and self-study that will help Visionaries better communicate and develop other skills to make them more effectively creative. Include these plans in their performance evaluation.

9. Encourage time-outs and play. When you notice that Visionaries are getting bogged down in the facts or otherwise stressed, encourage them to take a break or to go for a walk. You can also help by asking, "In what other ways can we look at this?"

SUMMARY

The Visionary's creative talent brings vision and far-reaching imagination to any challenge or problem. It allows the team to avoid staying stuck with too narrow boundaries. The Visionary looks at long-range trends and patterns. The Visionary talent gives the team an eye to the future and an uncanny sense of what can possibly happen. These ideas and images are based on a variety of known data from many different sources and data they often don't know how they know. Visionaries add much to the creativity of the organization through their insight into the future and their unusual perspectives and connections. Further developing the ability to effectively communicate ideas and to work with details and a group will heighten a Visionary's creative contributions at work.

SELF-ASSESSMENT

How does this talent impact my life as a dominant or auxiliary talent?

_____

_____

_____

If this is not my dominant or auxiliary talent, how do I demonstrate the use of this talent?

_____

_____

_____

How could I have used this talent in the past?

_____

_____

_____

How can I use this talent in the future?

_____

_____

_____

What do I need to do to better manage a Visionary team member?

_____

_____

_____

CHAPTER SEVEN

THE PILOT

ESTJ: AUXILIARY CREATIVE TALENT—NAVIGATOR

ENTJ: AUXILIARY CREATIVE TALENT—VISIONARY

The Pilot steers the ship through difficult waters and develops strategies to guide it toward new lands.

Pilots have many important creative contributions to make at work. A Pilot is a take-charge type of person. Through their organizational skills, Pilots make sure that what needs to happen will happen. One Pilot described her creative talent as "moving things ahead in a different way." Pilots tend to be proactive and action oriented. Part of their ability to get things done is creating excitement on the team and driving it forward with a passion. They add energy to the work atmosphere, so much so that their clients and associates can have a hard time keeping up with their rapid pace and high energy.

Pilots are adept at organizing projects and people, and they love to plan. They usually have an agenda for their meetings. They like to first define goals, objectives and priorities, key deliverables, and roles and responsibilities. They figure out the logical steps of what needs to be done first, then second, all the way to completion. They break the problem down into logical, manageable pieces. Their plans have regular checkpoints; they use checklists. Pilots often use a structured problem-solving approach, decision trees, or cost–benefit analysis tools to fortify their conclusions. They make sure that the team stays focused on those goals and priorities as they pursue creative solutions to problems and challenges.

PILOT	Results and Contributions

- Clarification of goals and responsibilities on projects and change initiatives
- High-energy team leadership
- New and different strategies
- Innovative organizational designs
- Making things happen through inventive, tough-minded problem solving
- Logical categorization of ideas and issues
- Focus on progress, improvement, efficiency, productivity, and results in change initiatives
- Thoughtful questions and challenges to conventional thinking

Pilots are usually very outgoing and articulate. They enjoy talking and express themselves very well. In fact, at times they can be outspoken as they openly share their concerns and questions. Their stories and conversations are usually brief and to the point, organized and analytical, and grammatically and stylistically correct. The goal of the story or conversation is to explain and teach.

The Pilot's creative talent provides logical frameworks and formulas to discover, analyze, and solve the problems encountered in the external world. Pilots are creative in the way they take a decisive, objective, and tough-minded problem-solving approach to their work and the world around them. The questions they tend to ask during creative problem solving illustrate their logical approach. These include the following:

- What's our charter?

- Do we know the purpose of our team and what we want to accomplish?

- What are the roles and responsibilities?

- Where are the boundaries of the challenge? How are we going to go about developing strategies?

- Which strategic planning model will work best here?

- What system will we use to evaluate the pros and cons and consequences?

- How do we want to work together?

- How can we start to collect information?

The approach outlined by a minister with this talent is a typical way of creatively addressing a problem:

> I would want to know a time frame. . . . I would want to set up a plan to guide our efforts. I would not be opposed to some of the ideas related to knowing the purpose and values, but I would want us to move on without getting bogged down in only ideas. . . . I need to take action and to have direction. . . . I find that in problem-solving situations I focus more on the goal or outcome than on the process. I enjoy brainstorming ideas and gathering perspectives, but a limit needs to be imposed so action plans can be implemented.

Pilots tend to be skilled at defining a creative strategy for moving forward and providing the direction and a sense of urgency. Part of a Pilot's strategy may include careful experimentation. Reflecting the Pilot talent, a CEO of a financial services organization said, "You try things, but don't risk a lot of money. And so if they fail, you haven't lost much. And while you're trying them, you run them like an investment. Pay attention to the expense and keep learning." He went on to add: "First, you have to understand the lay of the land and fashion a strategy, and then you have to implement the strategy. See what the reaction is. Get feedback. . . . It's free form . . . but everything is conscious."

One strength of the Pilot that can significantly help the creativity of the organization is the ability to synthesize information to propose new combinations and new ways of looking at the situation. This ability to analyze and synthesize is built on a solid knowledge base; Pilots bring expertise to the effort. Said one manufacturing executive with a Pilot talent,

> One of my favorite sayings is the one from Pasteur: "Chance favors the prepared mind." You really need to do your homework and understand your business. If you're always thinking about where it might be, you recognize the opportunity when it comes along, and you seize it. I think that's what creative thinking is all about. It's breaking everything down into categories and doing analogies and classification.

At their best, Pilots excel at clarifying what the real issues and conflicts are, defining terms to make sure that the real confusion isn't over definitions. They compare and contrast, separate the issues into logical groups, categorize, and then find the key differences. Their goal is improvement and progress. Pilots frequently ask, "How can we do this better?" They may be very critical and find all sorts of gaps in plans or analysis. They focus their attention on causes and effects analyzing a situation with "if this, then that"–type thinking. They are thus especially helpful in the problem-definition, fact-finding, planning, and implementation phases of projects. They pick up the nonsequiturs, the gaps in the knowledge, the flaws in the reasoning, and the problems with assumptions. They keep the team honest in its analysis.

The auxiliary talent of Pilots influences the type of data they use for their arguments, questions, and decisions. They may have the introverted data-collecting talent of either the Navigator or the Visionary as their auxiliary talent to balance their extraverted decision-making Pilot talent. When the Navigator is their auxiliary talent, the facts that hit their radar screen will be detailed, concrete, and specific. With this combination, Pilots are deliberate, practical, and systematic. Their focus is on standard operating procedures and rules to ensure appropriate and careful analysis of the data. They want factual documentation and clear-cut rationales. Once they have determined what needs to be done, they may become inventive and resourceful in the way they manage the implementation of the effort and achieve immediate, visible, and tangible results.

With an auxiliary talent of the Visionary, Pilots are more directed at what *could be* than at *what is*. Such Pilots tend to focus on the future and taking a strategic, systemwide view of the problem or situation. They tend to continually look at possibilities and challenges beyond the present, obvious, or known. They are intellectually curious about new ideas and tolerant of theory. They have a taste for more complex problems, as well as insight, vision, and concern for long-range possibilities and consequences. One executive with this combination said,

> I need lots of sources of expertise, people from different venues, diverse reading. I am not a detail person. . . . I have to force myself to make sure I go deep enough that I feel comfortable. I much prefer to get all the data, the inputs, and ideas, and then I'm very good at synthesizing, cutting through, and even rearranging it all in a creative way.

With either auxiliary talent, Pilots are skilled at breaking down complex situations into their important parts to make them more understandable and manageable. One Pilot describes his version of a creative manager as one who knows the business well enough to recognize when something has changed and whether it's a mistake or whether there really is something new that's coming in:

> Creative managers are those people who stand facing an infinite number of facts that are always going by them. They know which ones to seize and bring down. The chosen facts generally are the ones that are different from the normal pattern. Then creative managers put them into some kind of cohesive package that makes it possible to run the operation for the better.

Pilots know how to challenge a team to achieve objectives and find creative solutions. One Pilot, head of the U.S. subsidiary of a British firm, refuses to accept the word *can't* at work. Another Pilot, a top executive in a professional services firm, says, "I quite often see my role as playing devil's advocate. I'm not afraid to question conventional thinking." An entrepreneur with this talent sees himself as a strategic facilitator. He helps people organize their thoughts, think about the goal, and work to get as close to the finish line as possible. A CEO with this talent talked about the role he takes on in his manufacturing firm. He goes around asking,

> Where are we? What are we doing? Why are we doing it? How can we do it better? . . . Does this make sense in the overall picture of things? Are we really taking advantage of the things we can take advantage of? Does it make sense that we're going after this market? Is the return worth the reward? Or is the return worth the expense?

Because of their focus on improvement and progress, Pilots are usually open to change. According to one Pilot, a top executive in a bank, "I like change; I think that if you don't change, you're going to get rolled over." He added,

> I'm creative in that I always think that something can be improved. I'm never satisfied with what others have done. I am always improving on things. Even on jokes. When I retell the joke, it could be quite a bit different. There's always that level of trying to improve upon what's been done and have it fit our organization and our environment.

As one entrepreneur described his job, he indicated that his role is to keep pushing. He wants to know, "How are we looking at making this company a better place? What can we do to get bigger? What are we going to do to improve us? Where are we strong? How can we capitalize on our strengths?" According to him, "If you think things through, then you can avoid many problems. You can come up with creative solutions that are unique or different from what other people can come up with."

During change initiatives, Pilots make sure that things get done. They are adept at planning, laying out tasks, and dependencies. By charting out and carefully estimating all the pieces necessary to execute a plan, the Pilot, like the Inventor, can help the team overcome a key block to getting creative results: lack of well-thought-out plans.[1] Said one Pilot,

> My big concern is how we migrate. . . . A lot of people don't spend enough time and thought on migration. . . . That's probably a lot harder than coming up with the vision. I think I have that pragmatic side that helps get things done. . . . In implementing what I've done, I've tried to be creative. I think that it's all in the implementation; it really is. The best ideas can fail if they're not implemented properly. And there are more or less creative ways to implement.

To facilitate implementation, Pilots also bring their speaking and presentation skills to the creativity of the team. They can make logical, compelling presentations to management on the team's or the project's behalf. Their presentation will be clearly organized, with the appropriate charts and tables. They will not fear management's questions because they will have prepared themselves to logically answer any arguments.

The creativity of Pilots can be seen in innovative organizational designs and structures and new and different strategies and programs. The concept of management by objectives would be a Pilot design. The framers of the U.S. Constitution, with its focus on principles and truths, probably had this creative talent. Examples of Pilots are Alfred P. Sloan, Jr., who as president of General Motors in the 1920s redesigned its management structure, and Margaret Thatcher, prime minister of Great Britain in the 1970s and 1980s, who led a fundamental reconfiguration of social, economic, and political forces in her country.[2]

OBSTACLES

Several issues can get in the way of the Pilot's creative contribution. The possible blocks include their interpersonal skills, difficulty dealing with the qualitative side of issues, and seeing everything as a decision to be made. After reviewing some of the key blocks, you will find strategies for overcoming them in the next sections.

PILOT	Blocks to Optimal Creativity

- Dampening the creativity of others
- Direct approaches to communication and conflict
- Reliance on selected facts, jumping to conclusions too quickly, and failure to collect sufficient data
- The "tyranny of the or"
- Tendency to take charge too soon and need to control
- Critical questioning attitude
- Difficulties dealing with people issues
- Biases of their auxiliary talent to details or larger patterns
- Being overanalytical and seeing everything as a problem or a decision to be made

Pilots tend to think out loud, and that process can have a dampening effect on the creativity of the group, particularly if they sound definitive when they mean to be tentative. Such an approach, instead of opening up the discussion to more ideas and perspectives, can end up bowling people over.

In situations where multiple perspectives are being considered and evaluated, conflict may occur. Pilots often appear very certain of their ideas and opinions and thus sometimes seem to be dogmatic, or know-it-all experts who don't listen to others. They may be impatient and too quick to move on and may not let everyone have a chance to speak or participate. These types of behavior can dampen discussion of differences as creative approaches are explored.

Pilots often believe that "if you put the facts and the right information in front of them, reasonable people will come to the same conclusion." Such a statement doesn't really recognize the different ways of interpreting the same set of facts. Nor does it recognize that their creative problem-solving process can limit the data Pilots take in. Pilots tend to first define the model and then find the data. For example, in researching a project, they will define the hypothesis and then collect the data. If they are not careful, the hypothesis can frame their perspective and limit what they see.

Pilots may fail to collect a broad enough set of data in their decision-making process. They may rely too much on certain data, particularly quantifiable, objective data. They may be trapped by assumptions, at times adhering to prior beliefs about data, despite evidence to the contrary. Sometimes they rely too much on problem-solving or decision-making methods that have always worked in the past to generate alternative solutions. They tend to ascribe a regularity and structure to data and sometimes see life as a series of all-or-nothing propositions. In this case, they may become subject to the "tyranny of the or," where it is very difficult to accept paradox—two seemingly contradictory forces or ideas present at the same time—and to avoid choices that are either A or B, but not both.[3]

In addition, Pilots' auxiliary introverted data-collecting talent can interfere with their creativity. If it's the Navigator talent, Pilots may focus too closely on details and hard facts. If it's the Visionary talent, they can miss the details and pay too much attention to trends and patterns.

Pilots frequently take charge too quickly and act too forcefully, with their drive to make decisions and have things settled getting in the way of finding creative alternatives. Pilots may be so eager to make decisions that they overlook symptoms or possible new ideas. There is often pressure to adopt the first workable solution just to get the problem resolved. The motivations to be pragmatic can be stronger than the urge to be innovative.[4]

Pilots may be very focused on truth, accuracy, critical analysis, productivity, and achieving goals to the point of sometimes appearing critical, too questioning, too detached, and "cold" in their communications. They may not be inclined to spend time personally getting to know their teammates, talking about why things need to change, or finding out how the change is working. Perceived lack of time and a need for control also can get in the way of involving more people in decisions—a failure that can lead to bad results. A study of failed decisions found that "managers reported avoiding participation because of its time requirements and the seeming loss of control that results."[5] Pilots may thus find that their perceived lack of enough time can get in the way of their creativity, for many reasons. One Pilot, however, admitted,

I don't have the time to do what I want to do. But then again, if I had the time, I'm not sure that I wouldn't generate work. Creativity requires a lot of effort. I don't think it comes naturally to me. I do the things I feel very comfortable with. And maybe I am hiding from being more creative.

Although Pilots do care deeply about people and their own ideals, they may find it difficult to express these feelings. It may also be difficult for them to take people issues into account. They may miss the political issues and agendas. They are somewhat uncomfortable with sentimentality and other feelings, particularly if these emotions are part of the decision-making process. Yet people issues can be major roadblocks, as one Pilot found out in a merger when he "totally missed the people issues, the culture, the attitudes, the things that really matter."

Having to be alone for long periods of time, dealing with raw emotions, or having to use their Pilot talent to excess may cause stress. In these stressful situations, Pilots may become oversensitive, often misinterpreting comments from others as personal criticism. Their feelings may very easily get hurt. Pilots may have outbursts of emotion, which they don't know how to handle. Or they may withdraw and become very sentimental. Pilots may feel incompetent and have trouble communicating what's going on since they have a hard time talking about their own values and emotions.[6] These issues can limit their ability to come up with creative ideas and solutions.

BOOSTERS

Depending on their particular situation, there are several steps Pilots can take to gain maximum benefit from their creative talent and improve the effectiveness of their creativity:

1. Trust your strengths. Make sure that the team recognizes the need for goals, objectives, and structure. Stressing deadlines and clear analysis are important contributions to a team's creativity. Let colleagues know when you are thinking out loud as opposed to making pronouncements about final decisions.

2. Develop greater self-awareness. Making a candid assessment of your strengths and areas that need your attention as a creative individual is a critical step toward greater self-awareness and creativity. Be honest

PILOT	Enhancing Your Creative Talent

- Trust your strengths
- Develop greater self-awareness
- Find the right creativity tools and techniques
- Take time to reflect
- Listen, open up, and see other perspectives
- Balance process and product
- Look for gray areas
- Build a team and measure your participation
- Define and practice your creative process

with yourself about blocks and barriers from your experiences, knowledge, and creative talents. Ask for and listen carefully to feedback from colleagues, friends, and family about your talents and what might be getting in the way. Be clear about what might be keeping you from being your creative best and making your greatest contributions.

3. Find the right creativity tools and techniques. Play with tools that work for your talent. Some examples are the following:

- Checklists take you systematically through a series of steps to look at the problem differently. Alex Osborn, the originator of the brainstorming concept in the United States, suggests that you look at how to adapt, modify, magnify, minify, substitute, put to other uses, rearrange, reverse, and combine the problem or situation.[7]

- A creativity approach that provides a structured process for making sure that the problem is framed correctly, for generating multiple alternatives and options, and for selecting the best solution can be helpful. Follow the process to avoid missing key steps. Work with the team to develop a joint process.

- The set of tools and techniques from the TRIZ toolbox, based on over fifty years of research and study of patents in the former Soviet Union and now available in the United States, might also appeal to you. This study defined a large number of principles and methods that had been used to solve problems and produce patentable solutions and inventive breakthroughs. TRIZ methods bring a systematic discipline, multiple approaches, and rules and guidelines for invention that can appeal to those with the Pilot talent.[8]

4. Take time to reflect. Pilots need to spend time reflecting and processing information internally so that they don't just accept the opinions of experts they respect. Don't be afraid to slow down and listen more. Giving yourself time to think things through to find out what is important and what makes sense in the situation—to yourself and to others—is a significant step forward in personal development and the building of more independent thinking. If necessary, make room for such reflection in your time or day planner. A minister with the Pilot creative talent said,

> If time is available before a deadline, I will mull over ideas, trying to see different perspectives. I find some of my creativity is tapped when I am detached from the actual task or events. I can feel too confined and blocked if forced to sit on top of a task until it is completed. If time allows, I am more creative when I back away from a task, relax, and let ideas bubble.

An executive with this talent said, "I get to the office early and dedicate the first two hours to work requiring creative thinking. I also schedule time away from the office to recharge." An information technology executive said, "I put aside quiet weekend time to reflect on where I'm going to spend my time next week and how I can provide value and improvements to ongoing activities." Another business leader said, "While I am driving, I am always thinking, always looking for ways to solve problems, do things better." Another form of reflection is "sleeping on it." As one Pilot said, "You can make leaps of understanding while you're sleeping, and you can wake up the next morning with insights. It's important to pay attention to them." Learning to use a journal and other forms of reflection may also help.[9]

5. Listen, open up, and see other perspectives. In situations where multiple perspectives are being considered and evaluated, conflict may occur. Your approach to conflict, being direct and challenging, may not be appreciated by everyone and can dampen discussion and exploration of alternatives. Be careful how you word your questions so that team members feel you are open to their ideas and input. Instead of asking "Why?" ask open-ended questions such as "In what ways might we . . . ?" or "What if . . . ?" One college administrator with the Pilot talent recommended the following technique:

Often, in order to break down barriers and constraints that are in place, I need to think about what would the outcome be if I did this? Or who says I can't try another technique to achieve what I perceive to be realistic goals? I think the "What-if" question can be very fruitful and can provide a number of alternative solutions to both simple and complex decisions.

Use your auxiliary talent of the Navigator or the Visionary to slow down your decision making and make time for gathering and processing information, as opposed to always acting on it, and to help you involve others in the decision-making process. Count to ten before speaking up. Use your auxiliary talent to get out of your head, away from your typically intellectual endeavors to analyze and organize the world. Access your auxiliary talent in order to balance your tendency to reach conclusions too quickly. See the chapter on the Navigator (Chapter 4) or the Visionary (Chapter 6) for more strategies.

6. Balance process and product. Getting results is a critical piece of the creative process. However, it is not the only piece or purpose. Pilots often focus too much on the resulting product, as opposed to the means that got the team to the end result. Balancing the two is important for creativity. Commitment comes when people feel they are being heard and their needs are being met. Take time to objectively identify the causes of a conflict—in perception, assumptions, or decision-making criteria—as a step for adding to the collaborativeness of the team. Develop the patience you need to allow everyone to contribute to the discussion.

7. Look for gray areas. Another growth area for Pilots involves overcoming the tendency to see everything as a problem to be solved, a decision to be made, or an either-or situation. One executive commented on how easy it is to get sucked into "the vortex of mind-boggling decisions." Pilots are very good at defining a process and finding solutions. The fear is that, like carpenters who see everything as nails to be pounded with a hammer, they see the world as one giant problem to be solved. Not everything needs to be resolved immediately, and systematic problem solving is not always the best answer. Sometimes you may need to let situations unfold. One Pilot suggests using meditation to facilitate this building of patience and openness.

Part of a Pilot's strength is breaking down the complex into its component parts. To do this, Pilots categorize and find differences. This ability is helpful, but it can become too easy to see only the differences.

Remember that you cannot always logically and intellectually structure and manage the world around you. In addition, not every situation is black and white. You need to discover how to deal with the fuzziness of life. The world is becoming more and more complex. Life's challenges are not as clear as they once were; too many variables are imprecise, vague, and interdependent. They can't all be put in yes-no or either-or frames and then neatly solved. Learning to deal with this multivalent, ambiguous world is a major challenge. It is, of course, essential to boosting your creative contribution since finding both-and alternatives usually results in more creative solutions. Books on "fuzzy logic" may help.[10]

8. Build a team and measure your participation. In addition to calling on your auxiliary talent to gather more data, you might also find it helpful to team with others with different talents to avoid some of the common problems you may face in addressing challenges. Checking out and questioning assumptions with others will also help in making sure that the problem is stated correctly. By including others in the discussions and decisions, you bring new perspectives to the problem as well as garnering support for the final solution. This "team" can be a trusted friend or colleague, a significant other, or an actual team at work. As one Pilot acknowledged,

> I've come to truly appreciate diversity of views. It helps me hold lots of paradoxical views at the same time. The diversity of our group's approaches and the willingness to live with the differences make our group incredibly resilient and adaptable. The lesson I'm learning is that one must be rested and in balance to truly benefit from diversity. When one is stressed, the tendency is to fall into old judgmental patterns.

Letting go of the need to control the decision and determining where your involvement best serves the team's objectives are also important steps to take. Said one manufacturing business owner, "I have to be careful because I know that I don't think the way other people think. And I often want my way; I want people to try to see things my way. But even if I know it's the right decision, I can't force them to do it. I have to get them on board." Monitoring your involvement also frees you to be more creative and helps develop your associates' creativity.

9. Define and practice your creative process. Pilots who consciously follow a process they have developed with practice rarely complain of not having enough time to be creative. Said one Pilot, "I know I can be creative because I've done it so many times in the past. It never occurs to me that I don't have time to be creative. Once I know something needs to change, I go at it." His process includes articulating a framework for the problem and then including others who have a more meticulous, structured approach. It also includes letting go of his ego to include others in finding the solution. Another Pilot puts a problem aside and works on other projects while her unconscious processes the problem. One manager with a well-developed Pilot talent defined his preferred problem-solving technique:

> There are several well-ordered steps, from defining the problem statement and the rules of the meeting, identifying the symptoms and potential solutions, looking at the problem from the angle of making it worse, or denying that it existed, and then finding new potential solutions. I usually end up with a traditional set of solutions to the problem as well as with an additional set of innovative/creative type solutions. . . . I have used this technique on numerous occasions. Not only does it generate lots of good ideas, but it's also fun and it builds teamwork.

To stretch and grow your creative results and contributions even further, here are some additional strategies for Pilots:

1. Watch for biases from your auxiliary talent. Be sure that you are collecting both factual data and possibilities, for the current situation and the future. Stay open to big ideas, a broad view, and possible connections. Be careful to focus on details and to stay grounded in reality. If your auxiliary talent is that of the Visionary, be particularly careful to include others in your process if you are coming up with big leaps of action and change. Charting out the small steps and dealing with the people issues are critical to success. Review the chapter on either the Navigator (Chapter 4) or the Visionary (Chapter 6) to learn more about the blocks and barriers of your auxiliary talent and ways to overcome them.

2. Consider the people side of issues. The people side of the situation and the interpersonal issues in teamwork are important elements to consider. Pilots are great at analyzing problems, asking questions, and describing, examining, and critiquing the situation. Keep in mind that the logical way doesn't always apply. Learn to be more expressive and aware of the people involved in the effort. Appreciate and give time to the arguments and perspectives of your colleagues. Put yourself in their shoes. Spend some time before meetings checking in with people. Watch how you ask questions to be sure that you are soliciting viewpoints and keeping a discussion going. Practice the PPC approach in responding to ideas (what are the pluses about the suggestion, what are the potentials and what are the concerns?)[11] to avoid appearing too critical. In addition, consider all political issues.[12] Remember that "there is no substitute for clear thinking or for diplomatic action. Both thoughtful idea development and adroit idea promotion are essential."[13]

3. Work with your values and feelings. Be careful to balance the needs of others with the demands of the tasks or project in order to make a truly effective, well-thought-out decision. Books on emotional intelligence can provide some valuable insights on this area as well.[14] Review some of the tools recommended in the chapter on the Poet talent (Chapter 10) to see what additional insights they can bring. Give yourself time alone to attend to your own needs. A retreat to sort out your needs, priorities, and emotions can be helpful to your own development and to your creativity. You don't want to spend your life settling problems, reorganizing companies, and stating things clearly only to find out that you have missed the real meaning of life. Discover what is truly important to you and what really matters in your life. Using the "morning pages" from *The Artist's Way* is a possible technique.[15] Writing letters to yourself or to a child to explain what's going on inside you is another approach.

As a result of this introspection, you may feel more human, begin to recognize your limits, and appreciate the need for deep relationships. These reflective experiences—by bringing new, more subjective perspectives and by showing you the power of emotions—may help boost your creativity and imagination. They may also help you access your unconscious.[16]

4. Make your thoughts visible. Techniques used by some of the well-known creative geniuses in history can expand a Pilot's understanding of the problem. Drawing a picture of the problem or writing a metaphor for the problem can give a very different perspective.[17] Use diagrams, maps, or mind mapping, a technique in which you represent your thoughts using bubbles of key words and then organize those bubbles into a web of connecting lines in all directions.[18] Another technique is to build a collection of pictures from magazines and then randomly select a picture to stimulate your thinking on the problem.[19] Pilots who report using such visual techniques indicate that they come up with major breakthrough ideas this way.

5. Build some time for play into your life. Pilots are often told to get out of their head, find out what others are up to, and express themselves in ways that other people can understand. You need to do this and to consciously bring more fun and humor into your life. Although your work is often your joy, you still need to participate in the joy and adventure outside of problem solving and teamwork. Take time for yourself, to just take a walk or a swim or do something enjoyable, even frivolous.

HOW YOU CAN HELP A PILOT

If you work with Pilots, there are several steps you can take to boost their creativity:

1. Set the right structure. Make sure that they have enough structure to feel comfortable but that there is room for exploration and reflection. Make sure that they have sufficient challenge. Give them a job for which creativity is needed. Agree on clear goals and objectives. Make sure that people issues are considered, as well as more quantitative goals. Talk about the processes they will use to achieve the goals. Identify key stakeholders and how they will participate in the problem-solving or decision-making process. Discuss circumstances and political issues and their ramifications and explore how to incorporate these issues into the project's plan.

PILOT	Maximizing Their Contributions
• Set the right structure	
• Remind them about people issues	
• Help them find the shades of gray	
• Encourage them to take time to reflect	
• Help them learn to delegate	
• Make sure that they are exploring possibilities	
• Build a development plan	
• Watch for symptoms of stress and suggest time-outs	

2. Remind them about people issues. Help them work through political issues. Give them opportunities to teach others how to lead so that they can pass on their skills. Help them be more patient during change. Not everything or everyone has to move at their pace. Be sure that they are handling conflict as an open, collaborative, and creative process, as opposed to squelching it. Ask them about their own reactions, particularly during change.

3. Help them find the shades of gray. Ask questions that probe the process they used to come to conclusions. Provide different perspectives by playing devil's advocate. Be sure they take the time to ask the following questions:[20]

- Have we heard from everyone?
- What's important to each person on the team? How can we find a way to include it in the decision?
- What will fit best with the values of the organization?
- What will be fair to the people who are affected?

4. Encourage them to take time to reflect. Make sure that they take time to consider what they really think and to process the information internally. Ask questions that cause them to pause and consider issues more carefully.

5. Help them learn to delegate. Pilots are driven to get things done *now*. In the rush to results, they may be neglecting the development of their staff. This inability to give up control may be severely inhibiting the creativity of the organization. One possible strategy to make sure that Pilots are encouraging their staff to grow is for them to identify their successor as well as appropriate development plans for all their staff.

6. Make sure that they are exploring possibilities. To ensure that Pilots have considered many different alternatives in their problem-solving process, ask them questions to challenge their conclusions. Have them look at the problem from multiple perspectives, using the tools and techniques suggested.

7. Build a development plan. Encourage Pilots to take courses in interpersonal skills development, including courses in listening, facilitation skills, and team leadership and delegation. Several good suggestions for interpersonal skills development can be found in the books on emotional intelligence.[21] Consider hiring the right personal coach for a

Pilot who needs help with interpersonal skills. Incorporate these programs, workshops, and self-study courses into a Pilot's performance plan. Make sure that evaluation criteria include both the process and the results.

8. Watch for symptoms of stress and suggest time-outs. Under stress, Pilots may become rigid, overbearing, oversensitive to criticism or self-doubt, and strangely emotional. Encourage them to take vacations and to sleep on problems, as opposed to trying to solve them when they are under stress. Suggest that they let go of control, enjoy the moment, and remember that they don't need to do everything right now.[22]

SUMMARY

Without a Pilot, the team can start to flounder and waste valuable resources. Pilots provide structure, leadership, goals, and objectives. They get things going and keep the team working together toward the goals. They ask tough questions and challenge the team to see the situation differently. Pilots come up with new designs for working together and new strategies for getting things done. They provide energy, enthusiasm, and a positive attitude for the team. Through their careful, analytical thinking and their strong ability to focus, they can help ensure that the right problem is being addressed and that an implementation plan is developed and followed. Pilots can optimize their creative contributions to the organization by developing their interpersonal skills; making sure that they take time to look at different perspectives, ideas, and opinions; and strengthening the ability to lead more participatively.

SELF-ASSESSMENT

How does this talent impact my life as a dominant or auxiliary talent?

_____

_____

_____

If this is not my dominant or auxiliary talent, how do I demonstrate the use of this talent?

_____

_____

_____

How could I have used this talent in the past?

_____

_____

_____

How can I use this talent in the future?

_____

_____

_____

What do I need to do to better manage a Pilot team member?

_____

_____

_____

CHAPTER EIGHT

THE INVENTOR

ISTP: AUXILIARY CREATIVE TALENT-ADVENTURER
INTP: AUXILIARY CREATIVE TALENT-EXPLORER

Inventors provide the tools and insights that enable reframing of problems and discoveries of new solutions.

The contributions of the Inventors' creative talent come from their keen, questioning, and penetrating minds. Inventors are logical, rational, detached, and objective problem solvers. They share a similar thinking approach with Pilots, but more of an Inventor's analysis goes on internally, in a much less public way. Through introspection and internal reasoning, Inventors organize and clarify their ideas. They appear to have an internal framework that they have built through years of critical analysis. It's like a blueprint, a model, a "genetic code," or a "map of the mind," which they continue to update with new knowledge.[1] It helps them keep all their ideas categorized and prioritized. It ensures the integrity of their solutions and concepts. They seem compelled to analyze and clarify external events, experiences, ideas, and information against their personal framework to make sense of the world. Said one Inventor,

> I spend a lot of time thinking about stuff. I'm always looking at the angles and the odds, and what it is and why it works this way. It's kind of an innate, natural curiosity. I have an ability to tune out the rest of the world and go off into my own little world, and you couldn't penetrate it. It's a sense of introspection that allows me to get comfortable thinking about things and not knowing all the answers, but having fun looking for the answers.

INVENTOR	Results and Contributions

- Unconventional theories and models for analysis and synthesis of facts, ideas, and concepts
- Unusual and thoughtful solutions to problems through identifying what makes things work and through objective, impartial analysis
- Inventive ways to get around constraints
- Tough, unrelenting critique to get to the highest levels of effectiveness
- A quick understanding and intellectual curiosity that can speed the creative process
- Insightful questions that cause paradigm shifts in perspective
- Integrated solutions where everything fits

Inventors are quite self-reliant and independent in their thinking and in their work style. They appear to be guided very much by their own opinions and convictions. They often prefer to work alone. They are reflective, quiet, and detached. Stories from Inventors are brief and to the point. Organized and analytical, they are grammatically and stylistically correct. The goal of their conversations and writing tends to be to explain, clarify, and teach.

Inventors are usually flexible and tolerant of a wide range of behaviors and opinions. They like to play with new facts and ideas and find out how things work. Through their skepticism and constant challenging, Inventors bring new insight to any problem or situation. They may even invent new words or terms or reinterpret old ones to describe what's going on, since they often find language limiting. They like to be on the leading edge of new tools and techniques. One individual with the Inventor talent had a high-speed Internet connection through a cable link into his home long before anyone else did—just to be able to play with it. Said one Inventor, "I have always been a tinkerer. When I was four or five years old, I took a flashlight apart because I was curious. I remember taking my watch apart because I was bored in class in junior high." Another explained the creative insights she gets from examining what makes things work:

I remember as a child being reprimanded by my teacher for my behavior. She would give me assignments to write thousand-word compositions about what goes on inside a Ping-Pong ball or what happens when a leaf falls from a tree. I was lucky to have had a teacher who, in trying to give me a sense of self-control, would give me these hard tasks. I would rise to the challenge. In order to rise to the challenge, you have to be creative.

Relentlessly pursuing the truth, Inventors use an almost scientific approach to analyzing and solving problems and identifying what makes things work. Their insightful questions and careful processing of facts surrounding the problem situation usually produce paradigm shifts in a group's thinking. The results are often ingenious plans and solutions to all sorts of problems. They are especially good at challenging tacit assumptions, thus helping to really define the true scope of the problem or challenge. They can work things through and find elegant solutions so that everything makes sense. According to a CEO of a nonprofit organization reflecting this talent,

> The place that I have to use creativity the most is when I need to help trigger a shift in thinking. It's my job to figure out when we need to make a course correction, figure out how to jolt us, raise our awareness, and expose us to new stuff. I try to do the cutting-edge reading and introduce the ideas into our strategy and into our thinking. You've just got to keep doing something different so that the organization doesn't get stale.

The Inventor's ability to ask tough questions is valuable to a team and an organization. Inventors enjoy problem solving and tend to be intensely curious; they ask questions, and if the answers don't make sense, they will explore more. Said one Inventor, an association executive director, "My driving question in relation to any problem solving is 'Why?' If I know why, I then know what is to follow." Another Inventor described her role this way:

> I test thought processes, playing devil's advocate. I try to get [my associates] to think about things differently. I won't give employees answers. Instead, I'll say, "Let's talk about how you get to the answer." I will allow them to learn. It's all about challenging people to think for themselves.

Inventors make sure that the group's thinking is organized and that ideas hold up against the facts. Inventors have little patience for muddled thinking. They are often heard saying, "This isn't consistent with . . . ." In addition to asking "Why?," an Inventor may ask the following questions throughout the creative problem-solving process to encourage discussion and build new insights:

- What is the gap between what should be and what is?

- What needs improvement?

- How can we look at this differently?

- What if we tried to reverse, subtract, divide, add, multiply, combine, rearrange, and exaggerate?

- What are the positives and negatives of the problem?

- Which aspects of the problem are controllable? Which aren't?

- What's right and what's wrong about our approach?

- Where are the holes?

- What is the worst possible thing that could happen? How are we prepared to address that issue?[2]

Reflecting the Inventor talent, a CEO of a large financial institution described his creative results:

> This job requires you to have the ability to step back and conceptualize with the board about what the issues are, and then develop some hypothesis or some framework for saying, "Here's how I think we should deal with all these challenges." Developing a conceptual framework of what's important and a conceptual vision of the direction takes some amount of creativity, especially if it's not how people think about things. You have to find the things that don't fit and then figure out if you need to ask, "Does this work? Does this make sense?"
>
> It then turns very creative, when the world is changing and you have to twist your point of axis. Then you have to get others who don't necessarily agree to follow your logic. They have to be prodded because they often aren't willing to even go through the steps because it doesn't jibe with how they thought of the world before. All those processes are what I would call creative.

Although Inventors see the challenge differently, from quite unusual viewpoints, the kinds of problems and solutions to which they tend to apply their analytical skills depend on their auxiliary perceiving talent. This talent, as their extraverted way of dealing with and managing the external world, is usually well developed. With the Adventurer's talent,

Inventors tend to focus on the objective and impersonal details and specifics of what is presently happening and on material that is tangible and concrete. They tend to be careful, realistic observers of life around them. They quickly bring order out of confused, unorganized facts. They know what can and cannot be done. Inventors with this auxiliary talent constantly search for additional information and want to apply the information to achieve efficient results. They want to experiment and learn by doing since they are eager to be fully involved with life. They prefer variety and the freedom to freelance their talents to make sure that they can have an impact on others.

If their auxiliary talent is that of the Explorer, Inventors are more intellectually curious and concerned with theory. Their focus is on more complicated projects where imagination, ingenuity, and long-range planning are required; they are more comfortable with ambiguity. They are concerned about the integrity of their models. They are more interested in analyzing a problem and discovering where the solution lies. With the Explorer as their auxiliary talent, Inventors are concerned about knowledge for the sake of learning and building competence. More focused on possibilities than on practicalities, they are more concerned with the design and its interaction with the surrounding conditions than they are with the implementation of the solution.

With either combination of talents, Inventors contribute thoughtful analysis that helps with the team's definition of the challenge, in their exploration of alternatives, and in the implementation plan for any new initiative. Said the association executive director,

> I want to understand the situation and get it right and with the minimum of effort. I don't want to mess around or redo anything. Once I've done it, I want to be finished with it. There's nothing worse than putting in time and then finding that you've missed something critical or misunderstood what is being required of you. So getting the issues and desired outcomes clearly defined and agreed to is critical. If someone wanting something isn't clear, I can sometimes get almost obsessive asking, "Do you want this or that?" or "Are you sure you don't want . . . ?" I need to get the task clearly defined [about] what you want, how you want it, and, very importantly, when you want it!

Inventors are sufficiently skeptical and can foresee all sorts of difficulties. Because of their inner model, they seem able to predict where discrepancies will fall out. They look at probabilities and the logical consequences of any of the planned actions. Since a key block to getting creative results is underestimating the critical steps, finding missing pieces, and setting priorities,[3] Inventors have much to add to the creativity of the organization by charting out dependencies and all the pieces necessary to execute the plan.

Inventors are also creative in ways that make things work. The division head Inventor went on to say,

> I have always tended to challenge . . . and find creative ways to get around obstacles, rules . . . and find ways to make it work. . . . If there's a rule that says you can't do something, then I'll rise to that challenge. It's constantly pushing and challenging. Some of it was just a desire to challenge, a rebelliousness . . . or it's more challenging the norm. If it looks as if it's a straight line from A to B, I'll look at it differently to see if I can draw the line another way.

Said the association executive director,

> What I would be looking for in a challenging situation is a good outline of the facts, some options, pluses and minuses for us to question, discuss, think about. In that situation I would ask questions to clarify statements, tease out ambiguities, and check that they had done their homework based on my knowledge of that and other similar situations. I would ask, "Have they considered this?" "What are we trying to achieve here?" "What's our priority?"

Inventors may be seen as risk takers, but they don't necessarily see their approach as risky. Said one Inventor,

> What happens in my creative approach is that I try something different, and it works. Then I'll try it again, and it works again. I'm told I'm a high risk taker. I don't think of myself as taking high risks. It's just that I've managed to move my boundaries out so that I don't think of it as high risk. And the more I do it, the easier it gets.

Through their independence, flexibility, and curiosity, Inventors are likely to produce many creative results. Some examples of well-known individuals who may have had this talent are the architect Frank Lloyd Wright, the writer Ayn Rand, and the scientist Albert Einstein. In their relentless pursuit of explaining the meaning of life and finding guiding principles, the philosophers Immanuel Kant, Friedrich Nietzsche,[4] and Simone de Beauvoir also displayed this creative talent.

Since they can get bored with routines, Inventors are usually comfortable with change. Solving problems and exploring challenges stimulates them. In fact, they tend to see change as part of the normal process of life.[5]

Inventors also contribute to the creativity of a team through their ability to handle conflict. They are calm, thoughtful, and reasonable. In the heat of debate, they usually keep an impersonal, objective, and analytical stance. Their quiet composure helps the team work through conflicts and disagreements in a very productive way.

OBSTACLES

As with all the creative talents, Inventors have several challenges that can get in the way of their creative contribution. Possible blocks include focusing on objective data, ignoring emotional issues, procrastinating, and using either-or thinking. After reviewing some of the key blocks, you will find strategies for overcoming them in the next sections.

INVENTOR	Blocks to Optimal Creativity

- Concentration on impersonal, objective data, often overlooking the people side of the issue
- Ignoring emotional needs and values
- Biases of their auxiliary talent to details or larger patterns
- Dichotomous or either-or thinking
- An overdetached approach to conflict
- Procrastination and postponement of decisions
- Lack of focus and organization
- Minimal concern for schedules and deadlines
- Preference for freedom and variety

In their interpersonal relationships, they can sometimes appear to be formal, aloof, and distant. Their questioning style can seem to come from distrust and can be intimidating. Since Inventors prefer to understand a situation and want to think through their position before going to new ground and sharing it with others, they don't tend to readily share their thoughts. They can appear to have already made up their mind without taking any input from the group. They can seem to be single-minded about their views, to the point of appearing rigid, skeptical, cold, and negative. Because they are often nonconforming, are hard to read, and appear to be indifferent, their contribution to the team can sometimes be limited.

Inventors may have to struggle with their relationships with people and with sharing their inner ideas and models. They may fail to consider the emotional and personal needs of the people involved in the challenge or problem. They may not see that other people may have trouble understanding them. Inventors sometimes fail to see the impact of their decisions on others. Expecting their good ideas to take root on their own, Inventors sometimes fail to see that their ideas may need to be nurtured with others.

In their analysis of facts and evaluation of ideas, Inventors sometimes come to conclusions without having enough good data and information. They at times dismiss facts and ideas that don't easily fit into their inner model or that seem irrelevant. They may unduly favor quantifiable alternatives. They may also rely too much on selected methods, ones that have worked well for them in the past, to generate alternatives. Such methods can produce unconscious biases and filters that hinder creative decision making. Their auxiliary extraverted data-collecting talent can also cause biases and filters. If it's the Adventurer talent, the data Inventors see can be specific and sense based. If it's the Explorer talent, Inventors may ignore such data and see only trends and patterns.

The fuzziness of problems may challenge Inventors. They generally want problem statements to be clear and unambiguous, yet this is often not possible. They are usually convinced only by careful reasoning, logic, and verifiable data. They may get so caught up in their head that they start believing that their reality is the only reality. They may also retreat into introversion in times of conflict. If they do decide to address differences, they may appear competitive, seeing results as win-lose situations. If they are not careful, they may see life as a series of all-or-nothing, either-or propositions. In this case, they may become subject to the "tyranny of the or," where it is very difficult to accept paradox—two seemingly contradictory forces or ideas present at the same time—and to avoid choices that are either A or B, but not both.[6]

Another possible roadblock to Inventors being their most creative comes from their lack of concern for schedules and deadlines. As one consultant with the Inventor creative talent put it when describing a typical problem-solving approach, "After I was finished with my research and analysis, and I had procrastinated as long as I thought was manageable, I would conclude on the best options for the business." Another Inventor, an advertising executive, described a rather important upcoming meeting with his boss: "I have a great feeling in my head about what I want to say. At roughly 1:45 P.M. today, I will put it down on paper for our 2:00 P.M. meeting!" An Inventor may often be referred to as the "absent-minded professor." Such habits can hamper creative contributions.

Because Inventors are so independent and so organized, at least in their internal world, they often don't see the need for external structure. As team leaders, they don't always see that others may appreciate more formality. In fact, in their own external world, where goal orientation is not usually their first priority, they could probably use more discipline and structure. Their curiosity and preference for freedom and variety may cause Inventors to spread their interests and pursuits too thin. Said one Inventor, "There really isn't enough time to follow all the paths and roads, and I hate to close off doing things." This tendency may cause them to take on more projects than they have time for. Said another Inventor,

> If I don't stay focused, it hinders [my creativity]. I have a hard time seeing the forest through the trees. It's really a balance in figuring out when to stay focused and build a wall around what it is you're trying to do. Otherwise, you'll be scatterbrained all over the lot. [Being creative for me involves] staying focused. It's also periodically stepping back and trying to get the big view.

Being around people who are expressing strong emotions may cause Inventors stress. When other people aren't sensitive to their need to think things through and be alone, if they feel limited or intruded upon, or if they have to spend too much time with people, Inventors may get very emotional; they are uncomfortable in that situation. They may become hypersensitive to relationships and react excessively to criticism. They may also become overly self-critical.[7] One Inventor talked about being stifled by her boss, who kept putting up obstacles to her success:

> If I get very frustrated about not being able to do something, I become my own worst enemy in setting up obstacles. When I feel stifled, then I need to put myself in the right mind-set so that I approach it positively with the intention of winning, as opposed to negatively reacting or saying something dumb.

At other times, stress may cause a different reaction in Inventors. They may start to emphasize logic to an extreme and may get paralyzed with analysis. Life becomes even more black and white than it normally is for them.[8] All these reactions can interfere with Inventors' creative contributions.

BOOSTERS

Depending on their particular situation, there are several steps Inventors can take to gain maximum benefit from their creative talent and improve the effectiveness of their creativity:

1. Trust your strengths. Make sure that the team recognizes the need to question assumptions, to define the problem correctly, to develop a model for their decision-making process, and to pursue different angles of the challenge. Take the time you need to express yourself.

2. Develop greater self-awareness. Making a candid assessment of your strengths and areas where you need to focus attention as a creative individual is a critical step toward greater self-awareness and creativity. Be honest with yourself about blocks and barriers from your experiences, knowledge, and creative talents. Ask for and listen carefully to feedback from colleagues, friends, and family about your talents and what might be getting in the way. Be clear about what might be keeping you from being your creative best and making your greatest contributions.

3. Find the right creativity tools and techniques. Play with tools that work for your talent. Some examples include the following:

- Checklist-type tools such as Scamper that systematically take you through a series of steps to expand creative possibilities.[9]

- Brainwriting, in which team members write down their ideas, share them, and build on the ideas of others in silence. This tool gives Inventors time to think a problem through and come up with interesting alternatives.

- A problem-solving approach that provides a structured process for making sure that the problem is framed correctly, for generating multiple alternatives and options, and for selecting the best solution (see Chapter 11). Work with the team to develop a creative process. Trust and use the process to avoid missing key steps.

INVENTOR	Enhancing Your Creative Talent

- Trust your strengths
- Develop greater self-awareness
- Find the right creativity tools and techniques
- Learn about downtime
- Open up to the possibility of many different ways to look at problems
- Access your auxiliary talent
- Learn to express your ideas
- Balance the process with the result
- Define and practice your creative process
- Organize your information

- The set of tools and techniques from the TRIZ toolbox, based on over fifty years of research and study of patents in the former Soviet Union and now available in the United States. This study defined a large number of principles and methods that had been used to solve problems and produce patentable solutions and inventive breakthroughs. TRIZ methods bring a systematic discipline, multiple approaches, and rules and guidelines for invention that may appeal to individuals with the Inventor talent.[10]

4. Learn about downtime. It's important for Inventors to stop thinking and analyzing. Every now and then you need to take a time-out. To produce new insights and designs, let your ideas incubate. Find ways to integrate into your life creative forays that appeal to mind, body, and soul. One Inventor finds physical activity helpful to relieve stress. Another, an advertising executive, is taking voice lessons, plays hockey, and writes plays to access the other sides of himself. Change your activities and make sure that you have enough space to get back to your introspective self. Letting go of overwhelming responsibilities may also help. One Inventor described her recharging process:

> I watch soap operas at night. That's my dead cell introverted time. It requires no thought process. If I'm energized, I can be creative. If I'm not, I can't. My way of energizing and rebuilding those inner stores is to turn off my brain cells and do nothing. I do that through the dumb stuff I watch on TV. I find that dead brain cell time is when I get my juices renewed and my

inner energy levels back up. It clears the cobwebs and clutter out of my brain. Then I can be creative again.

5. Open up to the possibility of many different ways to look at problems. Many of life's problems are too complex to be stated in black-and-white terms. Not every problem can be solved using logical steps and analysis. Like those with the Pilot talent, you can benefit from learning to deal with ambiguity and fuzzy problems. Instead of first focusing on defining the problem, work to frame it out more generally and view getting to clarity as part of the creative process. Instead of asking "Why?," try asking "How?" Check out books on "fuzzy logic," such as *Fuzzy Thinking*.[11] One Inventor finds ways to get out of being herself, to change what she calls her default settings, or the typical ways she tends to react to people and situations. By taking different perspectives on a challenge or problem, you can reframe your more typical either-or/win-lose response to conflict.

6. Access your auxiliary talent. Learn to deliberately access your auxiliary talent of the Adventurer or the Explorer to investigate alternative perspectives and different solutions. This auxiliary talent may also help you keep from jumping to conclusions too quickly. Focus on data gathering to balance your analytical approach to life and to keep your thinking relevant. You need new ideas to promote productive thinking. See the chapters on these talents (Chapters 3 and 5) to get additional strategies on tapping into their power.

7. Learn to express your ideas. Be more willing to share your thinking processes, insights, and conclusions with others. Learn to give brief updates and to communicate your rich insights. Developing your listening, communicating, and relationship skills helps with your teamwork and allows you to clearly communicate your thoughts and concerns. Ask questions that encourage discussion and the building of new insights. Opening up more to others may also help in promoting creative discussion and dialogue. One Inventor, a successful consultant, talked about learning to trust his ability to generate ideas on the spot in order to "externalize an essentially internal process. I get more and better ideas faster by talking about them with others. Actually, as I talk about insights and feelings, they start to congeal or coalesce into concepts and ideas."

Practice public speaking through Toastmasters clubs, the National Speakers Association, or similar organizations. You can access your extraverted side through the auxiliary talent of either the Adventurer or the Explorer. You need the external orientation of your auxiliary talent to help you get out of your head and to share more of your ideas.

8. Balance the process with the result. In their external world, Inventors often tend to focus on the process, as opposed to the result or deadlines. Said one, "To me the reward is in what I learned and how I went through the process more than in what the outcome is." This approach can lead to procrastination in making decisions, especially if the Inventor's auxiliary perceiving talent is too well developed. Frank Lloyd Wright showed many of the traits of the Inventor talent in his approach to designing his famous Falling Water home for Edgar Kaufmann. The client had to wait six months in frustration for any results from Wright. Finally, Kaufmann phoned the architect and said he was three hours away and wanted to meet with him to go over the blueprints. In those three hours, Wright produced the extraordinary design that had been working its way through his mind over the past six months.[12]

One Inventor described a similar process:

> I work very well under pressure. If I have something to do, like a speech, I will often not sit down and write it until literally the eleventh hour. But that doesn't mean I haven't been thinking about it. I internalize it, I digest it, and then I just sit down and produce it. So it gives the appearance of producing stuff in a rapid cycle time. It actually is a longer cycle time than what one physically sees. You won't have seen my brain cells working, whether I'm lying in bed at night just thinking about things.

Taking care that deadlines are set to ensure that results get produced is important to an Inventor's creativity. Time-management techniques are also important. Let go of the need to seek the truth and move to resolution within appropriate time frames. Learning to plan backward can be a useful technique. Pinpoint the final due date for the project and, working back from that final date, establish critical milestones. Then, be sure to make the key milestone delivery dates. Post the schedule where you can see it. Get started now on the first deliverable.[13]

9. Define and practice your creative process. It is important for you to learn to define and trust your own process. As one Inventor, a successful author and consultant, put it, you may not want to let the solution crystallize too quickly. Part of his process is going through a series of questions to turn ambiguity into clarity while also appreciating some of the randomness of possible answers. Another Inventor indicates that she needs to spend time up front defining for herself what the problem is. She then consults with people who have the knowledge and experience to help her, pulls together the facts, gets away from the problem, explores options, does other things, comes back, thinks it through some more, clarifies, and then moves forward.

Having a process that you know works effectively can be a great boost to your self-confidence. Trusting in a process that has proven to produce creative results in the past may help overcome angst-filled negative thinking and fears of failure that can frighten off creativity. Knowing that you can produce creative results may also help you overcome concerns about not "writing the great symphony" every time. As long as you win some, you can lose some as well.

One systems integration specialist practices what he calls "iterative analysis," his process for getting to solutions. Other Inventors might choose to talk the problem over with others and play with ideas before forming conclusions. Make sure that you have gathered enough information before coming to final decisions. That successful author and consultant defined his process as follows:

> I start inductively, metaphorically, or visually with the problem. I will generate options, pick my favorites, and look for patterns or "solution" characteristics of the best options. Then I will generate additional options based on those patterns or characteristics. Then it's a question of picking the best of those options and working with them from there.

10. Organize your information. Another technique that may be helpful to Inventors is to find a way to deal with and organize all their accumulated information. One Inventor described her accumulation of ideas from observations, magazines, books, and conferences "where someone is talking about best practices. Somewhere down the line, I'll see an application where I can use the ideas. I have this repository of junk that I keep stuffing in my brain. I need to drill a hole in it and let it come out of my internal database." Finding a way to organize and quickly access this information is key to creative contributions and to ensuring that you can take action as well as think, analyze, and conceptualize.

To stretch and grow your creative results and contributions even further, here are some additional strategies for Inventors:

1. Make your thoughts visible. Techniques used by some of the well-known creative geniuses in history can expand an Inventor's understanding of the problem. Drawing a picture of the problem or writing a metaphor for the problem can give a very different perspective.[14] Use diagrams, maps, or mind mapping, a technique in which you represent your thoughts using bubbles of key words and then organize those bubbles into a web of connecting lines in all directions.[15] Another technique is to build a collection of pictures from magazines and then randomly select a picture to stimulate your thinking on the problem.[16]

2. Pay attention to the impact of your auxiliary talent. Take care that your auxiliary talent isn't blinding you to certain facts and details or bigger trends and possibilities. If your auxiliary talent is that of the Adventurer, recognize that your attention is usually on getting immediate results for the short term. Therefore, take time to consider the long-term implications of your decisions. You may also want to consider developing your ability to synthesize and integrate facts since this ability is a key characteristic of effectively creative individuals. If, instead, your auxiliary talent is that of the Explorer, then you need to ground yourself in reality, to avoid squandering your energies in pursuit of impossibilities. You may be avoiding important details. You may also need to simplify a solution that has become too complex. See the chapter on the Adventurer (Chapter 3) or the Explorer (Chapter 5) for more information.

3. Learn to balance objective, impersonal data with feelings and relationships. Recognize the different perspectives that come from those with the Harmonizer and Poet creative talents. We all need validation, not because we are weak and insecure but because we are human. Learn to express appreciation for others, to focus on the positive contributions first. Recognize that the data you observe may not address the people side of situations and challenges. You may need support in dealing with people, political issues, and agendas. Ask questions such as the following:[17]

- Have we heard from everyone?

- What's important to each person on the team? How can we find a way to include these things in the decision?

- What will fit best with the values of the organization?

- What will be fair to the people who are affected?

Take time to consider what matters emotionally to another person. Figure out the personal needs of the people involved in the challenge or problem. Team with someone you trust, who preferably has a different talent, to talk out ideas. Start meetings by asking how people are feeling. Take time to consider the impact of decisions on others. Pay attention to the stories and needs of others and use your extraverted auxiliary talent to interact and to be persuasive. By letting people in on your process and by working on the relationship side of teamwork, your contribution to the creativity of the organization can grow.

According to a successful consultant and project manager, by listening to others, finding out where they are coming from, and then going to that place with them, she has been able to "create miracles." By taking time to work with the team, she finds the both-and solution and the common ground, where "it's always most creative." A technique she has developed to help her out when she is not being sensitive to group needs is to have a colleague give her a prearranged signal to slow down and listen.

4. Develop your ability to get in touch with your deeper feelings. Learn to express your emotions and develop deeper connections with people. Network with others to get more used to interacting and hearing from other points of view. Reading books on emotional intelligence may provide some insights on these issues.[18] Writing in a journal or writing poetry may put you in touch with your own values.[19] Such connections with your feelings can help you access your unconscious. The tools and techniques recommended for the Harmonizer (Chapter 9) and the Poet (Chapter 10) may also help you access your unconscious.

5. Have some fun and learn how to avoid emotional and physical burnout. Inventors tend to work hard and enjoy their work. They sometimes lose sight of the fact that they are human and need nourishment for the body and soul. Said one Inventor, "I think you burn out very quickly, you lose effectiveness very quickly, unless you have some fun doing it. Fun is an important component for me." Some Inventors get involved in volunteer activities as a way to reach out to others, explore different perspectives, and relieve some frustration that they feel in the routines of work. Said one Inventor, "Getting involved in nonprofits gave me a creative outlet. It allowed me to keep perspective so I didn't shoot myself in the foot." Another, a banking executive, commented about his membership on the board of an arts group: "It's nice to be associated with that group. When you hear them talk . . . you see some guy with an orange crewcut and wearing a flannel robe and combat boots, and it does sort of break your point of view." Discover what fun is for you and make time for it; let unimportant issues go. Said one Inventor,

> Risking that stuff will fall through the cracks and won't crash is very important. . . . Just make the time. If I have to, I will force myself. Cancel a meeting that I didn't need to be at. Sit in my car for an hour. If I find I don't spend enough time thinking, it's a real problem. Once I can think and mull a problem over, then I can get to that leap between mulling it over and understanding it and then coming to the creative solution.

HOW YOU CAN HELP AN INVENTOR

If you work with Inventors, there are several steps you can take to maximize their creative contributions to the organization:

1. Check to be sure that structure is truly needed. Inventors need freedom from rules and procedures. Sometimes structure is not important because the Inventor has developed ways to manage time and projects. Recognize that deadlines can sometimes work to inspire creativity at the last moment. Learn to trust their process if they have been able to deliver.

2. Set mutually agreeable schedules and deadlines. Set expectations about results; discuss the goals and milestones. Decide which

---

INVENTOR	Maximizing Their Contributions

- Check to be sure that structure is truly needed
- Set mutually agreeable schedules and deadlines
- Provide the personal space they need to be the most creative
- Ensure that their teams include diverse talents
- Make sure they have spent enough time gathering data and considering all angles
- Give them time to express their thoughts and feelings
- Encourage development of their project-planning, time-management, and interpersonal skills and abilities
- Watch for symptoms of stress

processes will be used to reach results, but let Inventors achieve the objectives on their own. Make sure they have sufficient freedom and challenge. Check on progress and ask for brief updates at regularly scheduled meetings.

3. Provide the personal space they need to be the most creative. Find ways for them to have private time and space to work most effectively. If this is not possible in the workplace, then explore ways for them to have the reflective time they need (such as working out of the home, providing white noise, or wearing earphones).

4. Ensure that their teams include diverse talents. Be sure that Inventors have some people on the team whose opinions they respect. A good mix of talents ensures that the strengths of an Inventor are maximized. Make sure the team has the training and support it needs to get the benefits of talent diversity and the differences of perspectives and opinions that can result.

5. Make sure they have spent enough time gathering data and considering all angles. Ask questions such as "In what ways might we look at this differently?" to explore how broadly they have considered different angles and perspectives. Include a discussion of the political and people issues in project-planning sessions and in regular briefings. Explore with them their perspectives to be sure that they are seeing the gray in situations.

6. Give them time to express their thoughts and feelings. Inventors may need more time to disclose their perspectives on the problem. They may also not be ready to share alternative solutions. Give them time to reflect and then ask questions to encourage them to voice their opinions.

7. Encourage development of their project-planning, time-management, and interpersonal skills and abilities. Build courses, workshops, or independent study for improvement in these areas into their performance plan. Several good suggestions for interpersonal skills development can be found in the books on emotional intelligence noted earlier. Consider hiring the right personal coach for an Inventor who needs help with interpersonal skills.

8. Watch for symptoms of stress. When Inventors start showing signs of stress, such as uncharacteristic emotional outbursts or analysis paralysis, suggest time-outs and time to play. Suggest a change of scenery or activities, and lighten their workload, if possible.[20]

SUMMARY

Inventors are excellent problem solvers and valuable contributors in any work effort. They are questioning, independent, and unconventional. They are curious about new ideas, flexible, and tolerant of others. They can be fun and quite playful in their curiosity and in their quest for the truth. Through their support of the exploration of the facts and possibilities, they help the team arrive at innovative solutions to problems and make important contributions to the creativity of the organization. Further development of their social and organizing skills and their ability to find "both-and" solutions will help them be more truly and effectively creative.

SELF-ASSESSMENT

How does this talent impact my life as a dominant or auxiliary talent?

_____

_____

_____

If this is not my dominant or auxiliary talent, how do I demonstrate the use of this talent?

_____

_____

_____

How could I have used this talent in the past?

_____

_____

_____

How can I use this talent in the future?

_____

_____

_____

What do I need to do to better manage an Inventor team member?

_____

_____

_____

CHAPTER NINE

THE HARMONIZER

ESFJ: AUXILIARY CREATIVE TALENT–NAVIGATOR
ENFJ: AUXILIARY CREATIVE TALENT–VISIONARY

**Like a first mate, social director, and cook, the Harmonizer
makes sure the crew's needs are met and channels their efforts
as they pursue new directions and creative solutions.**

Some of the Harmonizers' major creative contributions at work come from their concern for people and their ability to establish a supporting and encouraging environment for the creative efforts of others. Their high energy level and enthusiasm add vigor to any team effort. They are action and results oriented and have strong social and organizational skills. Harmonizers provide caring leadership through change. Optimistic and positive in their approach to life, they create good feelings and harmony among the team members. They focus on reconciling conflicting views and finding creative solutions to people issues and relationship problems. Since achieving creative results often "depends on a group of people working together who are not used to working together,"[1] Harmonizers can make major contributions to the organization's creativity.

Relationships with others are very important to Harmonizers. They enjoy getting to know people and their individual gifts and talents. They do their best work with others because they find much synergy in team efforts and through conversation. The Harmonizer's ability to build networks and alliances with a wide variety of people is an important asset in

HARMONIZER	Results and Contributions

- High-energy team leadership
- Innovative solutions to problems and new programs that help customers, employees, or community
- A nurturing, energetic team environment that brings out the best in people
- Diverse and effective communication strategies
- Different perspectives through concern for context and circumstances
- Successful resolution of political problems that can impede change and innovation
- Heightened self-esteem for team members

any organization's innovation initiatives. One business unit head with this talent commented on her creativity:

> I like to gather resources no matter how remote their application to my immediate area they may be. I cultivate a wide network of acquaintances because you never know when you will need to call on someone's expertise. When I have a problem, I use my "database" to find the people, information, and knowledge I need. I also reciprocate.

At times the Harmonizer's contributions are not considered creative since they are focused on human relationships, as opposed to more tangible problems. They often have to be reminded that being sensitive to human relations is a valuable gift that raises the creativity level of the whole organization. One CEO of a large financial institution commented on the importance of the Harmonizer talent:

> I have changed my definition of creativity over time. In the old days, I used to think you were creative maybe once or twice a year at best and the main task was analytical. I used to think, "If you would just leave me alone in a dark corner, I can solve the problem." I don't think that's how organizations work today. I believe you have the opportunity to be creative much more often in terms of interpersonal interactions with people.

One Harmonizer, a top business leader in the telecommunications industry, at first felt that he did not fit into any definition of creativity because he believed that "creative people have the ability to get from point A to point F without necessarily going through B, C, D, and E. They create; they introduce new elements." His strengths, instead, have always included

> an ability to both get along with people and bring them along. It's an ability to figure out how to be someone whom people are prepared to follow because you appear to know what you're doing. I would say, drawing on this big canvas of what is creativity, my creative abilities lie in the area of broadly defined interpersonal skills, where you bring lots of different folks together, get them to work together, and make them feel valued. But that's not what people normally think about.

Because Harmonizers are very responsive to people's needs, they can bring out the creative potential of the team and help team members achieve their very best. They appreciate the unique creative gifts and talents of others and are willing to invest time and effort into the growth and development of the team. One Harmonizer said, "I can't be creative sitting in my office if I don't empower people who work with me to be creative too, to be able to take risks in being creative." As one entrepreneur said, "Finding good people is what creativity is all about. And great people attract great people. You just need to give them incredible freedom to try things out."[2] Another Harmonizer, this one the CEO of a family-owned business, said,

> I really want to develop people, and it's important for me that people feel a part of the team and be satisfied with the job. If it's true that management is getting things done through and with people, then being successful in business and in a lot of other endeavors in life is much more dependent on your ability to influence and interact with other people.

Harmonizers give team members the recognition and appreciation that they need. This support and encouragement helps team members develop a stronger sense of their creative selves. Such a sense can lead to more confidence in being able to deal with changes in the world and more self-esteem, which may in turn result in even greater levels of creativity.[3]

Harmonizers strive to build a culture where people like to work. They can structure the environment so that individual and group needs are met and creativity flourishes. They want the team to work well together, to collaborate and cooperate as they get things done. Their ability to organize the team and establish roles and norms for the group process based on shared values is very important for creativity. Such structure and norms allow the team to be more expansive. Because the members feel comfortable exploring all sorts of options and alternative solutions in a safe, nurturing environment, the creative output of the group will grow. Commented a CEO of a family-owned business, reflecting the Harmonizer talent,

> The first thing you have to do to get a large group of people to focus on and achieve an objective is communicate what the objective is, so that everybody has a common understanding of that vision. Then every employee has a framework for knowing how to make intelligent choices. That's how you build an organization where people can be risk takers and have a sense that they can experiment and try things.

Harmonizers are also skilled at getting others to look beyond what's happening, to see different perspectives, and to develop their own creativity. One Harmonizer defined her creative contribution as

> being honest with my feedback, by not withholding ideas or constructive criticism, by being willing to initiate new ideas or put them forth for discussion. I contribute by being a good leader, by challenging and supporting my staff, by helping them initiate ideas and solve problems.

Having excellent verbal skills, Harmonizers usually express themselves easily and are willing to be open and share their thoughts and feelings with others. They use their talent for expressing themselves to inspire the potential and the heart of their listeners and to build trust and common understanding.[4] Their language tends to be more personal; their stories are full of people and focus on relationships, emotions, and values. The goal of their stories and conversations is to reach out and touch someone. To achieve creative results, Harmonizers use their excellent communication skills to build support for innovation initiatives.

The Harmonizer's creative process tends to involve defining the issues and possible direction, discussing the problem with people, and then finalizing a decision. One Harmonizer commented on her process:

> I'd think about the issue and have an idea of the various directions I could take. I'd talk to a number of people with different perspectives and get their

ideas and thoughts. I might put together a task force to brainstorm. I see my
role with this group as that of facilitator. I keep the process on track without stifling creativity. I capture the ideas. I make sure everyone has an opportunity to participate, and I help the group prioritize and come to consensus
(if that is important, which sometimes it isn't). At the end I revisit my original thoughts and adapt and amend and discard as needed before making a
decision about direction.

Harmonizers are very accomplished at helping with the implementation of new initiatives. They make sure that people concerns are included in the process of gathering information and making decisions.
They often can visualize a situation and want to consider its impact on
the people involved. One CEO talked about making the decision to buy
a new truck. His partner had analyzed the costs and benefits and had
come up with two options. But the CEO looked at one of the choices and
said, "That thing looks too big. When that's backing into somebody's
driveway, they're going to get all upset and think that you're cracking their
asphalt!"

Harmonizers are aware of how important it is to help people deal
with resistance and move on into the future, so they will use their communication skills to describe the future to help overcome resistance. Not
satisfied with passive understanding, they want people to understand
why the change is needed and what is going to happen. They are adept
at building coalitions and acceptance for change. They want to honor and
celebrate the change and bring in new rituals to be sure that it takes root.
Harmonizers coach the organization through the change. Questions they
ask include the following:[5]

- Who or what is involved or not involved?

- Who will be affected and how?

- How will customers, employees, and stakeholders react?

- What's appropriate for everyone involved?

- How will the changes affect relationships among people?

- Who might contribute special strengths or skills?

- How do we get everyone on board in order to implement the change
  or initiative?

One consultant with the Harmonizer talent talked about her new assignment to lead a team that was having a hard time accepting their new role and having to sell its services:

> The change had been thrust upon them. I spoke with each team member individually and then had team forums where we dealt with the issues of transition from their past role and capabilities to the new role, expectations, and capabilities. Each team member had to make a decision about his or her commitment to full participation in the new structure. Then we went through a business-planning process to reach a common vision and purpose that united the team.

Harmonizers can be very creative in dealing with the political situations that inevitably arise out of innovation initiatives. Managing political agendas is critical to successful change; to succeed in getting changes implemented, a team needs to contend with conflicting agendas of peers and peer organizations, shifting power grids, and environmental forces for which there is only partial information. "Dealing well with politics requires preparation and learned skills. Politics isn't about winning at all costs. It's about maintaining relationships and getting results at the same time."[6] In referring to her strengths, one executive with the Harmonizer talent said, "I use my skills to influence and convince. Sometimes you can catch more flies with honey." In turning a bank around, a CEO, reflecting the Harmonizer talent, commented on how important it was to build trust with the regulators:

> [You have to establish] the right kind of relationship. . . The key is to get them to say, "We trust this person's judgment [so] that on a day-to-day basis he won't do anything improper and inappropriate." If you go in and fight these guys, you don't win. . . . The objective is to figure out, not necessarily what in some empirical, utopian context is right or wrong, but what is this regulator's problem and how can I make him feel as if his problem is getting appropriately addressed.

Harmonizers have a great deal of insight into and understanding about people. Their auxiliary talent influences how this insight takes shape. If their auxiliary talent is that of the Navigator, they will be practical, realistic, and matter-of-fact. They excel at dealing with specific customer problems and want to chip away at those problems in order to find a better solution. They will be curious about new facts, especially if they relate to people. With the Navigator talent, they usually have firsthand, tangible knowledge of people and situations on which they base their decisions. They encourage the development of step-by-step plans and procedures to ensure that situations are resolved.

If Harmonizers' auxiliary talent is that of the Visionary, the focus shifts from facts and today's reality to possibilities about the future. These Harmonizers are more interested in theory and vision. They have the imagination to come up with new possibilities beyond what is present, obvious, or known. Their goals at work are more focused on benefiting people and society. They will be seen as a catalyst for drawing out the best in people and known for their creative insights about people. They are very curious about new ideas and are stimulated by the possibilities of improving the world.

No matter what their auxiliary talent is, Harmonizers make a significant contribution to the creativity of the organization through their ability to recognize the importance of context in any particular situation. Seeing the gray in the world, they know that strict formulas do not work with most of the complex problems we face today, given all the inevitably interdependent variables. The people side of these issues often compounds their complexity. The answers are rarely yes or no. As the preceding quote from the banking executive regarding the regulators shows, Harmonizers seem capable of managing through that fuzziness and ambiguity. By helping others interpret problems from many different perspectives, they encourage the group to find new and different solutions to the challenge. Such an ability is a major contributor to the generation of creative solutions, since consideration of both-and solutions generates more creative ideas than either-or thinking.

Examples of possible Harmonizers are Eleanor Roosevelt, whose humanitarian efforts helped create different solutions to people problems during the Depression and World War II, and Mahatma Gandhi, who developed innovative methods of peaceful resistance and nonviolent political revolution.[7] Others are Martin Luther King, Jr., and Maya Angelou, both of whom have made major contributions through their ability to reach out to others. Another example is Mary Parker Follett, one of the first management consultants in the United States, who in the 1920s and early 1930s advocated replacing bureaucratic, hierarchical institutions with group networks and alliances. Her clear message that relationships matter, voiced eighty years ago, still holds true today.[8]

OBSTACLES

As with all the other creative talents, several blocks can get in the way of the Harmonizer's creativity. These include their overidentification with others, jumping to conclusions, and concern for consensus. After reviewing some of the key blocks, you will find strategies for overcoming them in the next sections.

HARMONIZER	Blocks to Optimal Creativity

- Boundary management issues
- Overidentification with others and need for approval
- Making incorrect assumptions and jumping to conclusions
- Failure to gather sufficient information
- Biases of their auxiliary talent to details or larger patterns
- Need for control and failure to listen
- Concern for consensus
- Difficulty seeing the disagreeable side to people or issues
- Dislike of having to deal with conflict

Their concern for people can be a block as well as a boost in Harmonizers' attempts to be more creative. For example, boundary issues can challenge Harmonizers and may limit their independence in creatively solving problems and making decisions. Harmonizers can overidentify with others and give the needs of others too high a priority. Said one CEO of a family-owned business,

> I come from a background of social work and mental health. The goal in social work is to help people find out what they want to achieve and then help them achieve it. In business, the goal tends to be to help people achieve what the organization needs to have done, not what they want to do. So I might actually spend too much time trying to be sure that people are feeling good about what they are doing and not enough time focusing on the goals of the customer or the business.

In addition, Harmonizers may sometimes depend too much on the ideals, conventions, and customs of the group and organization. Wanting to be accepted by others, they can be too concerned about what is proper and expected. Said one Harmonizer, "I would probably be more creative if I were more iconoclastic. I get a lot of ideas that I don't push that hard because I'm interested in building consensus and I am very sensitive to criticism. I want approval for what I am doing." This goal may lead to conventional behavior and a failure to question the group's opinion. Harmonizers may react too easily to the mood of the group and fail to reflect on their own interpretations, opinions, and needs. Their language can be lengthy and confusing because they try not to hurt anyone's feelings or want to address everyone's concerns.

In conflict situations Harmonizers tend to focus on reconciliation of conflicting parties rather than conflicting facts or issues. In the process they may fail to generate new ideas. They often prefer positive, confirming alternatives that they believe people want. They may inappropriately favor alternatives coming from certain trusted or respected individuals. Their decisions may focus on solving people problems but not necessarily address other critical organizational issues. They may deny the existence of conflict, disagreements, and ugly facts. They can find conflict that develops from creative differences troublesome. Said one retail business owner,

> My decision making is colored too much by those considerations about people. I worry too much about how other people feel, to the point where I'm concerned about how I'm going to make a vendor feel when I do something, where other people would just make the tough decision.

In addition to giving too much weight to other people, Harmonizers have some other challenges to their creativity and decision making. By nature, they prefer making decisions; they like to feel that things are settled. Thus, they may fail to take the time to listen to all the facts or to search for new and different ideas and solutions. The family-owned business CEO went on to say, "I can easily overread the situation and then overreact to it. Then erroneous assumptions about cultural biases and feelings can inhibit my creativity and my actions, if I don't test them out."

The auxiliary talent of Harmonizers can get in the way of their creativity. If it's the Navigator talent, Harmonizers may overlook trends, patterns, and possibilities as they work at solving problems and getting results. They can be overly concerned with the present or the past. If their auxiliary talent is that of the Visionary, details and reality can be overlooked as they pursue vision and ideals. They may ignore the present reality and focus only on the future and all its possibilities.

Harmonizers may also want to control situations and people. Such a need can lead to rigidity and even extend to perfectionism. Said the retail business owner, "I have this need to make everything perfect. We have to have a product that I can be proud of. But that lengthens the time it takes to either get it to the marketplace or have it actually be used in the company. And I have such a hard time letting go of that."

Stress inhibits the creative contribution of Harmonizers as much as with any other talent. Harmonizers may be especially stressed if they feel that they are misunderstood, not trusted, or not taken seriously. Such stress may also develop if they are alone too much or if they are being pressured to conform to a view with which they really don't agree. In any of these cases, they may get caught up in convoluted logic or negative and either-or thinking. They may become cold, theatrical, mechanical, and calculating. Their thoughts may turn destructive. They may also withdraw from their usual social self, becoming pessimistic and depressed. Harmonizers may become compulsively obsessed with finding the absolute truth. They can start to doubt themselves, worry, or feel guilty and then push for harmony, no matter what the cost. They may support the current structure uncritically and fail to see wider possibilities in life.[9] All these factors can limit their perspective and hamper their creativity.

BOOSTERS

Depending on their particular situation, there are several steps Harmonizers can take to gain maximum benefit from their creative talent and improve the effectiveness of their creativity:

1. Trust your strengths. Be sure that the team focuses on the people issues and the political considerations during change and innovation efforts. Also make sure that the team looks at the context surrounding a situation to explore alternative solutions, beyond either-or thinking. If the situation you are facing calls for time for you to listen and then reflect before coming up with new thoughts or making decisions, let the group know that you will need time before voicing your opinions and conclusions.

2. Develop greater self-awareness. Making a candid assessment of your strengths and areas where you need to focus your attention as a cre-

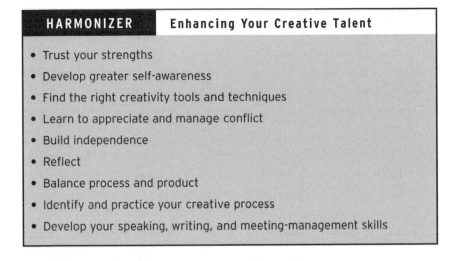

| HARMONIZER | Enhancing Your Creative Talent |

- Trust your strengths
- Develop greater self-awareness
- Find the right creativity tools and techniques
- Learn to appreciate and manage conflict
- Build independence
- Reflect
- Balance process and product
- Identify and practice your creative process
- Develop your speaking, writing, and meeting-management skills

ative individual is a critical step toward greater self-awareness and creativity. Be honest with yourself about blocks and barriers from your experiences, knowledge, and creative talents. Ask for and listen carefully to feedback from colleagues, friends, and family about your talents and what might be getting in the way. Be clear about what might be keeping you from being your creative best and making your greatest contributions.

3. Find the right creativity tools and techniques. Several tools and techniques play to a Harmonizer's strengths and boost their creative results:

- Many creative ideas come from groups inside and outside the organization. Such groups recommended by Harmonizers to help boost creativity include "consumer focus groups to get some good input as to how customers feel about the way the company has been servicing them. Of course, one immediate reaction is you don't want to do that because you don't want to hear what they're going to tell you about your company, but you need to."

- Setting up a board of trusted advisors may also be helpful. Another Harmonizer set up advisory boards and used them differently than they had been used in the past: "We use them as focus groups, for discussions about products, as well as about the strengths and weaknesses of the organization. It's really our own think tank."

- Another tool that may work for Harmonizers is Empathic Design, a process in which "designers, engineers, marketers, and team leaders immerse themselves in the environment in which potential customers live and work."[10] Walt Disney used similar techniques, personally identifying with the characters in his films, with his audiences, or with visitors, to come up with all sorts of creative ideas.

- Along the same lines is a technique called role playing, in which you pretend to be someone else, living or dead, and ask how he or she sees the problem or how he or she would solve the problem.[11] You might want to develop a list of people you can regularly call upon in your mind, as sort of an imaginary board of trusted advisors.

- Visual tools might also work for Harmonizers, both privately and in a team. Examples would be mindmapping—a technique in which you represent your thoughts using bubbles of key words and then organize those bubbles into a web of connecting lines in all directions[12]— or just putting all your ideas on paper and seeing if patterns, connections, and themes emerge.

4. Learn to appreciate and manage conflict. Part of the creative process involves exposing different assumptions and perspectives and making sure that they are thoroughly explored. Too much focus on harmony may keep the group from exploring all ideas. It can lead to groupthink, in which everyone begins to think alike or focuses on traditional lines of inquiry. Such an approach may keep the team from reaching an in-depth understanding of the real situation and a genuine appreciation for various alternatives. Be sure that your desire for approval and harmony doesn't get in the way of reaching optimal solutions. The following are some ways to avoid this:

- Look at conflict as a means to bring out the best in people. Find a conflict-management or mediation course that emphasizes the role of conflict in establishing good working relationships and generating more productive decisions.[13]

- Use a creative problem-solving approach to conflict (see Chapter 11 for more details).

- Follow the lead of this Harmonizer, who learned to creatively deal with conflict. He approached conflict without being *ad hominem*. Without effectively saying, you're a jerk for believing in what you believe, or you're stupid for not believing what I believe. . . . You want to respect the other person. You may disagree, but you still want him or her to understand that this is over here, this argument we're having about this subject. It doesn't really have anything to do with my affection, regard, or respect for you.

- While keeping good relationships in mind, take the time to look at facts and step back to get the big picture.

5. Build independence. To ensure optimal results and creative solutions, develop the ability to balance the needs of others with your own needs and values. Consider making decisions based on what something is worth both to the group or community *and* to you. Develop and express your own opinions even if the group disagrees with them. Build independence and be willing to ask bold questions without fear of losing the group's acceptance. Learn to be more objective and to set limits on how much you let others dominate or invade your life.

6. Reflect. Find the time and space for more introspection and reflection. Consider keeping a journal.[14] As you examine circumstances and the situation on your own, you can develop more independence in your decision-making process. Said one CEO,

> I find that probably more than most other people I have to go through the processing of my feelings, to make sure everything is okay. If I'm in an all-day meeting, I'm exhausted when I get home. After dinner, I go upstairs and lie down, and I mull over and over everything that happened.

Consider scheduling time-outs for yourself, even putting them in your day planner. Take time to ponder. Don't be the first to express an opinion; let others in the group speak first. Listen, really listen, to what they have to say. One Harmonizer suggested,

> I remove my body from the microconcerns that I have on a day-to-day basis. Then I am much more open to ideas popping into my head. . . . I go to a lot of conferences. They may not teach me anything, but I come back with great ideas and feel refreshed. There is a saying by Leonardo da Vinci that we should really get away from where we are, because to remain constantly at work means we do not see things clearly.

7. Balance process and product. Because Harmonizers may be quick to jump to conclusions and to act on assumptions that can turn out to be wrong, balance your decision-making talent with your auxiliary perceiving talent, of either the Navigator or the Visionary. Spend more time paying attention to all sorts of data, not just memorable data or data relating to people, and looking squarely at the facts, even those that you wish were not true. You may need to look at reality or at possibilities in a situation before making a decision. Don't be so quick to decide about options or the problem itself. Such a preference can stifle the creativity of the group. Of course, at the same time, make sure that the team eventually does find closure and that you have not put off coming to conclusions because you are afraid to hurt people's feelings about moving on.

Focus on developing the creative talents in others. Ask them for alternatives, and let them decide. Hold off solving the problem yourself. Learn to let go. Doing so could provide the time you need to be more creative! Review the chapter for either the Navigator (Chapter 4) or the Visionary (Chapter 6) for more ways to stimulate use of your auxiliary talent.

8. Identify and practice your creative process. Knowing what to do to develop different and valuable results greatly facilitates creative contributions. Review the creative problem-solving process in Chapter 11 and consider adapting it to work for you. Such a process will ensure that you both diverge and explore alternatives and converge around next steps. You may want to investigate other techniques for organizing and storing your creative ideas. Exhibiting the organization of typical Harmonizers, a school admissions director indicated that she "writes ideas down and slips them into the appropriate file to use later. When it comes time for meeting with that group, editing that article, or changing procedures, I try to see where this can be utilized." Another Harmonizer uses mind-mapping techniques to organize her thoughts and ideas. Another Harmonizer commented on her creativity:

> I'm creative mostly at home or at leisure. While I walk, I allow my mind free range and often that is when I find a solution to problems or conundrums. When I do housework or watch television, I often come up with ideas or thoughts that lead to solutions or processes that I want to pursue. Stuff pops into my head when my mind is not fully engaged in what I'm doing. Maybe that's why I have trouble thinking about work as creative because my mind is almost always fully engaged while I'm there.

9. Develop your speaking, writing, and meeting-management skills. Another area for development for Harmonizers is in the articulation of their opinions and in giving and receiving feedback. To be effective in making points in creativity discussions, practice being brief and more concise in your conversations and presentations. Be sure that you are focusing your thoughts and opinions and getting said what you want to say and what needs to be said. Clarifying your communications may add to your creativity through a heightened ability to gain acceptance of your ideas in a larger group. Developing a briefing document[15] or executive summary may help you organize your thoughts before a meeting or written or verbal presentation. Publishing and sticking to an agenda for meetings may help ensure that meetings get results. Designate a timekeeper and facilitator to be sure that you stay on target.

To stretch and grow your creative results and contributions even further, here are some additional strategies for Harmonizers:

1. Practice critical thinking. Harmonizers need to incorporate more critical, analytical thinking in their creative decision-making process and to develop their ability to make tough decisions if the lack of such abilities is getting in their way. Although understanding context and people issues is very important for successful innovation and change, these are not the only criteria for decision making in organizations. People issues must be balanced against business needs for effective creative results to be achieved. Critical problem-solving tools, techniques from the Total Quality Management toolkit, such as force-field analysis for evaluating positive and negative forces impacting decisions, or process-mapping systems may help boost your creativity by providing analytical perspectives.[16] They can help you analyze a challenge and come to conclusions, even without everyone's agreement.

You may also develop your own criteria and techniques for looking at the pros and cons of a situation and possible solutions, for asking if-then questions, and for exploring the consequences of any actions you might decide to take. Follow a standard creative problem-solving process that takes you logically and systematically through the steps involved and gives time for both divergent and convergent thinking.

2. Watch out for biases from your auxiliary talent. Your auxiliary talent can impact your creativity by limiting or biasing the data you take in. With the Navigator auxiliary talent, you may be focusing on facts and data and ignoring trends and possibilities. With the Visionary auxiliary talent, you may be ignoring the present or the past and focusing too much on possibilities. You may be seeing things from too complicated a point of view. To build your creativity, take both a big-picture view and a snapshot of grounded reality, paying attention to details and realities. See the chapters on the Navigator (Chapter 4) and the Visionary (Chapter 6) for more information on what to do about these biases.

3. Practice relaxation techniques. Some techniques that may help you be more creative include seeking a change of scenery, exercising, listening to music, and reflecting in a journal about what has happened. You sometimes need time alone to get back to your center. Use your auxiliary talent to explore possibilities and options and to support reflection in your search for what really matters to you and what really makes you feel alive. One Harmonizer described how he renewed his creativity through music: "Music for me is more of a refuge than a thinking place. It's just a space to relax, clear my mind so that I can think." Another Harmonizer needs the ocean or her garden to rejuvenate her creativity.

4. Access your unconscious. Use of logical, analytical thinking tools may help you get in touch with your unconscious. Check out the tools and techniques recommended for the Pilot (Chapter 7) or the Inventor (Chapter 8) for more ideas and for support in accessing your unconscious. Explore puzzles and games that require logic and strategy.[17] Using these tools may help you out of stressful situations. They may also bring new knowledge about yourself, knowledge that can further improve your creative contributions. You may find less need for total harmony and start to feel more confident about your own thinking. You can gain objectivity and clarity about your own goals.[18]

HOW YOU CAN HELP A HARMONIZER

If you work with Harmonizers, there are several steps you can take to maximize their creative contributions to the organization:

1. Set the right structure. Make sure that Harmonizers have enough structure to feel comfortable but that there is room for exploration and reflection. Give them a job that challenges them and calls for creativity. Agree on clear goals and objectives. Make sure that quantitative goals are

HARMONIZER	Maximizing Their Contributions

- Set the right structure
- Help them set boundaries
- Show them appreciation
- Allow them time to process change
- Help them build their conflict-management skills
- Encourage development of their listening and data-collecting abilities
- Work with them on developing their analytical abilities
- Work on a development plan
- Recognize signs of stress

considered as well as people issues. Talk about the processes they will use to achieve the goals.

2. Help them set boundaries. Make sure that their management style includes the proper amount of delegation since Harmonizers are prone to want to exercise more control than a team may need. If they complain about constantly being interrupted to deal with problems, suggest that they have scripts available, such as "I am working on a project that requires my full concentration. Can we schedule a time to meet later today?"

3. Show them appreciation. Let Harmonizers know how much you appreciate their perspectives and how much these perspectives add to the creativity of the organization.[19] Validate them. Value their insights and listen to them. Allow them to express their feelings in a safe environment. Build a relationship with them, one anchored in mutual trust and respect.

4. Allow them time to process change. Harmonizers may be somewhat reluctant to change because of possible negative impacts on others or possible conflicts with their own values regarding relationships. Give them the support they need to work through their concerns. Allow time for them to consider all aspects and allow enough time on a project for all sides to be heard.[20]

5. Help them build their conflict-management skills. Help Harmonizers find a conflict-management course or one on giving and receiving feedback in ways that build the effectiveness of the team. Encourage them to reflect and then voice their opinions. Understand that their silence does not necessarily mean agreement. Touch base with them privately to find out what they feel are the critical issues. Be careful about asking "Why," questions, which can be intimidating. Instead, ask, "What are your feelings on this problem?" or "What do we need to do to ensure success?"

6. Encourage development of their listening and data-collecting abilities. Ask questions to explore their decision-making process. Questions such as "In what ways might we?" or "What are the pluses, potentials, and concerns of this issue?" can explore the extent of their data-gathering efforts.

7. Work with them on developing their analytical abilities. If this is a potential limitation to their success, help them be more analytical or team them with someone for whom this is a strength. If they have to go it alone, at the beginning of a project discuss and mutually establish goals and objectives and the criteria to be used in making decisions. Help them plan changes. Make sure that they are thinking things through and considering the pros, cons, and consequences of a decision. In a nonthreatening way, explore how they came to their conclusions.

8. Work on a development plan. Mutually work on personal goals to develop Harmonizers' presentation and delegation skills if these are issues that are impeding their ability to be effectively creative. Build such courses, workshops, and self-study into their performance plan.

9. Recognize signs of stress. When Harmonizers are under stress, they may become overcritical of themselves and others. Allow them time to vent, reflect, and regain their balance so that they can continue to be positive, creative contributors.[21]

SUMMARY

Without the Harmonizer, the team may suffer from lack of concern for people during the development and implementation of creative solutions. A nurturing, safe environment where team members' needs, values, and feelings are considered may also be missing. Through their support and high energy, Hamonizers help team members build the self-esteem they need to be truly creative. Harmonizers use their organizational skills to ensure that the team finds creative solutions. They also ensure that the team looks at context and circumstances, keeping them away from black-and-white thinking, instead focusing on integrating conflicting opinions. Their communication and political skills are extremely important in managing people through change. By focusing on proper boundary and conflict-management skills, finding support when analysis and critique are required, and making sure they have considered diverse points of view before making decisions, Harmonizers can become even more effectively creative.

SELF-ASSESSMENT

How does this talent impact my life as a dominant or auxiliary talent?

_____

_____

_____

If this is not my dominant or auxiliary talent, how do I demonstrate the use of this talent?

_____

_____

_____

How could I have used this talent in the past?

_____

_____

_____

How can I use this talent in the future?

_____

_____

_____

What do I need to do to better manage a Harmonizer team member?

_____

_____

_____

CHAPTER TEN

THE POET

ISFP: AUXILIARY CREATIVE TALENT–ADVENTURER

INFP: AUXILIARY CREATIVE TALENT–EXPLORER

Like the singer of sea chanteys, the Poet helps keep alive the vision and purpose of the voyage and keeps the crew's spirits buoyed.

Poets have many creative contributions to make at work through their focus on values—both their own and the organization's—through their sensitivity and concern for people, and through their unconventional perspectives. They add quiet grace and a sense of depth to any group in which they participate. Because they have usually taken the time to discover what's important to them, Poets have a strong and stable sense of who they are and what they stand for. They want to be sure that the organization is doing the right thing. They may be the ethical backbone of any group because of their high moral standards and the example they set in living by them. Poets ensure that a team finds meaning in the effort, stays focused on what really matters, and thus sustains its passion.

Poets see life in unconventional ways. They have a finely developed taste for beauty and sense of proportion. Their eye for the beauty of a design and the elegance of a solution often adds a new perspective to the situation. Poets are usually quite independent, flexible, tolerant of others, and self-aware.

Although they often prefer to work alone, they are usually good team players. Poets are nurturing and loyal to people and project efforts they care about. They feel committed to the group and make sure that their

POET	Results and Contributions

- An aesthetic appreciation for grace and elegance in solutions
- Building an environment of trust, respect, and support, a safe place for testing out new ideas and behaviors
- Independent and thoughtful perspectives on the challenge, addressing people-related values, context, and circumstances
- Serving as the team's ethical backbone
- Generation of new possibilities and options through reflection and incubation
- Articulation and portrayal of values, feelings, and perspectives, often through writing

responsibilities to the team are met. Their focus on people helps create a positive, affirming environment, one where creativity can flourish. They are concerned about how people will work together. Recognizing people's need for appreciation and validation, Poets praise the good that they frequently see. They affirm the value and uniqueness of the individual and are reluctant to categorize. Poets quietly support everyone in expressing their unique creativity. Through their nurturing encouragement, they can heighten the self-esteem of the individuals on the team and thus increase team members' creative contributions. Their ability to create an environment where people enjoy working and feel as if they are making a contribution can have very positive results in terms of reduced turnover of staff. Their support is also particularly helpful during change, when people feel disrupted, confused, and lost.

Said one Poet, a financial services executive,

> I try to inspire people by including them, educating them, and making it safe for them to be creative—that is, give them the benefit of their untested ideas, previous failures, "off-the-wall" stuff that might germinate into something wonderful. I also assign "design" tasks to junior, sometimes newly hired, people to come back with ideas. Their instructions are: no barriers, no time constraints, and no cost considerations.

Poets have much to contribute to the process of finding creative solutions to organizational challenges. In the discussion of alternatives, they are the champions of values and concern for people. For example, as one

Poet, an educational consultant, commented, "I will always look at what's best for the student." Poets are also good at reading body language and picking up signs that reveal hidden feelings and emotions. The questions they typically ask in addressing creative challenges are helpful in exploring facts and issues, evaluating alternatives, and planning for implementation. These questions may include the following:

- How does everyone feel about this issue?

- How does this fit into the organization's values?

- How does it fit with the team's values and those of the team members?

- Who might gain or lose from the situation? From the solution?

- How will customers, employees, and stakeholders be affected?

- What's important to them?

- How will they react?

- Who might contribute special strengths or skills?

- How do we get them on board?

Poets contribute to the creativity of the organization through the ability to recognize the importance of context in any particular situation. When Poets look around them, they see a different world; they have a different perspective, based on context, people, and values. Said one consultant with the Poet talent, "I see the interconnectedness of the whole. I look at relationships. I see life in terms of 'more or less,' not 'either-or.' Things are more 'fuzzy,' less clear-cut." This evaluative process, which has been called "fuzzy logic" or fuzzy thinking,[1] is very important when dealing with complexity. It looks at facts as matters of degree. Facts, in this world of grayness, are multivalent, vague, or inexact.

Individuals with this creative talent are more likely to see nuances, context, and circumstances and are fairly fluid in assessing possibilities. Since they can see the gray in the world, Poets know that strict formulas do not work with most of the complex problems we face today. The people side of these issues often compounds their complexity. These days, the answer is rarely yes or no. Poets, like Hamonizers, seem to be capable of managing through that fuzziness and ambiguity. This attitude helps them see things very differently than do other members of the team.

Avoiding an all-or-nothing view of the situation, Poets tend to see other possibilities in the middle and beyond the boundaries that the team has set. They can also be comfortable managing in less rigidly defined and potentially more innovative ways, such as through using influence, borrowed resources, or matrix management.

Poets are usually adept at taking a more detached perspective on a challenge or problem. Very curious and tolerant of a wide range of diversity, they see the value in exploring contradictory points of view. They are nonjudgmental, understanding, and forgiving. They want to pursue a variety of options. They usually push the group to allow ideas to incubate and thus tap into the unconscious, a world that can be an incredible source of inspiration and imaginative insights. Poets can thus be very helpful in times of conflict. They make sure that the team reaches consensus through exploring areas of agreement and common ground and in finding ways to reconcile and accommodate conflicting points of view.

Poets bring flexibility in attitude, perspective, and behavior to a team effort. Because their preferred way of dealing with the external world is through a perceiving function, they tend to be concerned about having adaptable rules and responsive operating procedures. Poets chafe at limits to their freedom. They prefer less structure and somewhat fluid plans. Their experience has shown them that by plunging in, "following your hunches," a creative solution will emerge. They encourage their team members to stay open to find that creative solution, to let it emerge since answers are often not obvious right away.

When the team is planning the implementation of any effort, Poets appear to have an inner barometer that measures the impact of decisions on the people involved.[2] They will take politics, resistance, and ego issues into consideration when developing a plan. For example, they would be capable of anticipating the aesthetic, ideological, political, and moral objections to an affirmative action program.[3] By making sure that the team considers these types of issues and works to find common ground, Poets make a significant contribution to the success of the effort.

Poets' perspectives on challenges and their use of their dominant creative talent are influenced by their extraverted perceiving auxiliary talent of either the Adventurer or the Explorer. If Poets have the Adventurer as their auxiliary talent, they focus on the needs of the moment. They tend to live in the present and are quite flexible. Their attention is on knowing the details of people's lives. Their stories and communications are more focused on specific people and the details of the workplace. Poets with this combination of talents are concerned with reconciling facts and details, as opposed to ideas. They are more likely to use their hands to express themselves—in woodworking or sculpture, for example—because the work of their hands would likely be more eloquent than anything they could say. They may excel in fine craftsmanship, since they have discriminating taste and a sense of beauty and proportion. Their focus is on the team's decisions regarding implementation and the practicality of the solution. These Poets look for common ground to keep harmony, and they appreciate flexible decision rules. They add fun to the process, and they want freedom and space to set their own time frame.

If Poets have the auxiliary talent of the Explorer, their focus is on ideas, as opposed to facts and details. They are more concerned with the future vision than with the detailed implementation plan. Their imaginative and intuitive insights are focused on people, but they have a more global, long-range perspective, on the long-term exploration of growth opportunities and possibilities for individuals and society. Poets with this auxiliary talent want to truly understand the human experience. They need to have a dream before they can act; in fact, they are often seen as dreamers.

With either auxiliary talent, the creative contribution from Poets at work also comes from their powerful ability to write and communicate. This gift is particularly important at the start of any new initiative and during the implementation process. They help keep people informed about what is going on. They can communicate with others in human, clearly understandable terms since they are more in touch with the people side of issues. They bring their life experiences to bear to better understand and articulate the situation and make it real. Poets can make any effort fun and meaningful. Said the financial services executive, "I don't think of myself as particularly creative at work. What creativity I do demonstrate comes in my communications (speeches, arguments, selling my point of view, bringing a unique perspective)." She went on to say, "I've been told my speeches are funny, easily understood, educational, and down to earth. I seem to have a knack for adjusting my content, word choice, length, and degree of technical jargon to my audience in a somewhat expert fashion."

Poets use their writing to craft great stories and articles to express their ideals and to help the team reach its vision and goals. Their skills can be used during implementation of the chosen initiative to communicate to those involved the vision of what is going to take place and the reasons behind the changes. Some examples of well-known individuals who may have had this creative talent are the playwright William Shakespeare and the poets T. S. Eliot, Charlotte and Emily Brontë, and Emily Dickinson. All used their gifts and talents to vividly portray many of the deep, burning issues of life.

Their concern for values, their ability to communicate, and their loyalty to the organization help Poets define the rituals and stories that are so important in enabling a change to become part of the culture. This assistance ensures that the change is enduring and not just another fad.

OBSTACLES

Poets may be blocked from being more creative in a number of ways, many of which are related to their concern for people and values and to their lack of organization. After reviewing some of the key blocks, you will find strategies for overcoming them in the next sections.

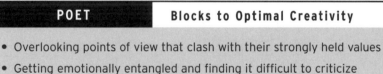

POET	Blocks to Optimal Creativity

- Overlooking points of view that clash with their strongly held values
- Getting emotionally entangled and finding it difficult to criticize others and give honest, direct feedback
- Avoidance of conflict
- Procrastination and indecision
- Biases of their auxiliary talent to details or larger patterns
- Keeping feelings and opinions private
- Lack of organization
- Excessive need to reflect and process

In their creative processes, Poets may exclude or ignore facts that they find incompatible with their own well-trusted and well-developed value system. Although they can often help the team deal with conflict, they may be uncomfortable with such disagreements if they are personally involved or if their values are attacked. They may also find it difficult to provide critical feedback to others because of their concern for hurting someone else's feelings.

Values and feelings can interfere with Poets' creativity in other ways. Their feelings may take too much precedence in some situations. They may get too caught up in context and circumstances. Their difficulty in setting boundaries and their responsiveness to meeting people's needs may lead to encroachments on their time and space. They may respond too easily to ideas and solutions with emotional appeal. Said a business owner, reflecting the Poet talent, "I'm kind of responsive to how I'm feeling, and sometimes I don't really feel like dealing with this stuff right away."

Since Poets are usually adaptable, they may sometimes appear to be indecisive about issues that don't really matter to them. Other people may not be sure where they stand on an issue. Poets prefer to keep on pondering, but at the same time, they can be somewhat intransigent on positions that really matter to them. Poets find it difficult to work to implement a solution unless they are committed to it and it fits into their value systems, and they don't change those value systems easily. In fact, they can be slow to change, particularly when they are comfortable with the way things are now, if the changes conflict with their ideals, or if personal losses or relationships are involved.[4]

A Poet's decision-making process takes place internally; Poets tend to manage their external world with their auxiliary talent—the perceiving talent of the Adventurer or the Explorer. This extraverted perceiving talent is usually well developed to facilitate their working in the external world. A very well developed auxiliary talent can cause Poets to be less focused, organized, or disciplined externally when they need to maximize their creative contribution. For instance, Poets tend to start businesses without a business plan. One Poet remarked that she and her partner decided it would be fun to open a crafts store. "It just sort of happened." The business has succeeded, but they were lucky. An emergent attitude to new projects must be balanced against the need for some sort of plan that sets a direction.[5]

The auxiliary talent of Poets can cause other problems for their creativity. If it's the Adventurer talent, Poets may focus only on specifics in the here and now. If it's the Explorer talent, Poets may ignore such facts and pay too much attention to future trends and possibilities.

It can be difficult for Poets to share their thoughts and feelings. Like other individuals with introverted creative talents, they tend to be private and reflective. Therefore, people often don't see their complex inner processing of information. As with the Inventor creative talent, Poets can be hard to understand and hard to get to know; they are complex, and much is going on inside them. Poets need a great deal of time to process what they have taken in and decide how they feel about it all.

Depending on the situation, another block to a Poet's creativity is having to deal with objective, quantitative analysis. Because logical, systematic thinking does not necessarily come naturally to Poets, they may feel somewhat vulnerable in this respect. They can thus be blocked, and they may question their own competence. If they think that their intellectual capabilities are being threatened or if they think that others are smarter than they are, Poets may become stressed and start to see incompetence everywhere, in themselves and in others.[6]

Stress can affect a Poet's creativity just as with any other creative talent. With Poets, stress may result if their values are violated, if they have to spend too much time with people, or if they are tired. Stress can also be triggered when they feel unappreciated, when others don't live up to their standards and expectations, or when they have to listen to a great deal of negativity and criticism. Their stress may reveal itself as an obsession with the truth. Their analytical thinking, not normally their strong suit, may become very narrow and focus on only one or two key issues. They may start to split hairs and see everything in black-and-white terms, becoming negative, cynical, sarcastic, and even hostile. They may take action without thinking things through just to bring back some sense of order. Or they may take uncharacteristic control of the situation. They may start to organize things in some sort of orderly, logical, and linear fashion.[7] These reactions can severely limit their creativity and their contributions.

BOOSTERS

Depending on their particular situation, there are several steps Poets can take to gain maximum benefit from their creative talent and improve the effectiveness of their creativity:

1. Trust your strengths. Be sure that the team focuses on personal and organizational values, the people issues, and the political considerations during change and innovation efforts. Make sure that the team looks at the context surrounding a situation to explore alternative solutions and to find the gray areas in a world they may be seeing as black and white.

2. Develop greater self-awareness. Making a candid assessment of your strengths and areas where you need to focus attention as a creative

POET	Enhancing Your Creative Talent

- Trust your strengths
- Develop greater self-awareness
- Find the right creativity tools and techniques
- Learn to appreciate conflict
- Voice your opinions
- Be sure that you are open to possibilities
- Enhance your speaking and writing skills
- Set boundaries
- Practice good project and time management
- Define and practice your creative process

individual is a critical step toward greater self-awareness and creativity. Be honest with yourself about blocks and barriers from your experiences, knowledge, and creative talents. Ask for and listen carefully to feedback from colleagues, friends, and family about your talents and what might be getting in the way. Be clear about what might be keeping you from being your creative best and making your greatest contributions

3. Find the right creativity tools and techniques. Poets may find the following techniques helpful:

- Many creative ideas come from groups inside and outside the organization. Such groups include consumer focus groups, organized to find out how customers feel about the way the company has been servicing them, and advisory boards.

- Another tool that works for Poets is Empathic Design, a process in which "designers, engineers, marketers, and team leaders immerse themselves in the environment in which potential customers live and work."[8] Walt Disney used similar techniques. By personally identifying with the characters in his films, with his audiences, or with visitors, he came up with all sorts of creative ideas.

- Poets can explore the technique of role playing, in which you pretend to be someone else, living or dead, and ask how he or she sees the problem or how he or she would solve the problem.[9]

- Poets, with their private, introspective nature, may also want to explore brainwriting, in which team members write down their ideas, share them, and build on the ideas of one another in silence.

- Visual tools, such as mind mapping and storyboarding, in which the problem is displayed in pictures or diagrams, might also work for Poets, both privately and in a team.[10]

4. Learn to appreciate conflict. Part of the creative process involves bringing to light different assumptions and perspectives and making sure that they are thoroughly explored. Conflict of opinions, objectives, and assumptions is inevitable in the creative process. As an objective third party, Poets can often help others out of conflict. Be careful that your concern for consensus is balanced against its dangers. Too much focus on harmony may keep the group from exploring all ideas. It can lead to groupthink where everyone begins to think alike. Such an approach might keep the team from reaching an in-depth understanding of the true situation and a real appreciation for various alternatives. Don't let your desire for approval and harmony get in the way of reaching optimal solutions. Techniques to avoid this include the following:

- Look at conflict as a means of bringing out the best in people. Check out books and workshops for a conflict-management approach that emphasizes the role of conflict in establishing good working relationships and leading to more productive decisions.[11] Or use a creative problem-solving approach, as outlined in Chapter 11.

- Consider taking a mediation course as a way to deal with conflict.

- While keeping good relationships in mind, take the time to look at facts and step back to get the big picture. Whenever possible, one Poet makes sure that she prepares, rehearses, and thinks through all the details before she steps into a potential conflict arena.

5. Voice your opinions. Learn to express your concerns and feelings sooner rather than later in the creative process. Share your thoughts and opinions with others more openly and in a reasonable amount of time so that the team can benefit from them. Access your auxiliary talent to get the right balance between the world around you and the world inside you. Your auxiliary talent, whether that of the Adventurer or the Explorer, can provide you with a channel to get outside yourself and allow you to express your feelings, ideals, and inner certainties to others.

6. Be sure that you are open to possibilities. Your auxiliary talent of either the Adventurer or the Explorer can help you get out of internally processing and evaluating information against your value system and help you open up to alternative ideas and bring fresh perspectives to your life. Check out the tools recommended for your auxiliary talent in Chapter 3 (the Adventurer) or Chapter 5 (the Explorer).

7. Enhance your speaking and writing skills. Another area for development for Poets is how they articulate their opinions and give feedback. Poets may be gentle and unassuming. These attitudes when reflected in communications can detract from the message you want to convey at work. A Poet's communications may be very personal, flowery, and poetic. Although you don't want to lose your unique talent, you may want to evaluate it to be sure that you are making yourself heard and understood in the workplace in order to maximize your creative contribution.

To be more effective in making points in creativity discussions, practice being brief and more concise in your conversations and presentations. Focus your thoughts and opinions and say what you want to say and what needs to be said. Clarifying your communications can add to your creativity through a heightened ability to gain acceptance of your ideas in a larger group. Developing a briefing document[12] or executive summary may help you organize your thoughts before a meeting or a written or verbal presentation. Try practicing your presentation skills in a safe environment, such as a volunteer activity or a Toastmasters club, or get involved with professional groups that offer opportunities for speaking engagements.

8. Set boundaries. Another area for development may be learning to set boundaries and not getting too involved with seeing things from other people's perspectives. If you are not careful, you can lose your own perspective. Step back and take an objective view of the situation to avoid getting too focused on how it fits into your values and to avoid merging with others. If possible, team with someone who is skilled at keeping boundaries clear and intact.

9. Practice good project and time management. Poets are internally well organized, but they may not be as organized and focused in the external world. This is particularly true if they have overdeveloped their auxiliary extraverted perceiving function. If this is the case with you, you may need to develop strong project-management practices in order to stay on track. Following a standard creative problem-solving process that takes you logically and systematically through the steps involved and gives time for both divergent and convergent thinking may also help (see Chapter 11). Learn to plan backward to be sure you meet your deadlines. Calculate the final due date for the project and establish critical milestones working back from that final date; then make the key milestone delivery dates. Post the schedule where you can see it, and get started right away on the first deliverable.[13] Although working under pressure can be stimulating to Poets, waiting until the last minute may result in missed opportunities and lost resources. A flexible plan that does not constrict but still gives focus and some measures of progress may also be helpful.

10. Define and practice your creative process. To be consciously creative, you need to be aware of your own process; practice and refine it to help you be more creative. One Poet in need of inspiration takes a new notebook and a new pen and then gets on the train for no other purpose than to be open to creative ideas that he knows will start to flow. As another example, the financial services executive with the Poet talent indicated the following:

> I am not terribly creative off the cuff. I tend to ponder the challenge, frequently in my subconscious, and develop ideas (approaches, solutions, speeches, or introductions) over a period of a day or two. In this process, I also tend to rehearse my delivery (what words I will use, what rebuttals are available for anticipated challenges, or whatever). On major issues, I will sometimes consult with trusted peers and employees prior to going into my subconscious pondering. This preparation usually provides a broader perspective from which I can select fodder for my internal deliberations. Sometimes this step also provides cautions that I must consider.

To stretch and grow your creative results and contributions even further, here are some additional strategies for Poets:

1. Practice critical thinking. To broaden your contributions, you may want to incorporate more critical thinking into your decision-making process and develop your ability to make tough decisions. Understanding context and people issues is very important for successful innovation and change, but these are not the only criteria for decision making in organizations. People issues must be balanced against business needs for effectively creative results to be achieved.

If you can't team with someone who has this strength, you may have to develop an approach for it on your own. Tools that show you how to evaluate pros and cons and possible consequences may boost your creativity by helping you look at a challenge from more analytical perspectives.[14] Experiment with courses in business planning and analysis. You may also develop your own techniques for establishing criteria and objectives, for looking at the advantages and disadvantages of a situation and possible solutions, for asking if-then questions, and for exploring the consequences of any actions you might decide to take.

2. Open up to the world of logic to balance your creative talent. As you become more comfortable in your analytical abilities, you may enjoy order in the external world and have less concern for hurting the feelings of others. By adding logical analysis to your skill set, you may heighten your creative contribution and not let your idealism get in the way of results. Spend time writing down your experiences and detailing the pros and cons of choices. One business leader reflecting the Poet talent spends time writing down his reactions since he feels he's "more logical when I write than when I'm talking."

3. Access your unconscious. Such use of logical, analytical thinking tools may also help Poets get in touch with their unconscious. Try accessing your unconscious for inspiration and new ideas by playing chess or other analytical games. Check out the tools and techniques recommended for the Pilot (Chapter 7) or the Inventor (Chapter 8), such as Scamper, for more ideas and for help in accessing your unconscious. Using these tools may help you out of stressful situations. They may also bring new knowledge about yourself, knowledge that can further improve your creative contributions. You may find less need for total harmony and start to feel more confident about your own thinking. You may gain objectivity and clarity about what your own goals and objectives are.[15]

4. Watch for biases from your auxiliary talent. Your auxiliary talent can impact your creativity by limiting or biasing the data you take in. You may be focusing on facts and data and ignoring trends and possibilities, or vice versa. Look at both current reality and future possibilities when you are gathering information. The chapters on the Adventurer (Chapter 3) and the Explorer (Chapter 5) have more information on these biases.

5. Find work you love, or love your work. Poets need to feel passionate about their work in order to be the most creative, more so than perhaps any other talent. If you can't change your work, volunteer to work with organizations whose causes you care about or take on work assignments that represent your areas of concern—for example, space planning, policy crafting, or offsite-meeting planning. This tactic allows you to have input and perhaps even have your personal objectives met, especially if no one else takes on the assignment.

HOW YOU CAN HELP A POET

If you work with Poets, there are several steps you can take to mazimize their creative contributions to the organization:

1. Check to be sure that structure is needed. Poets usually prefer freedom from rules and procedures. Sometimes structure is not important because the Poet has developed ways to manage time and projects. You need to recognize that sometimes deadlines can work to inspire creativity at the last moment. Learn to trust their process if they have shown the ability to deliver results as promised.

2. Provide the time and space they need to be the most creative. Find ways for them to have private time and space to work most effectively. If this is not possible in the work space, then explore ways for Poets to have the reflective time they need (for example, working out of the home, using white noise, or wearing earphones). Poets may need more time to disclose their perspectives on the problem. They may also not be ready to share alternative solutions. Give them time to reflect, and then ask questions to encourage them to voice opinions. Make sure that they have spent enough time gathering data and considering all angles. Ask questions such as "In what ways might we look at this differently?" to explore how broadly they have considered different angles and perspectives. You might want to ask Poets for their opinions and/or encourage them to write out their perspectives.

3. Make sure they are engaged and motivated. When Poets are passionate about their work, their creativity jumps. Help them see how their values and their work are linked. Find them the right assignments.

4. Recognize their sensitivity and show them appreciation. Let Poets know how much you appreciate their perspectives and how much these perspectives add to the creativity of the organization.[16] Value their insights and listen to them. Allow them to express their feelings in a safe

POET	Maximizing Their Contributions

- Check to be sure that structure is needed
- Provide the time and space they need to be the most creative
- Make sure they are engaged and motivated
- Recognize their sensitivity and show them appreciation
- Allow them opportunities to express their uniqueness
- Help them build their conflict-management and communication skills
- Help them define objectives, set boundaries, prioritize, and plan
- Encourage critical thinking
- Build objectives for improving new skills into their performance plan
- Watch for symptoms of stress

environment. Build a relationship with them, one of mutual trust and respect. Poets may need some time to process change to see if it fits in with their value systems. Give them the support they need. Respect their need to consider several points of view and allow enough time for all sides to be heard.[17]

5. Allow them opportunities to express their uniqueness. Let Poets use their fine taste and sense of aesthetics to personalize their work space to make themselves and others feel more comfortable. Find a place for them to use their strengths and help others.

6. Help them build their conflict-management and communication skills. Help Poets find a conflict-management course or a course on giving and receiving feedback in ways that build more effective relationships in a team. Encourage them to reflect and then voice their opinions. Understand that their silence does not necessarily mean agreement. Touch base with them privately to find out what they feel are the critical issues. Be careful about asking "Why?" questions, which can be intimidating. Instead, ask, "What are your feelings on this problem?" or "What do we need to do to ensure success?" Suggest courses to improve the organization and conciseness of their written and verbal presentations.

7. Help them define objectives, set boundaries, prioritize, and plan. Although Poets may chafe at structure, they can still benefit from some mutually agreeable schedules and deadlines, with regular reviews.

Make sure that you are clear on both priorities and the plan for action. If Poets have a concern about constantly being interrupted to deal with problems, suggest that they have scripts available, such as "I am working on a project that requires my full concentration. Can we schedule a time to meet later today?"

8. Encourage critical thinking. Help Poets plan out changes. Make sure that they are thinking things through. Explore different possible alternatives. Help them investigate the consequences and the pros and cons of decisions.

9. Build objectives for improving new skills into their performance plan. Work with Poets to identify skills—such as critical thinking and project, time, and conflict management—that may need improvement or support or that may be interfering with their creative contribution. Build courses, workshops, or independent studies in these areas into their performance plan.

10. Watch for symptoms of stress. When Poets start showing signs of stress, such as being overcritical of themselves and others or withdrawing, suggest time-outs and time to play. Let them have the space and privacy they need to return to their balanced self.[18]

SUMMARY

The Poet's creative talent provides a reflective perspective for making decisions based on personal values that are usually people focused, quietly supportive, and nurturing. Without a Poet's creative talent on the team, the team's effort might suffer from a lack of focus on people issues, lose some grace and beauty, and fail to incorporate values into the problem-solving and decision-making processes. The team also may not stay open to see contextual issues and additional opportunities as they emerge. To bring out the best in Poets, the team needs to respect the unique perspectives Poets bring and allow them the time and space they need to make their contributions. If Poets take the time to listen to information that may conflict with their values and to speak out, share opinions, and learn to manage conflict, they can optimize their creative contributions to the organization.

SELF-ASSESSMENT

How does this talent impact my life as a dominant or auxiliary talent?

_____

_____

_____

If this is not my dominant or auxiliary talent, how do I demonstrate the use of this talent?

_____

_____

_____

How could I have used this talent in the past?

_____

_____

_____

How can I use this talent in the future?

_____

_____

_____

What do I need to do to better manage a Poet team member?

_____

_____

_____

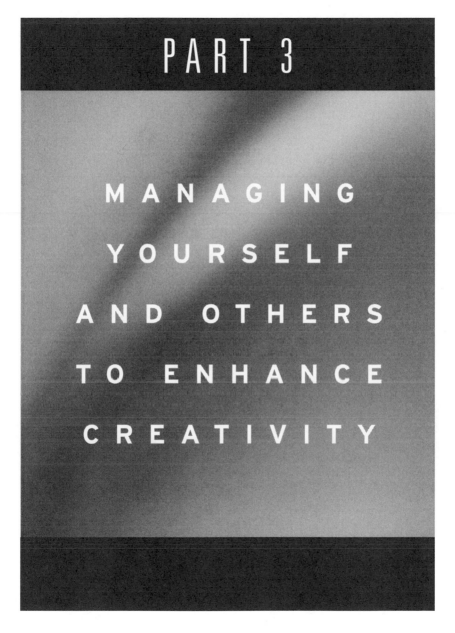

PART 3

MANAGING YOURSELF AND OTHERS TO ENHANCE CREATIVITY

CHAPTER ELEVEN

STRENGTHENING CREATIVITY IN TEAMS

The key to competitiveness is innovation, and the key to innovation is people. Taking care of people, therefore, is the essential way of taking care of business.

—Randall L. Tobias, chairman and chief executive emeritus of Eli Lilly and Co.[1]

Leveraging the strengths of the eight different creative talents to achieve the greatest benefit for you personally and professionally requires figuring out how to integrate them into teamwork and into your life. This chapter addresses what you need to do to maximize the contributions from different talents when you're working on a team. The next chapter will help you look at ways to optimize your own talents in your life.

Contrary to what popular press articles claim, managing creativity in organizations is not all about letting go. According to Robert Lutz, CEO of Exide and former vice-chairman and president of Chrysler,[2] "Real creativity has nothing at all to do with casual days. The absence of discipline and standards doesn't drive creativity. In fact, it's almost the opposite."

Teams that produce extraordinary results work well together and have a climate of mutual trust and respect, effective communication, and commitment to growth and learning. They also have processes that take advantage of the different creative talents. The effectiveness, productivity, and creativity of the team are all heightened by processes designed to creatively solve problems, facilitate constructive conflict resolution, and successfully implement solutions. As long as such processes don't take on a life of their own, they can speed up idea and product development and produce better solutions for customers and clients. When processes are designed with flexibility, customer service, optimal time to market, and product excellence as the goals, they do not add bureaucracy but instead provide guidance and learning and save time in the long run.[3] Such processes can also ensure that your team balances planning with execution, idea generation with delivery—critical issues in today's world.[4] In fact, "most of what happens in successful innovations is not the happy occurrence of a blind flash of insight but, rather, the careful implementation of an unspectacular but systematic management discipline."[5] A director of a highly successful nonprofit organization similarly remarked:

> Structure liberates creativity. Artists of all mediums learn this from the beginning of their training. A trained painter is required to learn how to paint from the primary colors first, before using any other colors. Innovation without boundaries, structure, or discipline will simply be a lot of fuzzy ideas that are never fully realized. An organization's structures will either release everyone's creativity or inhibit creative people.[6]

In the following pages are some points for team members to consider in evaluating how well they are working together and what changes they need to make to ensure that the team can translate the different talents and great ideas into creative results and solutions.

BUILD A CLIMATE OF TRUST AND MUTUAL COMMITMENT TO LEARNING AND DEVELOPMENT

Taking advantage of the different talents on a team calls for more than just putting them together on a project. A team where creativity blossoms has a safe environment marked by openness, deep appreciation for individual differences and needs, a certain amount of intellectual playfulness, mutual trust, respect for others' abilities, and a willingness to challenge others' ideas.[7] On such teams, members share information and fully air differences in assumptions and interpretations. As team members, you want to ensure that the team benefits from the diversity of its members' backgrounds, skills, knowledge, and creative talents.

According to Peter Drucker, an organization cannot, of course, overcome all weaknesses. "But it can make them irrelevant. Its task is to use the strength of each [individual] as a building block for joint performance."[8] To turn individual building blocks into extraordinary joint performance and achieve the benefits from that diversity, you need to promote open communication, deep appreciation for individual differences and needs, and a safe climate. Team members need to feel secure in raising and sharing new ideas and constructively challenging each other. As one leader said, "Creativity flourishes in an open environment where people aren't afraid to think out loud."

Talents take on heightened significance in a team setting. Awareness of the talents and appreciation for them can help the team members find new strengths, build on each other's strengths, and make even greater contributions. The talents provide a framework for growth and development. Understanding the talents can also help the team work better together and communicate more effectively.

After learning about their creative talents, the first step for team members is to develop a chart that inventories the mix of talents available to the team. The team can see if some talents are more heavily represented than others and which ones may be missing. It can then consider the impact that the mix of talents may have on the team's performance. What will help creativity flourish? Do you have enough fact finders and possibility promoters, historical and systemwide views, analytical thinkers and people perspectives? Do you have enough idea generators as well as implementers?

With this inventory and assessment, the team can then focus on how to compensate for missing talents. You may not be able to or even want to recruit new members. Instead, you can look to team members to grow and develop. Can someone on the team stretch and learn? If you're missing a dominant talent, maybe someone for whom it's an auxiliary talent can commit to adding that perspective. Or other team members may want to step up to new roles as part of their own development. Team members are all distinct individuals and bring their own unique selves, their education, background, and idiosyncrasies to their talents. They have their own needs and ambitions that will color their talents. The team wants to avoid stereotyping or limiting team members for any reason, including creative talents.

In planning sessions, team members should discuss what they require for the team and for themselves—what kind of structure, environment, and experiences will work best for them, given their talents, personal preferences, and organizational goals and constraints. Then they should agree on the kinds of support they can give one another.

Look over the sections on helping the talents maximize their creative contributions in the chapters in Part 2; a summary chart is also included at the end of this chapter. Opportunities to learn and and expand your skills repertoire motivate creative performance. Team members who play to one another's strengths figure out how to match work assignments with individual skills, knowledge, creative talents, and development plans. You want to take care not to create so large a challenge that team members feel overwhelmed. Through the right support and the right job assignments, however, a team can push the frontiers of the members' skills and help them develop new competencies.[9]

With knowledge of the talents on the team, team members need to commit to supporting one another's attempts to be more creative. Successful experiences at being creative and positive feedback build on one another. Individuals who believe that they are creative are generally not afraid to dive into a mess and figure out how to get out of it. All team members must agree to treat each other as talented individuals and to commit to growing and learning in order for talents to prosper. Mutual encouragement of new ideas and a commitment to the team members as individuals strongly influence the creativity of the team.[10] The willingness of team members to see mistakes as learning experiences and as part of the creative process boosts team and individual development.

As team members stretch and grow, the team should build recognition of achievements into its daily routines. Celebrating small wins and first steps can go a long way toward building group and individual creativity. Team members can encourage one another to get out of their zones of comfortable, steady habits and produce creative results. Some team members need this encouragement more than others, but everyone benefits from regular and frequent feedback. Supportive and constructive feedback regarding innovation attempts builds self-confidence and encourages more innovation.[11] Figure out how to give each other feedback—in constructive, caring, and honest ways and without treating issues, as that Harmonizer said, "ad hominem." Using knowledge of the talents and the language of the MBTI instrument can depersonalize the situation and aid in opening up feedback discussions.

FOSTER COMMUNICATION

Besides providing a framework for growth and development, the talents can also promote better teamwork by helping team members look at how they communicate and interact with one another. The ability to listen and to communicate allows creativity to flourish. Supporting creativity on a team means making sure that team members' opinions, thoughts, and feelings are heard and are valued.

As illustrated in Chapters 3 through 10, your creative talents can affect your communication with others. Your preferences can limit the time you spend really listening to and interacting with others. With a dominant introverted talent, such as the Navigator, Visionary, Inventor, or Poet talent, you may listen well but share your opinions with others reluctantly. You may be more inclined to privately process the information you have received. You may withhold observations and perspectives until you are comfortable voicing them. The team may lose the benefit of your opinions and the direction they can provide.

On the other hand, if you have a dominant extraverted talent, such as the Adventurer, Explorer, Pilot, or Harmonizer talent, you may find yourself talking more frequently than you listen. You may overwhelm team members with your energy and ideas. Keeping your talent in check will take advantage of the different perspectives on the team and will help ensure that everyone's ideas are heard.

Even with good listening skills, your talents can serve as filters and affect the diversity and breadth of information to which you pay attention and can keep some information from even hitting your radar screen. These filters can keep you from benefiting from the individual differences on your team. You may not be open to information that is different from what you are used to hearing and seeing. The Pilot or Inventor talent may not pay attention to information about people. The Harmonizer or Poet talent may ignore data about costs, benefits, or bottom-line consequences. Navigators and Adventurers may focus on facts and details, whereas Visionaries and Explorers may totally fail to see those facts. Unless you are aware of these biases, you may see only one side of the picture. The team should consider how the talents affect the way it communicates and discuss how to improve team interactions.

Good questioning skills as well as good listening skills facilitate team interactions. Your creative talents can also affect how you ask questions and can impact the breadth and diversity of the answers. In addition to biasing you to only one side of the issue, your talents can limit the perspective you get, depending on the type of questions you ask. Team members with the Pilot or the Inventor as their dominant or auxiliary talent may find themselves asking closed-ended questions that elicit yes or no answers. Such questions can close off discussions and the free flow of ideas and alternatives. On the other hand, the type of questions that Explorers and Visionaries tend to ask—such as "What would happen if . . . ?" or "How might we . . . ?"—tend to encourage exploration, as do requests like "Describe it to me," "Tell me what you want to happen," or "Help me understand what you need to do about this." "How?" questions are less intimidating than "Why?" questions and will elicit more information, positive thinking, and insight. Such questions can also help the team deal more effectively with differences of opinion.

In its interactions and communications, your team needs to build a culture of possibilities so that team members will put forth new and different ideas. Statements such as "That won't work!" and "That's a dumb idea!" or a culture of criticism and cynicism can put a damper on enthusiasm and creative passion. The team should not allow put-downs or power plays. Instead, it should convert negative comments into opportunity finding through the use of "In what ways might we . . . ?" questions. Those team members with the Inventor or Pilot talent may quickly point out flaws. Practice turning this perspective, which is certainly useful in planning for contingencies, into a constructive discussion. The team can use every member's talents and questioning skills to transform obstacles, problems, and issues into opportunities.

One team in a small entrepreneurial architectural firm won an award after designing a work space for an Internet start-up company even though their final budget was a fraction of the original proposal. Another team, in a security software company, was faced with severe staffing constraints; like many companies, they just couldn't find enough good people. These constraints led them to make changes in many of their business processes, which allowed them to eliminate unnecessary systems and to do more with fewer people. Those are just two examples of what a team can accomplish by "possibilitizing" a challenge.[12]

Good communication skills and a positive attitude can help the team derive maximum benefit from its diversity and manage the conflict that inevitably comes from such diversity. Finding a creative way for the team to resolve conflict can make the difference between spectacular success and miserable failure. Good listening and questioning skills can help the team avoid symptoms of poor group decision making, such as groupthink, running on "automatic pilot," and conflict avoidance.

Team members should make sure they share all perspectives and opinions and hear the voices of team members with different creative talents. They can use their knowledge of talents to explore and break through differences in assumptions, filters, and biases. Team members should get to the root of the disagreements and determine whether a conflict is caused by divergent assumptions, understanding of the facts, evaluation criteria, or desired outcomes. Harmonizers and Poets may find the lack of harmony uncomfortable, but it's only a step along the way toward a truly creative and collaborative solution. One way to ensure everyone's contribution in a discussion is to make such participation a part of the team's operating guidelines. You might want to go around the room and ask each member if he or she agrees with the decision or problem as currently stated or has concerns. Another technique is for each team member to assign a number equating to the degree of agreement. The team can then explore the different ratings.

Using talents and good communication skills enables a team to deal effectively with tough issues and differences in perspectives. Commitment to learning and growth can ensure that all team members maximize their contributions. A possibilitizing culture supports the team's use of its diversity in creative talents to achieve extraordinary performance.

FIND THE RIGHT CREATIVE PROBLEM-SOLVING PROCESSES, TOOLS, AND TECHNIQUES

According to one leader from a financial services organization,

> The issue for leaders in the new workplace becomes how to stimulate groups of people throughout the organization, wherever they might be, to jump across boundaries, to raise their hands when they think they see a better approach or when they think the organization is going down a path that doesn't make sense. . . . You sit around the table with five or six people and you try to get a process going where there aren't sacred issues and where the mix of people around the table is quite complementary, where you can develop a fact base and you think about problems in a way that is free of biases or emotion. Then you try to come up with alternative solutions, rather than just one deterministic solution. That's the way you manage. That's the way you attack problems. That's the way you play the competitive game.

Having a flexible and systematic approach to problem solving and decision making can increase the effectiveness and creativity of solutions and decisions and help your team play the competitive game. Such an approach also promotes team learning.[13] The right problem-solving process helps the team discover what the challenge or situation really is all about. It can help the team successfully resolve conflict. The right process includes idea-generation tools as well as techniques to support convergence and provide focus for selecting among alternatives so that the team can move forward to resolve the situation. It allows time for reflection and learning. Finally, the right process takes advantage of the different creative talents and allows for stretch and growth. It encourages open discussion of different perspectives without forcing through decisions.

The right process will change over time as the team adds new learnings and experience. Although the steps may seem cumbersome at first, they do get easier with practice and as the team modifies the process with use. To ease the concerns of those uncomfortable with the formality or with some of the steps, setting time frames for each step may be helpful. Time limits can be especially valuable for those who might prefer to move on before exploring alternatives or for those who would rather spend their time generating alternatives and never move on. Team members with talents that prefer process to product can help keep options open until it's time to converge on the next steps, and then those focused on results can help drive the team to successful conclusion.

The steps that the team needs to address, depending on the problem, include the following:

1. Figure out the problem or challenge. Since the definition of the challenge can determine the range of possible alternatives that will be explored, the team must ask the right questions and define the problem completely, accurately, and broadly enough. The team needs to gather as much information as possible because even accurate information, if only partially gathered, can result in disastrous decisions.[14]

As you learned in Chapters 3 through 10, individual differences in talents will impact how you become aware of problems, what kinds of issues you see, what types of data you take in as facts or reality. If the team gathers the appropriate facts and looks at the situation from a variety of perspectives, it can stretch boundaries and escape the trap of conventional thinking. The team must look at the history of the problem, as well as to the future, since past knowledge can provide stepping-stones to new insights.

Listen to facts and details from Navigators and Adventurers. These team members can focus the team on the component parts and details and will provide grounded facts and reality. Then, the team should listen to the possibilities and future trends from Explorers and Visionaries. Those team members can help the team see interdependencies, look at the larger system, integrate ideas across a wide range of disciplines, and generate lots of connections and possibilities about the nature of the problem. They can also help the team deal with the ambiguity of an often messy front end of a challenge.

Hold off moving on to the next step until you're confident that you have identified the right challenge. Don't let Pilots and Harmonizers jump to conclusions too soon. When the team is comfortable with the problem definition, it can access its decision-making talents to home in on the ideas it wants to pursue.

If the problem still lacks clarity after a set amount of time, the team needs to decide whether it's appropriate to spend more time exploring or whether it's possible to move on. To deal with a problem that is still fuzzy and amorphous, the team can set some boundaries and do some market tests and prototypes. It can try out some ideas and not waste time forever analyzing. Instead, it can develop a plan to reach more clarity.

2. Define goals and objectives. After defining the challenge as clearly as possible, the team needs to know what it wants to achieve in pursuing a solution. Spending time in this step will help avoid wasting energies later on. Although you want to keep these goals and objectives constantly in mind as you try to resolve the problem, you also need to continue reexamining these goals and objectives for ongoing validity since they can end up limiting the alternatives you generate.

When setting goals, the team should get the perspectives of all the talents since they will likely have different views on what the team is supposed to accomplish. In defining goals and objectives, get help from Inventors and Pilots. Also, be sure to consider the perspectives of the Harmonizers and the Poets.

3. Generate alternatives. Once the challenge has been defined and objectives clarified, the team must access its data-collecting talents again, to look at as many alternatives as possible. Make sure that the team uses creative tools and techniques that will twist paradigms, stretch imaginations, gather lots of different information, and eliminate blinders and habitual ways of seeing the situation. The team should incorporate use of the different techniques described in Chapters 3 through 10 so that everyone can contribute. As was pointed out in these chapters, one size does not fit all. Some tools work for certain creative talents, and other tools work better for other talents.

During this step of generating alternatives, the team should allow for as much playfulness and good humor as possible. Team members want to be inventive and nonlinear, to try unusual combinations and different tools, to tinker and mess around with ideas. The team may need to encourage Navigators and Adventurers to stretch during this step since they may not be as comfortable with it as Explorers and Visionaries are. The team should honor agreed-on time frames but at the same time avoid closing off the session too soon. Many great ideas come in the later stages of an idea-generation session.

Critical to success in generating alternatives is following the rules of brainstorming. Too often, too many ideas get judged, evaluated, and thrown away. Everyone should feel comfortable contributing his or her ideas and should feel that those ideas will be valued. The rules to follow are as follows:

- Set some general boundaries about the purpose of the session.

- Generate as many ideas as possible—the more ideas, the better. Quantity will lead to quality.

- Defer judgment. Hold off criticizing until the session is over and the decision is made to move to analyzing the ideas.

- Build on the ideas of others. Combine and improve on the ideas of your teammates.

- Encourage "freewheeling" of ideas—the wilder the idea, the better. It is easier to tame down than to think up.[15]

- Write down every idea verbatim to be sure that no idea or piece of an idea gets lost.

During this step, the team should make sure that all its members are producing a wide variety of alternatives and that the perspectives of the Harmonizer, Poet, Pilot, and Inventor are being heard. Harmonizers and

Poets bring up often-overlooked issues about people, values, and politics. Make sure that the Adventurers and Explorers let those with introverted talents contribute. Don't let them overwhelm the idea-generation session.

As the many different alternatives and options, facts, and possibilities are generated, Visionaries and Explorers can put the pieces together in unconventional, even unique, ways. Harmonizers and Poets can add the perspective of holding opposites and paradoxes open to find a way to combine and resolve contradictions.

The team should schedule time away from the effort to allow for those with introverted creative talents to process the ideas and for those with extraverted talents to reflect. Such incubation time can also facilitate the work of everyone's unconscious in providing inspiration and imaginative new ideas. Agree on a certain amount of time for such incubation, depending on the complexity of the problem. You may want to consider giving out notebooks in which people can jot down ideas during this time. Be sure to move on to the next step when appropriate.

The step of exploring alternatives is critical to the team's generation of wide-ranging solutions. It enables the team to move past compromise to integration. There is incredible value in resolving contradictions, as opposed to merely finding a compromise. Compromise doesn't usually solve the problem in the long run. A longer-lasting solution comes from one that integrates clashing needs and ideas. To find such a solution requires the generation of many different alternatives.

4. Select the best solutions. After generating alternatives, team members need to access their decision-making talents to pick the best solution(s). The team should systematically evaluate possible ideas against goals and objectives, perhaps by using such idea-selection tools as Nominal Group Technique or Affinity Diagrams.[16]

Selecting the best result, one that integrates conflicting sides, requires much creativity and may take time. The team should avoid letting time constraints drive it to leap on the first obvious solution. Commitment to fully exploring all options during this stage will be worthwhile in terms of the quality, elegance, and sustainability of the final choice.

To achieve an integrated solution, the team must recognize and appreciate the different ways the eight creative talents take in data and make decisions. To build an integrated, truly creative solution, the team should avoid taking an either-or view of the problem or situation. Instead, if it maintains an open mind, steps outside of the problem, and uses the team's creative talents to their fullest, it will find a "both-and" solution that satisfies all parties involved.

The next time you are stuck making a decision about alternatives, try to create a solution that integrates all sides. If it's a vacation you're planning, the integrated solution is not the mountains *or* the seashore; it's going somewhere that has both. In organizations, it's not losing employees because of long commutes when the company moves; it's finding telecommuting options or other solutions that enable you to keep good employees and still meet their needs. In product design, an example of an integrated solution was for razor manufacturers to come up with lubricated plastic holders, Teflon strips, or specially shaped blade carriers to solve the problem of having a razor sharp enough to cut the hair, but not so sharp as to harm the skin.[17] An integrated solution is not figuring out who gets the larger piece of the pie, whether at the dinner table or at work; it's creating a larger pie so that everyone gets a bigger piece.

It's possible that no "best" solution will emerge at this point because the team is faced with so many unknowns. To deal with such a situation, the team needs to determine what it does know and how it can deal with what it doesn't know. It may be hard for some talents to live with this lack of clarity, but it may be required for the team to move forward. The team may decide to iteratively try out some solutions as trial runs or prototypes before making a commitment to a final solution.

5. Plan and implement. To effectively plan and implement the chosen solution and obtain the desired results, the team should apply discipline to converge and focus. Planning and prioritizing next steps is just as important as generating alternatives. Again, each creative talent will have a different perspective to contribute. Look at the commonsense and fact-based specifics of Navigators and Adventurers to consider possible problems and then plan out what needs to be done. Navigators can identify possible resistance and help plan for ways to overcome it. Pilots and Inventors can look at contingencies, find ways to prepare for them, and make sure that many "What if" questions get asked so that the team can figure out how to manage the answers. Those team members with preferences for the Harmonizer or Poet talent can deal with communication and political issues.

Again, the team wants to balance planning with the need to move on. Some team members, especially those with Adventurer and Explorer talents, may want to jump in and just get going. That perspective is valuable for making sure that the team does not overanalyze or overplan but does move forward. However, the team still must take time to plan since doing so can save time and effort in the long run by making sure that important issues don't fall through the cracks and that significant rework is avoided. (See the next section for more details on implementation.)

6. Take time to reflect. Before concluding the problem-solving process, the team should take the time to learn from its experience. The team needs to schedule a review of personal and team performance if all members, individually and collectively, are going to improve. It should look at what worked and what didn't to ensure that energy is not wasted by making the same mistakes over and over again.

Although this step is often overlooked because of time pressures, it is a very important one. You need to rein in the drive to move on, which may come from Harmonizers and Pilots, to be sure that the team has time for introspection and learning. This step gets easier with practice. Make sure you have a mechanism for capturing the learnings and action items from the session.

Questions that need to be answered with appropriate note-taking include the following:

- What did you expect to accomplish in the problem-solving session?

- What did you accomplish?

- What explains the difference between expectations and reality?

- What did you learn?

- Were all perspectives of the different talents explored and used?

- How will you use the different creative talents more effectively next time?

- What can you do to speed the process next time?

The team can use this problem-solving process with conflict and any problem to achieve spectacular results. Using this collaborative approach and taking full advantage of its talents, the team will find that any problem can truly be the engine of creativity and learning.[18]

SELECT FLEXIBLE PROJECT-MANAGEMENT AND PRODUCT-DEVELOPMENT PROCESSES

Once the team has selected the best alternative solution to pursue, it needs to address several critical issues to ensure effective, smooth, and speedy development of the solution and its implementation. A recent survey of creativity and innovation in family-owned businesses showed that the challenge they face in the future is not the generation of ideas but rather the selection of the best ideas and their implementation.[19]

Flexible project-management and product-development processes increase the chances of team success in implementing creative solutions; they also ensure that the team concentrates on execution. With a strong focus on the customer and on product excellence, these processes can streamline the work, monitor progress and problems, and ensure that creative efforts are effectively channeled and innovative results are achieved.[20] They also allow the team to take full advantage of all the different skills and abilities of its members and their creative talents.

Several critical components will determine whether such processes produce winning results for the team:

1. Establish a project charter. A project charter establishes the project's purpose or mission and the benefits to be gained from the project effort. It defines roles and responsibilities, lines of authority, and project scope and boundaries. It includes major milestones, resource requirements, and risks and contingencies to be addressed. It outlines mutually agreed-on and clearly defined expectations about what is to be achieved, product specifications, and success measures.

The charter gives the team the structure it needs to channel its creative efforts and achieve success. Clearly defined goals and expectations provide focus and are important for a team's creativity. Short- and long-term goal clarity "is what harnesses the creativity of employees, focusing their creativity, and giving it direction."[21] Stretch goals can energize, inspire, and spur on creative efforts since everyone knows what they are trying to achieve. They can help set boundaries and keep efforts from being wasted. Well-conceived and articulated goals can also help you and your team track and measure progress. They provide checkpoints for any needed midcourse corrections. They provide boundaries for those talents who may need them. They provide direction for decisions that need to be made. As long as they are broad enough, goals will allow plenty of room for creativity.

Goals should be both results and process oriented. They should include some developmental goals as well, for teamwork improvement or individual development. Pilots or Inventors can help prioritize the goals if that's needed. Goals should address reality and the steps required to reach a vision and should be clear about expectations, as well as challenging. Use Navigators or Adventurers to keep the goals grounded. Use Explorers and Visionaries to be sure that the goals have enough vision and stretch and are aligned with the organizational culture. Use the perspectives of the Harmonizers and Poets to make sure that people issues and values are included. Including the perspectives from the different creative talents will ensure that all issues are addressed.

2. Focus on the client. Focusing on the client helps speed development and implementation and produces better results. Listening to clients, having them as active members of the project team, using their expertise in market research, and getting them involved in testing product designs or solutions are all formal ways to include clients and ensure the best, most innovative results. Including customers in the process can reduce duplicate steps, allow for concurrent tasks, and prevent downstream delays.[22] The team should make sure that the voice of the customer is heard through both informal channels and formal mechanisms.

Take advantage of those team members with dominant or auxiliary Harmonizer and Poet talents to ensure that clients are included in all steps. Use the tools recommended for those talents and for others, such as focus groups or other processes in which team members work with customers, to fully understand their needs.

3. Plan the project and its execution. Milestones in a well-documented plan are also critical to creative performance, heightening task motivation and creating a sense of order. They "serve as key targets that infuse team members with a sense of urgency and keep them focused on goals and objectives."[23] Having a road map helps track progress and measure success, both of which are critical for productive innovation. Planning for interdependencies and contingencies to manage risks is also important. When adjustments need to be made, a good plan keeps everyone alert. All the different creative talents can contribute their perspectives in designing a solid plan.

To creatively address changes that are inevitable, plans must be flexible but still give direction. They should include a certain amount of enlightened trial and error to make sure that the team is also learning by doing.[24]

4. Use creativity tools and techniques. The team should use the creative problem-solving process described above and the creativity tools and techniques defined in Chapters 3 through 10 when it faces problems during project execution. Too often, a team will set out on a course of action but end up solving the wrong problem, repeating past mistakes, or getting too attached to a solution that worked in the past. Using creativity tools and techniques all along the way will help the team out of such stalemates. The team can also use the tools to develop unusual ways to minimize risk and support the creative resolution of the challenge. Make sure that the project plan includes steps to incorporate these tools to stretch the thinking and imagination of all the team members.

5. Take time to reflect. As with problem solving, teams and team members learn from reflection and introspection about what worked and what didn't. Making time, however brief and informal, to review what the team learned during the project supports learning and growth for individuals and for the organization. (See the discussion on pages 205–206 for more details on this step.)

A FINAL WORD ABOUT TEAM LEADERSHIP

The discussion of what team members can do to promote creative and innovative results is *not* meant to imply that team leaders don't play a role in fostering higher creativity levels in a team. Rather, the discussion is meant to highlight the role of the creative talents and the key steps that team members can take to ensure that everyone is participating in and benefiting from the team's potential. The discussion is also meant to recognize that in many of today's organizations self-managed teams or rotating team leadership is becoming the norm.

Team leadership, however it is structured in your organization, plays a very important role in promoting creativity on the team. Anyone holding such a responsibility needs to understand how his or her behavior, expectations, and words can impact a team's performance. Supportive team leadership can ensure the survival of creative ideas from individuals and teams that sow the seeds of successful innovation. It provides the direction, consultation, and support that can be more critical for creativity and innovation than total freedom.[25]

According to Ben Zander, director of the Boston Philharmonic Orchestra, a leader is the "relentless architect of the possibility that others can be."[26] If you have team leader responsibility, your words and actions communicate your expectations for outstanding performance. Those expectations have a major impact on the creativity of team members.[27] The role of the team leader in building an environment where creativity flourishes is absolutely critical. According to research, what distinguishes an organization as a "veritable hotbed of creativity" is the quality of its leadership.[28] Whether the team provides its own leadership or gets it from one individual, such leadership can make a significant contribution to the team's extraordinary results.

SUMMARY

Teams that promote creative behavior and innovation are those that have members with diverse perspectives, talents, and skills. Having different creative talents on the team will result in better strategic decisions because of the mix of perspectives and the flexibility of approaches to problem solving and decision making that they provide.[29] Teams that know how to work well together and use superior problem-solving and project-management techniques react faster and are more resilient, productive, and efficient than teams without these mechanisms.

The factors that promote creativity and innovation in a team also drive outstanding profitability, customer service, employee retention, and organizational growth. They are the same factors that help certain companies outperform others by 30 to 40 percent.[30] They are also the same factors that contribute to building an organization where people matter and an environment that is truly a wonderful place to work.

By ensuring that everyone works well together, gets the maximum value from the talents, and treats one another with trust, respect, and support, your team can optimize innovation, employee retention, entrepreneurial behavior, and customer satisfaction.[31] By making sure that the right structure and processes are in place to channel and focus the team's efforts and to appreciate one another's talents, your team can maximize its creative contributions and use its strengths as building blocks for extraordinary performance.

MAXIMIZING TEAM TALENTS

Results and Contributions	Maximizing Their Contributions
ADVENTURER • Clever and satisfying solutions to customer and operational problems • Practical applications that recognize shape, line, color, and texture, which can be handled and taken apart • Adding fun, curiosity, adaptability, flexibility, and positive energy to the team • Imagination full of specific details: how things look, smell, taste, sound, and feel • Prompt, practical, and ingenious responses to crises and emergencies • Experimentation with the group, pushing it to find new solutions that work	• Provide an environment that brings out their strengths • Allow for fun and celebration • Give them mutually agreed-on goals and schedules • Help them organize their writing and their presentations • Challenge their processes • Build a diverse team • Work on a development plan • Recognize the signs of stress
NAVIGATOR • Practical adaptation, fine-tuning, and building on what others have done • Ability to fix things to make them work • Skill in helping people understand new products and services • New rites, rituals, and systems to make the change work • Imagination full of specific details, with an impressionistic, surrealistic perspective • Keeping the group or project grounded, focused, and on track • Understanding of and planning for possible resistance to new initiatives	• Structure the right environment • Provide focus and limits • Provide space and time • Show appreciation • Provide the information they need to process a change • Encourage an attitude of positive possibilities • Teach conflict management • Build a development plan • Watch for symptoms of stress and suggest time-outs
EXPLORER • Ability to see external patterns, trends, and relationships • Tireless generation, promotion, and initiation of new enterprises, new business ventures, and new ideas • Inspiring ingenuity and discovery in others • Imagination full of connections and associations • High-spirited team-building and successful change initiatives because of their enthusiasm, energy, and passion • Helping others push past what is accepted and expected • Possibility thinking to envision future	• Make sure that they have the right environment • Help them with timing issues • Assist them in developing sensitivity to others • Set goals and objectives • Explore the facts with them • Make sure that they take time to reflect before moving on • Help them find balance between the personal and professional worlds so that they don't burn out too quickly • Recognize signs of stress

MAXIMIZING TEAM TALENTS

	Results and Contributions	Maximizing Their Contributions
VISIONARY	• Provocative questions that challenge the group to find profound answers and big solutions • "Incasting" (versus forecasting)—working back from the future to develop plans • New designs and solutions through unusual connections • Imagination full of hard-to-describe images and futuristic possibilities • Multidisciplined perspectives • Penetrating, far-reaching insights into future trends • Ability to integrate, synthesize, and move the group forward	• Structure the right environment • Provide focus and limits • Provide space and time • Work with their ideas to ground them • Help them share their thoughts and ideas • Help them with managing conflict • Encourage the use of their decision-making talent • Work on development plans • Encourage time-outs and play
PILOT	• Clarification of goals and responsibilities on projects and change initiatives • High-energy team leadership • New and different strategies • Innovative organizational designs • Making things happen through inventive, tough-minded problem solving • Logical categorization of ideas/issues • Focus on progress, improvement, efficiency, productivity, and results in change initiatives • Thoughtful questions and challenges to conventional thinking	• Set the right structure • Remind them about people issues • Help them find the shades of gray • Encourage them to take time to reflect • Help them learn to delegate • Make sure that they are exploring possibilities • Build a development plan • Watch for symptoms of stress and suggest time-outs
INVENTOR	• Unconventional theories and models for analysis and synthesis of facts, ideas, and concepts • Unusual and thoughtful solutions to problems through identifying what makes things work and through objective, impartial analysis • Inventive ways to get around constraints • Tough, unrelenting critique to get to the highest levels of effectiveness • A quick understanding and intellectual curiosity that can speed the creative process • Insightful questions that cause paradigm shifts in perspective • Integrated solutions where everything fits	• Check to be sure that structure is truly needed • Set mutually agreeable schedules and deadlines • Provide the personal space they need to be the most creative • Ensure that their teams include diverse talents • Make sure they have spent enough time gathering data and considering all angles • Give them time to express their thoughts and feelings • Encourage development of their project-planning, time-management, and interpersonal skills and abilities • Watch for symptoms of stress

MAXIMIZING TEAM TALENTS

Results and Contributions	Maximizing Their Contributions
HARMONIZER • High-energy team leadership • Innovative solutions to problems and new programs that help customers, employees, or community • A nurturing, energetic team environment that brings out the best in people • Diverse and effective communication strategies • Different perspectives through concern for context and circumstances • Successful resolution of political problems that can impede change and innovation • Heightened self-esteem for team members	• Set the right structure • Help them set boundaries • Show them appreciation • Allow them time to process change • Help them build their conflict-management skills • Encourage development of their listening and data-collecting abilities • Work with them on developing their analytical abilities • Work on a development plan • Recognize signs of stress
POET • An aesthetic appreciation for grace and elegance in solutions • Building an environment of trust, respect, and support, a safe place for testing out new ideas and behaviors • Independent and thoughtful perspectives on the challenge, addressing people-related values, context, and circumstances • Serving as the team's ethical backbone • Generation of new possibilities and options through reflection and incubation • Articulation and portrayal of values, feelings, and perspectives, often through writing	• Check to be sure that structure is needed • Provide the time and space they need to be the most creative • Make sure they are engaged and motivated • Recognize their sensitivity and show them uniqueness • Allow them opportunities to express their uniqueness • Help them build their conflict-management and communication skills • Help them define objectives, set boundaries, prioritize, and plan • Encourage critical thinking • Build objectives for improving new skills into their performance plan • Watch for symptoms of stress

CHAPTER TWELVE

DEVELOPING YOUR PERSONAL ACTION PLAN

We always think we are now at the end of our discoveries. We never
are. We go on discovering that we are this, that, and other things,
and sometimes we have astounding experiences.

–Carl Jung[1]

In the final months of writing this
book, I had dinner with one of the participants in my original study.
As we discussed the incredible power that creativity brings to individuals
and to organizations, we started to explore the reasons why it is not being
tapped to its fullest potential. My dinner companion, a partner in a large
consulting firm, stated, "My experience in management has convinced
me that we don't focus enough on strengths. We need to start focusing
on developing people's strengths, as opposed to paying so much attention
to deficiences or weaknesses." She went on to say,

> Most of us are bright enough to become fair achievers in lots of areas. But
> that approach is flawed for a couple of reasons. First, it assumes that there's
> an ideal model for measuring us all against. I'm not sure such an ideal
> really does or should exist. And second, organizations need outstanding, cre-
> ative performances in a few areas, not just fair performance across the
> board. Part of being successful is knowing what you don't know and playing
> to your strengths, playing to other people's strengths, and combining them,
> so that the whole group puts all the pieces together.

That conversation struck a nerve for me. Having many times been compared to external "standards of excellence" or "best practices"—either by others or, worse, by myself—I know what it feels like to concentrate on what's missing. There are probably a variety of reasons why there hasn't been adequate focus on strengths. Whatever the reasons, however, it's time to shift your attention to using your unique talents to be the best that you can be and not trying to live up to some ideal that may not even exist.

In Chapter 11, we looked at the impacts of your creative talents when you're working with others to solve problems and deal with challenges. But teamwork, no matter how good, still begins with the strengths of the individual team members. In the end, you are responsible for your own life and how you develop your creative talents.

To capitalize on your talents, you must make an honest assessment of what they are and what you can do to further develop them. The more you learn about yourself and explore your creative talents, the more you will be able to consciously access them and confidently use them to consistently produce different and valuable results. As you get to know your talents, you'll see how to maximize your contributions. If you're great at building teams, get even better; find opportunities where this talent can make its maximum contribution. If you're terrific at coming up with far-reaching visions, find job situations that play to that strength.

Focusing on your particular strengths does not mean you can rest on your laurels since there is always room for improvement and growth. After identifying where your talents lie, you'll want to look at two other areas. You'll want to define the issues that may be getting in your way of being your creative best and the areas where your strengths may need assistance. From that perspective, you can then determine what you require for further growth, flexibility, and contribution.

Discover what can keep you from being your creative best. A focus on building your strengths is not an excuse for bad behavior or for ignoring problem areas if and when they are getting in your way. You want to address behavior that is causing a negative impact on others or on yourself. Look at the blocks and barriers that are identified for your talents (see the summaries at the end of this chapter) and determine which ones need to be eliminated or avoided. Perhaps it's the filters and biases from your talents. Or perhaps it's your preferences for extraverting over introverting or for data collecting over decision making. Whatever they may be, you'll want to develop a plan for managing or eliminating any obstacles that are getting in the way of your optimal creativity.

You also want to make sure that you are not letting any of your talents become a limitation. For example, a Pilot who excels at organizing and analyzing can find that strength becoming a limitation if it moves into overcontrol. The same is true for Harmonizers who let concern for others dominate their decision-making process and keep them from seeing other creative options, or for a Navigator who lets concern for details become a block for producing creative results. Talents that become obstacles need to be managed as well.

Finally, there will be areas that are not your strengths. You need to figure out how to compensate for areas where you need help. If you are in an organization, you can find others to support you and provide balance. As you flex and grow as a team, you can make even more contributions by combining talents to explore creative solutions. If you're on your own, you may have to do more for yourself. If you are not able to find colleagues, clients, family, and friends to help out, you may have to stretch and develop even more flexibility and capacity in those other talents. Remember that these other talents are available to you. You just have to work a bit harder to use them. You may never be entirely comfortable using them, but they are available to you as additional techniques in your skills toolkit to help you reach even higher levels of creativity.

After making a clear assessment of what you need to do to further build on your talents, there are three more issues to consider if you're going to optimize these talents and be more effective, productive, and creative: (1) defining the best processes, (2) having the right knowledge base, and (3) finding your passion.

DEFINING THE BEST PROCESSES

Defining your creative process, the steps you need to take and the tools and techniques you can use, is critical to improving your creative results. Knowing the process that works best for you to produce creative results makes obtaining those results much simpler. "No time to be creative" will disappear as an obstacle. Individuals who are clear on how to tap into their creativity rarely mention time as a barrier. That's because they know how to readily access their creativity and come up with new ideas. They know how to reframe questions, generate alternatives, and produce creative results. Said one executive,

It never occurs to me that I don't have time to be creative. If I see something that needs to be changed, I just go after it. I know I will find a creative answer, because I've done it time and time again. It gets easier and takes less time with practice.

Chapters 3 through 10 provided some suggestions for defining your process. (They are summarized at the end of this chapter.) These processes vary by talent and by individual. They range from formal systematic processes, such as a structured creative problem-solving process that might work for Pilots, to more informal trial-and-error improvisations that might work for Adventurers. You might want to look at the formal creative problem-solving process in Chapter 11 for larger problems and adapt it for your own use. For smaller issues, you need to spend some time finding out what can help you get more creative perspectives, access your unconscious, and uncover new insights. Find the techniques that work for you. These could include playing with children, going for a walk, or practicing visualization. Or they might involve getting on a train with a new notebook and pen or using mind mapping, or maybe working on your deck, mowing the lawn, jogging, or doing housework.

You also want to consider the environment in which you work the best. One playwright needs to have all his pencils lined up in a specific way to get his creative juices flowing. Other individuals need candles or music to optimize their creativity. You may need a totally organized office or a special room or chair. You may need people and noise around you, or you may prefer to be alone. You may prefer to develop ideas by yourself and then present them to the group to benefit from their insight. You must determine what works best for you given your talents, the problem, and the situation.

As you define your process, include steps that will help you move back and forth between your dominant and auxiliary talents to be sure that you are looking at situations, challenges, and problems most creatively. By moving back and forth between your dominant and auxiliary talents, you can collect all sorts of data and make better decisions. You can balance action and talk with reflection and introspection. You can let ideas incubate and then move on. Taking a bath, going for a walk, and brainstorming with others are all helpful techniques for freeing up your creativity. One consultant, who has a very well developed Pilot talent, finds she really has to struggle to let go of her structured decision-making talent to find the most creative solutions, especially under stress:

Often, if I keep on trying to solve the problem, nothing works. But if I go for a walk down by the ocean, all of a sudden, new ideas that provide a solution or new direction will just pop into my head—sometimes out of nowhere! Of course, I also need to look at what's really important and have to get past my inner critic to let ideas through.

Make sure to compensate for biases, filters, and blind spots caused by your dominant or auxiliary talent. You need to be gathering all types of information about facts, details, trends, and patterns; about people and culture issues; and about more quantifiable, objective costs and benefits. Your process should help you explore a wide range of alternatives. To come up with the best, most creative results, you need to allow yourself to see what you aren't looking for,[2] to avoid the perceptual shortcut of "I already know what I see,"[3] to stay open to new input, and to deal with conflicting information. Using checklists of questions to ask in new situations or having a colleague remind you may help.

Your process should also help you consciously access your decision-making talent to address the organizational side of creativity to achieve the results you want, especially if your dominant talent is the Adventurer, Explorer, Inventor, or Poet. Your decision-making talent can help you plan tasks, manage priorities, keep focused, and avoid wasting your creative energy and other important resources. Making lists, keeping journals and detailed notebooks, using project-management techniques, having regular idea or product quotas, and posting your project plan visibly are just some of the common practices highly creative people follow to provide the needed discipline.

Structuring your days and setting aside your best times for creative work are also key techniques for producing higher output. What time of day works best for you? The successful consultant with the Inventor talent found that he worked best writing his book from 11 P.M. until 2 A.M. He would then go to bed and be ready to be back at work on it again from 10 A.M. until 1 P.M. The sculptor Henry Moore also had a routine and set of rituals. He would get up at 8 A.M., be at work by 9 A.M., take a break at 10 A.M., and then work three more hours before lunch. Define what works best for you. By balancing your idea generation and data collection with this focus and organization, you'll be able to get things done and achieve the creative results you desire.

Defining and practicing your process provide many benefits. Developing your process builds confidence in yourself as a creative individual and in your ideas as having merit. By taking time to reflect on and digest information, you can make up your own mind regarding external standards and opinions. At the same time, with more confidence you'll tend to be more open to a variety of data, to deal better with conflicting opinions, and to more readily share your ideas and perspectives. You will come to trust your own judgment as you operate free from established expectations. Such confidence and independence will also help you be bold and thick-skinned when you need to be in the face of any resistance to your ideas.

As you become more familiar with and confident of your dominant and auxiliary talents, start to stretch into those that are less familiar to you, finding new sources of creativity—both consciously and unconsciously. Purposely trying out other talents can further develop your range of abilities to produce even more different and valuable results. Letting the unconscious support you can lead to new ideas and imaginative solutions. In addition to some of the tools and techniques described in the chapter on your dominant talent, such techniques as meditation, fantasy, relaxation, dreaming, prayer, visualization, journal writing, artwork, and movement will help you access your unconscious for inspiration and even guidance.

When you're defining your process, figure out how to keep yourself at your physical and emotional best. To build and maintain your competitive edge, find time to rejuvenate, play, incubate, rest, and relax. Find ways to celebrate your accomplishments. Being your creative best also requires figuring out how to deal with stress and to stay healthy, emotionally and physically. Chronic illness, emotional issues such as depression, poor nutrition, and feeling tired from lack of exercise and sleep can all limit your ability to deal with stress and be more creative. According to one sleep specialist, "Creativity is the first thing to erode when you need sleep. The ability to be creative lies in the frontal areas of the brain and those are the areas most sensitive to sleep deprivation."[4] Taking care of yourself, getting exercise, eating well, swimming, gardening, taking walks, or whatever works for you can have great benefits in not only a longer life but also a more creative one.

Finally, your process should address any personal fears and ego issues. Although the creative talents help explain much about the differences in individual creativity, they do not, of course, explain everything. They don't explain some of the more personal, emotional obstacles that can keep you from being your creative best. These personal obstacles come in many shapes and sizes, such as the need for approval, feelings of insecurity, negative messages from childhood, fear of failure, and power and control issues; but they can all limit your creativity. For example, a chaotic childhood may have led you to seek and find stability and to structure a lifestyle in which change and taking risks are seen as only rocking the boat. Creative endeavors may have no place in your desire to control your environment and hug safe shores. Or you may have given up on your particular creative gifts because they weren't honored or respected in your family or in your schooling. Other behavior might have received greater rewards. In defining your process, find out what might be limiting your creativity. As one executive put it,

> I would say that if anything were ever an obstacle for my creativity, the biggest obstacle would be myself. It's all where I set my boundaries and where I put my walls, and if I refuse to move them, then I've become the problem, as opposed to the solution.

Build into your process the steps for overcoming those personal blocks. Find friends to support your efforts to be more creative and overcome your need for perfection. Read books about those issues.[5] Learn to talk back to your inner critic. Find tools that help you deal with these emotional blocks since you don't want them to prevent you from discovering and using your creative talents.

HAVING THE RIGHT KNOWLEDGE BASE

Another step to take to further grow your creativity and be your creative best is to build the right knowledge base against which to apply your creative talents and process. Occasionally, you might be lucky and produce some new insight in a field unknown to you or ask a question that provokes an uncommon response or leads to new perspectives. To *consistently* produce different and valuable results, however, you need to apply your creative talent and the process you have defined against knowledge of and expertise in your product, your field, and your industry. Creating fine music requires a good "ear," knowledge of music theory and the techniques involved in writing music, and experience using different instruments. Producing great photographs call for a good "eye," as well as knowledge of the camera, photographic composition, and lighting techniques. In the field of management, knowing the basics of motivation leads to creativity in managing your associates.[6] Knowledge of your field allows you to create great Web designs; achieve breakthroughs in medicine, biotechnology, or telecommunications; or craft new child-care solutions, novel transportation services, or manufacturing process redesigns.

To build this knowledge base, you need to stay intimately involved with the details of what's going on in your field and your business and why it's happening. Get input from customers, associates, and other stakeholders. Your knowledge of the past and of experts and practitioners brings new insights and perspectives. As one business owner said, "You need to know what's in the box before you can work on getting out of it!"

If you don't have the requisite knowledge, you may not know whether a possible solution is appropriate and works to solve the problem. You may not even understand the key problems. To be effectively creative, you must continue to learn, study, and broaden your knowledge base and then turn knowledge into action. One artist from New Zealand described his creativity as "research" as well as art. He traveled, exhibited his art, talked with other artists about what they were doing, and subjected his work to often unfriendly critics—all to learn more about and further develop his own creativity. His works of art reflected his learning. He continues to grow as an artist and refuses to become stale.

In addition to knowledge, the right attitude about learning, particularly learning from mistakes, is also crucial. You need to risk a little in the process and continue to produce despite failures because mistakes can be fascinating learning experiences. As you grow and learn, you will build confidence and more trust in your ability to find new solutions.

As with so much else relating to creativity, knowledge and learning require balance since "sacred cows" and proven models in your field can also get in your way. In this case, learning and knowledge need to be balanced with unlearning. Proven ways to solve problems don't always continue to work. You can get too close to the problem, and your knowledge can blind you to new facts and developments. Established rules, shared assumptions, paradigms, and mental models that frame a particular field of knowledge—such as finance, law, or science—can influence your recognition of information. They can isolate you, insulate you from new information and facts, and make you rigid. New discoveries are often hard to make because it is so difficult to break out of established perceptual modes.[7] It's not only Navigators who fall in love with the things that they think are true and are reluctant to let them go; everyone tends to treasure well-worn and comfortable truths, even when they become old and shabby and lose their utility.[8] Everyone must figure out how to discard what's no longer effective to make way for new learning.

Sometimes you must suspend these frameworks and let go of your expertise to see things differently. Again, it's all about balance. You have to know enough to be smart but still be open to exploring new territory, testing knowledge, and investigating novel and unexpected facts. To truly benefit from your creativity, you need the right balance between knowledge and an openness to new information so that you can step back from the details and "helicopter up" to see the big picture, vision, or future. Be sure to ask questions such as "How would a cartoon character, a personal hero, or a movie character look at this issue?" Such questions, as well as using the other creative tools and techniques described in Chapters 3 through 10, can jolt you out of the same old thinking and get you back on your creative track.

FINDING YOUR PASSION

Finally, passion will drive you to use your talents, your process, and your knowledge to reach your creative potential. This passion can be a quiet love for your work and life or a roaring obsession with making a contribution. That New Zealand artist had to use his art to tell his story because he zealously believed in its importance. Entrepreneurs who are driven to create value in the marketplace see their work as much more than jobs. Says one founder of an Internet design firm, "If I thought this was a job, I'd be gone by now. . . . I don't want a job. That's 9 to 5 and boring. I want a challenge. I do this because I love problem solving."[9]

Your passion, almost obsession, can help you overcome all sorts of fears and barriers. Doing something that isn't part of your passion can drain you. One former manager, a Navigator, related how she had recently quit her job, despite her strong need for security and stability: "I suddenly realized how much energy my job was taking from me. I know that by releasing that energy, I will be able to find something that will allow me to redefine my contribution to the bigger world."

Life's circumstances may keep you from following your passion right now, but don't let that stop you from making a creative contribution in the world. Perhaps you could make developing your creative talents your passion for now and find a better creative outlet later. Or you could use your creative talents to make a greater contribution in your home or volunteer life.

Taking a different step, away from safe shores, to achieve your creative best requires courage. Your passion helps drive that courage. It gives you perseverance and a willingness to risk. It supports your boldness in asking tough questions and challenging yourself and others. It gives you the energy required to reach outside the norm. As an Australian Methodist minister exclaimed one Sunday, "An idea pursued with passion crackles with power."[10]

Creativity takes a lot of sweaty trial and error, many long hours, and hard work as you try to come up with new ideas and creative solutions. When you create, you don't act by rote. You have to work hard, mull, ponder, tinker, play, analyze, and decide. You need dogged persistence, commitment, patience, and passion to accumulate knowledge, to keep reaching onward, and to see something through all sorts of physical and emotional obstacles. Deeply etched messages from society or family, personal needs and fears, and even laziness can limit your creativity. Being creative often isn't easy; it takes boldness and daring, much like the discoverers of the fifteenth and sixteenth centuries possessed, to ask tough questions, to take some risks, and to brave the unknown. The status quo and routine are often much more attractive, despite the tremendous benefits of creativity. That's why persistence and passion, along with talent, a creative process, and knowledge, are so important.

CONCLUSION

Carl Jung believed that creativity is one of the primary instincts and motivating forces of life.[11] According to Jung and others, creativity brings with it awesome powers and capabilities. The benefits from being creative often defy measurement. Being creative can help you achieve extraordinary results at work—in a team or by yourself. It supports your drive to be more competitive, productive, and effective. It fosters the development of new attitudes and the breaking of old, useless mind-sets; it helps you think more expansively.

Developing your creative talents not only leads to more creative results and contributions at work, but also builds confidence so that you can handle the challenges of life and gives you a deeper level of resilience to help you cope with constant change. Developing your creative talents strengthens your capacity to adapt and to bend and bounce back more buoyantly. It builds a positive attitude so that you can deal with any of the uncertainties and complexities that appear as you change, grow, and age. Seeing yourself as creative is thus vital for a healthy and productive life.

Success in today's dynamic world requires the willingness to try new routes and to explore new worlds as you continue to reinvent yourself, your life, and your work. Figure out how to let your creative talents flourish so that you can truly realize their full benefits and value. One business owner said, "When I'm trying to be creative, I am trying to be the best that I can be, and to be able to say that I did the best with what I had as capabilities. It's all about my life." Think about it. How does it feel to say to yourself, "I am creative!"?

The journey toward reaching your creative potential is not a simple one. Sometimes, personal or professional circumstances in your life, such as layoffs, death, or other changes, force you to find your gifts and talents. Sometimes the disadvantages of having limited your choices become apparent as you grow through life, so you finally resolve to do something about them. Or maybe you just decide it's time to fulfill a lifelong dream. Whatever the reasons for starting the journey of discovery, it will be well worth it. Finding your creative potential and making creative contributions to the world are acts of "high courage flung in the face of life, the absolute affirmation of all that constitutes the individual, the most successful adaptation of the universal condition of existence coupled with the greatest possible freedom for self-determination."[12]

The journey, according to Jung, is "a lifetime's task which is never completed; a journey upon which one sets out hopefully toward a destination at which one never arrives."[13] Your challenge is to get started, to take the first step. In a commencement address at Mount Holyoke College, the writer Anna Quindlen quoted George Eliot as once having said: "It is never too late to be what you might have been." Then Quindlen added, "It is never too early, either. And it will make all the difference in the world!"[14]

✳

Discovery follows discovery; each both raising and answering questions; each ending a long search, and each providing the new instruments for a new search.

—J. Robert Oppenheimer

CREATIVE TALENTS PERSONAL DEVELOPMENT

Adventurer (ESTP, ESFP)	Navigator (ISTJ, ISFJ)
RESULTS AND CONTRIBUTIONS • Clever and satisfying solutions to customer and operational problems • Practical applications that recognize shape, line, color, and texture, which can be handled and taken apart • Adding fun, curiosity, adaptability, flexibility, and positive energy to the team • Imagination full of specific details: how things look, smell, taste, sound, and feel • Prompt, practical, and ingenious responses to crises and emergencies • Experimentation with the group, pushing it to find new solutions that work	• Practical adaptation, fine-tuning, and building on what others have done • Ability to fix things to make them work • Skill in helping people understand new products and services • New rites, rituals, and systems to make the change work • Imagination full of specific details, with an impressionistic, surreal perspective • Keeping the group or project grounded, focused, and on track • Understanding of and planning for possible resistance to new initiatives
BLOCKS TO OPTIMAL CREATIVITY • Focus on the external world in the short term • Obsession with the process and the joy of the moment • Impatience with inaction • Unwillingness to get into the deeper issues behind the situation or the conflict • Tendencies to be easily distracted and quickly discouraged • Failure to see the value of new ideas, theories, and possibilities • Lack of direction or appreciation for structure and deadlines • Biases of their auxiliary talent to certain types of data • Fear of the unknown and the unconscious	• Need to study and understand change and preference for the status quo • Perfectionism and obsession with details • Biases of their auxiliary talent to certain types of data • Problems expressing and articulating thoughts and feelings • Avoidance of conflict • Overcautiousness • Clinging rigidly to the plan • Need for control • Fear of the unknown and the unconscious • Lack of comfort with uncertainty
ENHANCING YOUR CREATIVE TALENT • Trust your strengths • Develop greater self-awareness • Find the right creativity tools and techniques • Develop your abilities to organize and structure project efforts • Find an approach to time management that works for you • Learn to reflect on what you are taking in • Slow your listening and reacting down • Access your auxiliary talent for its decision-making abilities • Recognize and practice your own creative process • Team with others who take a broader view of the situation	• Play to your strengths • Develop greater self-awareness • Find the right creativity tools and techniques • Find heroes, role models, and helpmates • Be careful with the details • Use your auxiliary talent to connect with people and share ideas • Use your auxiliary talent to help focus, to get outside your head, and to turn ideas and possibilities into reality • Define how you go about finding creative answers and practice the process • Work with a team • Overcome the need for control and perfection

CREATIVE TALENTS PERSONAL DEVELOPMENT

Explorer (ENTP, ENFP)	Visionary (INTJ, INFJ)

RESULTS AND CONTRIBUTIONS

Explorer (ENTP, ENFP)	Visionary (INTJ, INFJ)
• Ability to see external patterns, trends, and relationships • Tireless generation, promotion, and initiation of new enterprises, new business ventures, and new ideas • Inspiring ingenuity and discovery in others • Imagination full of connections and associations • High-spirited team-building and successful change initiatives because of their enthusiasm, energy, and passion • Helping others push past what is accepted and expected • Possibility thinking to envision future	• Provocative questions that challenge the group to find profound answers and big solutions • "Incasting" (versus forecasting)–working back from the future to develop plans • New designs and solutions through unusual connections • Imagination full of hard-to-describe images and futuristic possibilities • Multidisciplined perspectives • Penetrating, far-reaching insights into future trends • Ability to integrate, synthesize, and move the group forward

BLOCKS TO OPTIMAL CREATIVITY

Explorer (ENTP, ENFP)	Visionary (INTJ, INFJ)
• Irresistible pull of the external world • Unfocused energy and overextension of self • Tendency to be easily distracted and become impatient • Failure to address facts and details • Preference for idea generation over implementation • Overwhelming or silencing others • Biases of their auxiliary talent to certain types of data • Not understanding or appreciating facts, history, or resistance to change • Burnout and loss of their creative edge	• Neglect of relevant facts and details about people and things • Constant pursuit of new ideas • Perfectionism and need for mastery • Overly independent and private • Biases of their auxiliary talent to certain types of data • Reluctance to share ideas and information • Making the simple overcomplex • Possible single-mindedness and tunnel vision • Stubbornness and rebelliousness • Not taking care of themselves

ENHANCING YOUR CREATIVE TALENT

Explorer (ENTP, ENFP)	Visionary (INTJ, INFJ)
• Trust your strengths • Develop greater self-awareness • Find the right creativity tools and techniques • Find ways to capture ideas • Get help in organizing and executing ideas • Access your auxiliary talent for balance • Practice good time-management techniques • Reflect and grow • Become more conscious of and practice your own creative process • Learn to communicate with other talents	• Play to your strengths • Develop greater self-awareness • Find the right creativity tools and techniques • Be sure to capture your ideas • Review and reflect on those ideas • Use your auxiliary talent to help focus, to get outside your head, and to turn ideas and possibilities into reality • Use your auxiliary talent to connect with people and share ideas • Know and learn your creative process • Appreciate the team • Limit your search for information

CREATIVE TALENTS PERSONAL DEVELOPMENT

Pilot (ESTJ, ENTJ)	Inventor (ISTP, INTP)
RESULTS AND CONTRIBUTIONS • Clarification of goals and responsibilities on projects and change initiatives • High-energy team leadership • New and different strategies • Innovative organizational designs and structures • Making things happen through inventive, tough-minded problem solving • Logical categorization of ideas and issues • Focus on progress, improvement, efficiency, productivity, and results in change initiatives • Thoughtful questions and challenges to conventional thinking	• Unconventional theories and models for analysis and synthesis of facts, ideas, and concepts • Unusual and thoughtful solutions to problems through identifying what makes things work and through objective, impartial analysis • Inventive ways to get around constraints • Tough, unrelenting critique to get to the highest levels of effectiveness • A quick understanding and intellectual curiosity that can speed the creative process • Insightful questions that cause paradigm shifts in perspective • Integrated solutions where everything fits
BLOCKS TO OPTIMAL CREATIVITY • Dampening the creativity of others • Direct approaches to communication and conflict • Reliance on selected facts, jumping to conclusions too quickly, and failure to collect sufficient data • The "tyranny of the or" • Tendency to take charge too soon and need to control • Critical questioning attitude • Difficulties with dealing with people issues • Biases of their auxiliary talent to certain types of data • Being overanalytical and seeing everything as a problem or a decision to be made	• Concentration on impersonal, objective data, often overlooking the people side of the issue • Ignoring emotional needs and values • Biases of their auxiliary talent to details or larger patterns • Dichotomous or either-or thinking • An overdetached approach to conflict • Procrastination and postponment of decisions • Lacking focus and organization • Minimal concern for schedules and deadlines • Preference for freedom and variety
ENHANCING YOUR CREATIVE TALENT • Trust your strengths • Develop greater self-awareness • Find the right creativity tools and techniques • Take time to reflect • Listen, open up, and see other perspectives • Balance process and product • Look for gray areas • Build a team and measure your participation • Define and practice your creative process	• Trust your strengths • Develop greater self-awareness • Find the right creativity tools and techniques • Learn about downtime • Open up to the possibility of many different ways to look at problems • Access your auxiliary talent • Learn to express your ideas • Balance the process with the result • Define and practice your creative process • Organize your information

CREATIVE TALENTS PERSONAL DEVELOPMENT

Harmonizer (ESFJ, ENFJ)	Poet (ISFP, INFP)
RESULTS AND CONTRIBUTIONS • High-energy team leadership • Innovative solutions to problems and new programs that help customers, employees, or community • A nurturing, energetic team environment that brings out the best in people • Diverse and effective communication strategies • Different perspectives through concern for context and circumstances • Successful resolution of political problems that can impede change and innovation • Heightened self-esteem for team members	• An aesthetic appreciation for grace and elegance in solutions • Building an environment of trust, respect, and support, a safe place for testing out new ideas and behaviors • Independent and thoughtful perspectives on the challenge, addressing people-related values, context, and circumstances • Serving as the team's ethical backbone • Generation of new possibilities and options through reflection and incubation • Articulation and portrayal of values, feelings, and perspectives, often through writing
BLOCKS TO OPTIMAL CREATIVITY • Boundary management issues • Overidentification with others and need for approval • Making incorrect assumptions and jumping to conclusions • Failure to gather sufficient information • Biases of their auxiliary talent to details or larger patterns • Need for control and failure to listen • Concern for consensus • Difficulty seeing the disagreeable side to people or issues • Dislike of having to deal with conflict	• Overlooking points of view that clash with their strongly held values • Getting emotionally entangled and finding it hard to criticize others and give honest, direct feedback • Avoidance of conflict • Procrastination and indecision • Biases of their auxiliary talent to details or larger patterns • Keeping feelings and opinions private • Lack of organization • Excessive need to reflect and process
ENHANCING YOUR CREATIVE TALENT • Trust your strengths • Develop greater self-awareness • Find the right creativity tools and techniques • Learn to appreciate and manage conflict • Build independence • Reflect • Balance process and product • Identify and practice your creative process • Develop your speaking, writing, and meeting-management skills	• Trust your strengths • Develop greater self-awareness • Find the right creativity tools and techniques • Learn to appreciate conflict • Voice your opinions • Be sure that you are open to possibilities • Set boundaries • Practice good project and time management • Define and practice your creative process

FINAL THOUGHTS

If you have additional examples, stories, experiences, or other comments about the material in this book and any impact it has had on your life or work, or if you have any questions, I look forward to hearing from you. Please e-mail me at: lynne@lynnelevesque.com or check out my website at: www.lynnelevesque.com.

ENDNOTES

Chapter 1 (How Are You Creative?)

1. Carl G. Jung, "Psychological Factors in Human Behaviour," in vol. 8 of *Collected Works of C. G. Jung*, Bollingen Series XX (Princeton, NJ: Princeton University Press, 1971): 118.

2. Unless otherwise noted, quotations are from the author's conversations with clients, colleagues, and students and her research, including the dissertation study: Lynne C. Levesque, "Factors Influencing Creativity at the Top of Organizations" (Unpublished doctoral dissertation, University of Massachusetts at Amherst, 1996).

3. Nathaniel Branden, *Self-Esteem at Work* (San Francisco: Jossey-Bass, 1998).

4. Teresa Amabile and Regina Conti, "Changes in the Work Environment for Creativity During Downsizing," *Academy of Management Journal* 42, no. 6 (1999): 630–40.

5. Carl G. Jung, *Psychological Types*, in vol. 6 of *Collected Works of C. G. Jung*, Bollingen Series XX (Princeton, NJ: Princeton University Press, 1990): 433. See also Jung, "Psychological Factors."

6. Robert Reich, "The Company of the Future," *Fast Company* (November 1998): 150.

7. "Survey: Innovation in Industry," *The Economist* (22 February 1999): 5–28. See also Andrew Van de Ven, "Central Problems in the Management of Innovation," *Management Science* 32, no. 5 (1986): 592.

8. Alan M. Webber, "Danger: Toxic Company," *Fast Company* (November 1998): 152–61; and Jeffrey Pfeffer, *The Human Equation* (Boston: Harvard Business School Press, 1998).

9. Michael A. West and James L. Farr, "Innovation at Work." In *Innovation and Creativity at Work*, ed. M. A. West and J. L. Farr (New York: Wiley, 1990): 9.

Chapter 2 (Discovering Your Creative Talents)

1. Carl G. Jung, *Analytical Psychology: Its Theory and Practice* (The Tavistock Lectures) (New York: Vintage Books, 1968): 19.

2. Carl G. Jung, *Psychological Types,* vol. 6 of *The Collected Works of C. G. Jung,* Bollingen Series XX (Princeton, NJ: Princeton University Press, 1971): 393; Roger R. Pearman and Sarah C. Albritton, *I'm Not Crazy, I'm Just Not You* (Palo Alto, CA: Davies-Black, 1997): 11.

3. Alan Brownsword, *It Takes All Types!* (San Anselmo: CA: HRM Press, 1987).

4. See James Hillman, "The Feeling Function," in *Lectures on Jung's Typology* (Woodstock, CT: Spring Publications, 1971).

5. John Beebe (speaker), *A New Model of Psychological Types* (5 audiotapes) (Evanston, IL: C. G. Jung Institute of Chicago, 1988).

6. John Jacobi, *The Psychology of C. G. Jung* (New Haven, CT: Yale University Press, 1968): 24.

7. Gordon Lawrence, *People Types and Tiger Stripes* (Gainesville, FL: CAPT, 1993): 116.

8. See Darryl Sharp, *Personality Types: Jung's Model of Typology* (Toronto: Inner City Books, 1987): 91-92.

Chapter 3 (The Adventurer)

1. As quoted in Mary H. McCaulley, "The Myers-Briggs Type Indicator®." Paper presented at Understanding and Nurturing Creativity in People: A Focus on Cognitive Styles, Learning Styles, and Psychological Type, an International Conference hosted by the Center for Studies in Creativity, Buffalo State College, Buffalo, NY, April 28–30, 1997.

2. Michael J. Gelb, *How to Think Like Leonardo da Vinci* (New York: Delacorte Press, 1998): 95.

3. J. H. Van der Hoop, *Conscious Orientation* (London: Kegan Paul, Trench, Trubner, 1939): 29.

4. Adapted from Sue G. Clancy, "STJs and Change," in *Developing Leaders,* ed. C. Fitzgerald and L. K. Kirby (Palo Alto, CA: Davies-Black, 1997): 420–21.

5. Nancy J. Barger and Linda K. Kirby, "Enhancing Leadership During Organizational Change," in *Developing Leaders,* ed. C. Fitzgerald and L. K. Kirby (Palo Alto, CA: Davies-Black, 1997): 344–45

6. Carl G. Jung, *Psychological Types,* vol. 6 of *The Collected Works of C. G. Jung,* Bollingen Series XX (Princeton, NJ: Princeton University Press, 1971): 364; Naomi L. Quenk, *Beside Ourselves* (Palo Alto, CA: Davies-Black, 1993): 146.

7. Isabel Briggs Myers, with Peter B. Myers, *Gifts Differing* (Palo Alto, CA: Davies-Black, 1980): 100.

8. Naomi L. Quenk, *Beside Ourselves.*

9. See Bob King and and Helmut Schlicksupp, *The Idea Edge* (Methuen, MA: GOAL/QPC, 1998); and Michael Michalko, *Thinkertoys: A Handbook of Business*

Creativity for the '90's (Berkeley, CA: Ten Speed Press, 1991); and Bryan Mattimore, *99% Inspiration* (New York: American Management Association, 1994): 96.

10. See Michalko, *ThinkerToys;* and Mike Vance and Diane Deacon, *Think Out of the Box* (Franklin Lakes, NJ: Career Press, 1995).

11. Sandra Krebs Hirsh, with Jane A. G. Kise, *Work It Out* (Palo Alto, CA: Davies-Black, 1996): 120.

12. See Paula Martin and Karen Tate, *Project Management Memory Jogger*™ (Methuen, MA: GOAL/QPC, 1997); Robert Wysocki, Robert Beck, Jr., and David B. Crane, *Effective Project Management* (New York: Wiley, 1995); and J. Davidson Frame, *The New Project Management* (San Francisco: Jossey-Bass, 1994).

13. Hirsh, with Kise, *Work It Out,* 120.

14. Marilyn Wood Daudelin, "Learning from Experience Through Reflection," *Organizational Dynamics* (Winter 1996): 36–48.

15. Hirsh, with Kise, *Work It Out,* 211.

16. Michael Michalko, *Cracking Creativity* (Berkeley, CA: Ten Speed Press, 1998): 105–106.

17. Lenore Thomson, *Personality Type* (Boston: Shambhala, 1998): 155, 158.

18. Roger L. Firestien, *Why Didn't I Think of That?* (Williamsville, NY: Innovations Systems Group, 1998).

19. Check out the exercises in Peter M. Senge, Charlotte Roberts, Richard B. Ross, Byron J. Smith, and Art Kleiner, *The Fifth Discipline Fieldbook* (New York: Doubleday, 1994).

20. Creative Education Foundation: www.cef-cpsi.org or call (800)447-2774.

21. *Fast Company* magazine: www.fastcompany.com; Curtis Sittenfeld, "Be Your Own Futurist." *Fast Company* (October 1998): 42.

22. World Futures Society: www.wfs.org

23. See Sandra Janoff and Marvin Weisbord, *Future Search: An Action Guide to Finding Common Ground in Organizations and Communities* (San Francisco: Berrett-Koehler, 2000); and Harrison Owen, *Open Space Technology: A User's Guide* (San Francisco: Berrett-Koehler, 1997).

24. See Peter Russell and Roger Evans, *The Creative Manager* (San Francisco: Jossey-Bass, 1992); Michael Ray and Rochelle Myers, *Creativity in Business* (New York: Doubleday, 1986); and Doris J. Shallcross and Dorothy A. Sisk, *Intuition: An Inner Way of Knowing.* (Buffalo, NY: Bearly Limited, 1989).

25. Quenk, *Beside Ourselves.*

26. Ibid.

27. Paul D. Tieger and Barbara Barron-Tieger, *Do What You Are* (Boston: Little, Brown, 1992): 298.

28. Hirsh, with Kise, *Work It Out,* 69.

29. Senge et al., *Fifth Discipline Handbook.*

30. Quenk, *Beside Ourselves.*

Chapter 4 (The Navigator)

1. From data collected during the *Survey on Creativity and Innovation in Family Owned Businesses* (Cambridge, MA: Cambridge Center for Creative Enterprise, 1999). Summary available from the author.

2. James Newman, "Conundrum No. 1: What Is Introverted Sensation?" *Bulletin of Psychological Type* 17, no. 2 (1994): 17.

3. Thomas Penderghast, "Creativity in Organizations," *Bulletin of Psychological Type* 16, no. 2 (1993): 17.

4. As quoted in Mary H. McCaulley, "The Myers-Briggs Type Indicator®." Paper presented at Understanding and Nurturing Creativity in People: A Focus on Cognitive Styles, Learning Styles, and Psychological Type, an International Conference hosted by the Center for Studies in Creativity, Buffalo State College, Buffalo, NY, April 28–30, 1997.

5. Ibid.

6. Andrew Hargadon and Robert I. Sutton, "Building an Innovation Factory," *Harvard Business Review* (May–June 2000): 161.

7. "Innovator of the Year: Michael Largent," *National Home Center News* 25, no. 7 (1999).

8. As quoted in McCaulley, "The Myers-Briggs Type Indicator.®"

9. J. H. Van der Hoop, *Conscious Orientation* (London: Kegan Paul, Trench, Trubner, 1939): 32.

10. Adapted from Sue G. Clancy, "STJs and Change," in *Developing Leaders,* ed. C. Fitzgerald and L. K. Kirby (Palo Alto, CA: Davies-Black, 1997): 420–21.

11. Angelo Spoto, *Jung's Typology in Perspective* (Wilmette, IL: Chiron, 1995): 46.

12. Clancy, "STJs and Change," 416.

13. As quoted in "Eureka Moments II," *Discover* (October 1996): 84.

14. Robert W. Weisberg, "Problem Solving and Creativity," in *The Nature of Creativity,* ed. R. Sternberg (Cambridge, England: Cambridge University Press, 1988): 160–63

15. Nancy J. Barger and Linda K. Kirby, *The Challenge of Change in Organizations* (Palo Alto, CA: Davies-Black, 1995): 232.

16. Van der Hoop, *Conscious Orientation*, 32–33.

17. McCaulley, "The Myers-Briggs Type Indicator®."

18. French physiologist Claude Bernard, quoted in Anna Muoio, ed. "The Art of Smart," *Fast Company* (July–August 1999): 94.

19. Naomi L. Quenk, *Beside Ourselves* (Palo Alto, CA: Davies-Black, 1993).

20. See Bob King and and Helmut Schlicksupp, *The Idea Edge* (Methuen, MA: GOAL/QPC, 1998); Michael Michalko, *Thinkertoys: A Handbook of Business Creativity for the '90's* (Berkeley, CA: Ten Speed Press, 1991); and Bryan Mattimore, *99% Inspiration* (New York: American Management Association, 1994): 96.

21. Michael Michalko, *Cracking Creativity* (Berkeley, CA: Ten Speed Press, 1998): 140.

22. Ibid., 95–100.

23. See Michalko, *Thinkertoys*; and Mike Vance and Diane Deacon, *Think Out of the Box* (Franklin Lakes, NJ: Career Press, 1995).

24. Sandra Krebs Hirsh, with Jane A. G. Kise, *Work It Out* (Palo Alto, CA: Davies-Black, 1996): 43.

25. Roger L. Firestien, *Why Didn't I Think of That?* (Williamsville, NY: Innovations Systems Group, 1998).

26. Creative Education Foundation: www.cef-cpsi.org or call (800)447-2774.

27. *Fast Company* magazine: www.fastcompany.com

28. World Futures Society: www.wfs.org

29. See Peter Russell and Roger Evans, *The Creative Manager* (San Francisco: Jossey-Bass, 1992); Michael Ray and Rochelle Myers, *Creativity in Business* (New York: Doubleday, 1986); and Doris J. Shallcross and Dorothy A. Sisk, *Intuition: An Inner Way of Knowing* (Buffalo, NY: Bearly Limited, 1989).

30. Quenk, *Beside Ourselves.*

31. Dee W. Hock, quoted in Anna Muoio, ed., "The Art of the Smart," *Fast Company* (July–August 1999): 90.

32. Hirsh, with Kise, *Work It Out,* 69.

33. Barger and Kirby, *The Challenge of Change.*

34. Ibid.

35. Jeffrey Pfeffer and Robert L. Sutton, "The Smart-Talk Trap," *Harvard Business Review* (May–June 1999): 141.

36. Quenk, *Beside Ourselves.*

Chapter 5 (The Explorer)

1. Lenore Thomson, *Personality Type* (Boston: Shambhala, 1998): 209.

2. Naomi L. Quenk, *Beside Ourselves* (Palo Alto, CA: Davies-Black, 1993).

3. Alex Osborn, *Applied Imagination,* 3d ed. (Buffalo, NY: Creative Education Foundation, 1993): 156.

4. See Bob King and Helmut Schlicksupp, *The Idea Edge* (Methuen, MA: GOAL/QPC, 1998); and Michael Michalko, *Thinkertoys: A Handbook of Business Creativity for the '90's* (Berkeley, CA: Ten Speed Press, 1991).

5. Kathleen Howley, "Saving House Where Architect Lived, Worked." *Boston Globe* (12 December, 1999).

6. See King and Schlicksupp, *The Idea Edge*; and Michael Brassard, *The Memory Jogger Plus+®* (Methuen, MA: GOAL/QPC, 1989, 1996).

7. Michael Michalko, *Cracking Creativity* (Berkeley, CA: Ten Speed Press, 1998): 55ff.

8. Sandra Krebs Hirsh, with Jane A. G. Kise, *Work It Out* (Palo Alto, CA: Davies-Black, 1996): 120.

9. Ibid.

10. Michalko, *Cracking Creativity*, 51, 105–106.

11. See Nancy J. Barger and Linda K. Kirby, *The Challenge of Change in Organizations* (Palo Alto, CA: Davies-Black, 1995); Daryl Conner, *Managing at the Speed of Change* (New York: Random House, 1993); and Alexander Watson Hiam, *The Portable Conference on Change Management* (Amherst, MA: HRD Press, 1997).

12. Quenk, *Beside Ourselves*.

13. Ibid.

Chapter 6 (The Visionary)

1. Daniel Boorstin, *The Discoverers* (New York: Vintage Books, 1985): 159.

2. Lenore Thomson, *Personality Type* (Boston: Shambhala, 1998): 224.

3. Darryl Sharp, *Personality Types* (Toronto: Inner City Books, 1987): 85.

4. James F. Bandrowski, "Orchestrating Planning Creativity," *Planning Review* (September 1984): 18–23, 44.

5. Curtis Sittenfeld, "Be Your Own Futurist," *Fast Company* (October 1998): 42.

6. Nancy J. Barger and Linda K. Kirby, *The Challenge of Change in Organizations* (Palo Alto, CA: Davies-Black, 1995).

7. Roger R. Pearman and Sarah C. Albritton, *I'm Not Crazy, I'm Just Not You* (Palo Alto, CA: Davies-Black, 1997): 75.

8. Ibid.

9. Naomi L. Quenk, *Beside Ourselves* (Palo Alto, CA: Davies-Black, 1993).

10. Ibid.

11. A Mattimore Group technique, Stamford, CT, (203)359-1801.

12. See Ann Faraday, *The Dream Game* (New York: Perennial Library/Harper & Row, 1976); David Fontana, *The Secret Language of Dreams* (San Francisco: Chronicle Books, 1994); Maria F. Mahoney, *The Meaning in Dreams and Dreaming* (Secaucus, NJ: Citadel Press, 1966); Jill Mellick, *The Natural Artistry of Dreams* (Berkeley, CA: Conari Press, 1996); and Louis M. Savory, Patricia H. Berne, and Strephon Kaplan Williams, *Dreams and Spiritual Growth* (New York and Ramsey, NJ: Paulist Press, 1984).

13. See Paula Martin and Karen Tate, *Project Management Memory Jogger™* (Methuen, MA: GOAL/QPC, 1997); Robert Wysocki, Robert Beck, Jr., and David B. Crane, *Effective Project Management* (New York: Wiley, 1995); and J. Davidson Frame, *The New Project Management* (San Francisco: Jossey-Bass, 1994).

14. Jeffrey Pfeffer and Robert I. Sutton, "The Smart-Talk Trap," *Harvard Business Review* (May–June 1999): 140.

15. Sandra Krebs Hirsh, with Jane A. G. Kise, *Work It Out* (Palo Alto, CA: Davies-Black, 1996): 43.

16. Ibid., 223.

17. Quenk, *Beside Ourselves*.

18. See Michael Michalko, *Thinkertoys: A Handbook of Business Creativity for the '90's* (Berkeley, CA: Ten Speed Press, 1991); and Mike Vance and Diane Deacon, *Think Out of the Box* (Franklin Lakes, NJ: Career Press, 1995).

19. Julia Cameron, *The Artist's Way* (Los Angeles: Tarcher/Perigee, 1992).

Chapter 7 (The Pilot)

1. Paul Roberts, "The Art of Getting Things Done," *Fast Company* (June 2000): 164.

2. Howard Gardner, *Leading Minds* (New York: Basic Books, 1995): 8.

3. James Collins and Jerry Porras, *Built to Last* (New York: HarperCollins, 1994): 43.

4. Paul C. Nutt, "Surprising but True: Half the Decisions in Organizations Fail," *Academy of Management Executive* 13, no. 4 (1999): 84.

5. Ibid., 85.

6. Naomi L. Quenk, *Beside Ourselves* (Palo Alto, CA: Davies-Black, 1993).

7. Alex Osborn, *Applied Imagination* (Buffalo, NY: Creative Education Foundation, 1993): 175–76.

8. See G. S. Altshuller, *Creativity as an Exact Science* (Luxembourg: Gordon and Breach, 1995); *TRIZ Journal* at www.triz-journal.com; and TRIZ Consulting, Inc., at www.members.aol.com/zroyzen/triz.html

9. Marilyn Wood Daudelin, "Learning from Experience Through Reflection," *Organizational Dynamics* (Winter 1996): 36–48.

10. Bart Kosko, *Fuzzy Thinking* (New York: Hyperion, 1993).

11. Roger L. Firestien, *Why Didn't I Think of That?* (Williamsville, NY: Innovations Systems Group, 1998).

12. Daniel Goleman, *Working with Emotional Intelligence* (New York: Bantam Books, 1998); and Daniel Goleman, *Emotional Intelligence* (New York: Bantam Books, 1995).

13. Nutt, "Surprising but True," 88.

14. Goleman, *Working with Emotional Intelligence*; and Goleman, *Emotional Intelligence*.

15. Julia Cameron, *The Artist's Way* (Los Angeles: Tarcher/Perigee, 1992).

16. Quenk, *Beside Ourselves*.

17. Bryan Mattimore, *99% Inspiration* (New York: American Management Association, 1994): 75.

18. Michael Michalko, *Cracking Creativity* (Berkeley, CA: Ten Speed Press, 1998): 55.

19. For guidelines on these processes, see Michalko, *Cracking Creativity*; and Bob King and Helmut Schlicksupp, *The Idea Edge* (Methuen, MA: GOAL/QPC, 1998).

20. Deb Stratas, "A Thinker's Guide to Feeling Types in Meetings," *Bulletin of Psychological Type* 22, no. 8 (1999): 35.

21. See Goleman, *Working with Emotional Intelligence;* and Goleman, *Emotional Intelligence.*

22. Quenk, *Beside Ourselves.*

Chapter 8 (The Inventor)

1. Carolyn Barnes, "Rooms of My Mind: Introverted Thinking," *Bulletin of Psychological Type* 22, no. 1 (1999): 1, 3.

2. James F. Bandrowski, "Orchestrating Planning Creativity," *Planning Review* (September 1984): 18–23, 44.

3. Paul Roberts, "The Art of Getting Things Done," *Fast Company* (June 2000): 164.

4. Carl G. Jung, *Psychological Types,* vol. 6 of *The Collected Works of C. G. Jung,* Bollingen Series XX (Princeton, NJ: Princeton University Press, 1971): 393.

5. Nancy J. Barger and Linda K. Kirby, *The Challenge of Change in Organizations* (Palo Alto, CA: Davies-Black, 1995): 240

6. James Collins and Jerry Porras, *Built to Last* (New York: HarperCollins, 1994): 43.

7. Naomi L. Quenk, *Beside Ourselves* (Palo Alto, CA: Davies-Black, 1993).

8. Ibid.

9. Michael Michalko, *Thinkertoys: A Handbook of Business Creativity for the '90's* (Berkeley, CA: Ten Speed Press, 1991).

10. There are several resources for more information on TRIZ in the United States. A first start is checking out two websites: www.members.aol.com/zroyzen/triz.html and www.triz-journal.com. Or you can contact TRIZ Consulting, Inc., phone: (206) 364-3116, fax: (206)364-8932, e-mail: ZRoyzen@aol.com

11. Bart Kosko, *Fuzzy Thinking* (New York: Hyperion Books, 1993).

12. Meryle Secrest, *Frank Lloyd Wright* (New York: Knopf, 1992).

13. Sandra Krebs Hirsh, with Jane A. G. Kise, *Work It Out* (Palo Alto, CA: Davies-Black, 1996): 120.

14. Bryan Mattimore, *99% Inspiration* (New York: American Management Association, 1994): 75

15. Michael Michalko, *Cracking Creativity* (Berkeley, CA: Ten Speed Press, 1998): 55

16. For guidelines on these processes, see Michalko, *Cracking Creativity;* and Bob King and Helmut Schlicksupp, *The Idea Edge* (Methuen, MA: GOAL/QPC, 1998).

17. Deb Stratas, "A Thinker's Guide to Feeling Types in Meetings," *Bulletin of Psychological Type* 22, no. 8 (1999): 35.

18. Daniel Goleman, *Working with Emotional Intelligence* (New York: Bantam Books, 1998); and Daniel Goleman, *Emotional Intelligence* (New York: Bantam Books, 1995).

19. Marilyn Wood Daudelin, "Learning from Experience Through Reflection," *Organizational Dynamics* (Winter 1996): 36–48.

20. Quenk, *Beside Ourselves.*

Chapter 9 (The Harmonizer)

1. Paul Roberts, "The Art of Getting Things Done," *Fast Company* (June 2000): 164.

2. From data collected during the *Survey on Creativity and Innovation in Family Owned Businesses* (Cambridge, MA: Cambridge Center for Creative Enterprise, 1999). Summary available from the author.

3. Nathaniel Branden, *Self-Esteem at Work* (San Francisco: Jossey-Bass, 1998): 27; and personal communication with the author.

4. J. H. Van der Hoop, *Conscious Orientation* (London: Kegan Paul, Trench, Trubner, Ltd., 1939): 84–85.

5. Nancy J. Barger and Linda K. Kirby. *The Challenge of Change in Organizations* (Palo Alto, CA: Davies-Black, 1995): 108

6. Polly LaBarre, "The New Face of Office Politics," *Fast Company* (October 1999): 82.

7. Howard Gardner, *Creating Minds* (New York: Basic Books, 1993): 5.

8. Mary Parker Follett, "How Must Business Management Develop in Order to Become a Profession?" as excerpted in *Mary Parker Follett, Prophet of Management*, P. Graham, ed. (Boston: Harvard Business School Press, 1996): 276.

9. Naomi L. Quenk, *Beside Ourselves* (Palo Alto, CA: Davies-Black, 1993).

10. Dorothy Leonard and Walter Swap, "How Managers Can Spark Creativity," *Leader to Leader* (Fall 1999): 47.

11. Michael Michalko, *Cracking Creativity* (Berkeley, CA: Ten Speed Press, 1998): 44; and Bryan Mattimore, *99% Inspiration* (New York: American Management Association, 1994): 100.

12. Michalko, *Cracking Creativity*, 55.

13. Sandra Krebs Hirsh, with Jane A. G. Kise, *Work It Out* (Palo Alto, CA: Davies-Black, 1996): 90.

14. Marilyn Wood Daudelin, "Learning from Experience Through Reflection," *Organizational Dynamics* (Winter 1996): 36–48.

15. Mattimore, *99% Inspiration*, 104–108; see also Hirsh, with Kise, *Work It Out*.

16. See Bob King and Helmut Schlicksupp, *The Idea Edge* (Methuen, MA: GOAL/QPC 1998); and Michael Brassard, *The Memory Jogger Plus+*® (Methuen, MA.: GOAL/QPC, 1989, 1996). See also Robert Damelo, *The Basics of Process Mapping* (Portland, OR: Productivity, Inc., 1996).

17. Naomi L. Quenk, "Fun with Your Inferior Function," *APT XII Proceedings* (July 1997): 41.

18. Quenk, *Beside Ourselves.*

19. Barger and Kirby, *The Challenge of Change,* 259.

20. Deb Stratas, "A Thinker's Guide to Feeling Types in Meetings," *Bulletin of Psychological Type* 22, no. 8 (1999): 35.

21. Quenk, *Beside Ourselves.*

Chapter 10 (The Poet)

1. Bart Kosko, *Fuzzy Thinking* (New York: Hyperion, 1993).

2. Catherine Fitzgerald and Linda K. Kirby, "Applying Type Dynamics to Leadership Development," in *Developing Leaders,* ed. C. Fitzgerald and L. K. Kirby (Palo Alto, CA: Davies-Black, 1997): 288

3. Paul C. Nutt, "Decision Style and Its Impact on Managers and Management," *Technological Forecasting and Social Change* 29 (1986): 341–66.

4. Nancy J. Barger and Linda K. Kirby, *The Challenge of Change in Organizations* (Palo Alto, CA: Davies-Black, 1995).

5. See, for example, Henry Mintzberg, *The Rise and Fall of Strategic Planning* (New York: Free Press, 1994).

6. Naomi L. Quenk, *Beside Ourselves* (Palo Alto, CA: Davies-Black, 1993).

7. Ibid.

8. Dorothy Leonard and Walter Swap, "How Managers Can Spark Creativity," *Leader to Leader* (Fall 1999): 47.

9. Michael Michalko, *Cracking Creativity* (Berkeley, CA: Ten Speed Press, 1998): 44; and Bryan Mattimore, *99% Inspiration* (New York: American Management Association, 1994): 100.

10. See Michael Michalko, *Thinkertoys: A Handbook of Business Creativity for the '90's* (Berkeley, CA: Ten Speed Press, 1991); and Mike Vance and Diane Deacon, *Think Out of the Box* (Franklin Lakes, NJ: Career Press, 1995).

11. Sandra Krebs Hirsh, with Jane A. G. Kise, *Work It Out* (Palo Alto, CA: Davies-Black, 1996): 90.

12. Mattimore, *99% Inspiration.*

13. Hirsh, with Kise, *Work It Out.*

14. See Bob King and Helmut Schlicksupp, *The Idea Edge* (Methuen, MA: GOAL/QPC 1998); and Michael Brassard, *The Memory Jogger Plus+*® (Methuen, MA.: GOAL/QPC, 1989, 1996). See also Robert Damelo, *The Basics of Process Mapping* (Portland, OR: Productivity, Inc., 1996).

15. Quenk, *Beside Ourselves.*

16. Barger and Kirby, *The Challenge of Change,* 259.

17. Deb Stratas, "A Thinker's Guide to Feeling Types in Meetings," *Bulletin of Psychological Type 22,* no. 8 (1999). 35.

18. Quenk, *Beside Ourselves.*

Chapter 11 (Strengthening Creativity in Teams)

1. Randall Tobias, "Good for Workers, Good for Business," *Boston Globe* (21 December, 1998).

2. As quoted in "Life in the Fast Lane," *Inc. Magazine* (September 1999): 10.

3. Eric H. Kessler and Alok K. Chakrabarti, "Innovation Speed: A Conceptual Model of Context, Antecedents, and Outcomes," *Academy of Management Review* 21, no. 4 (1996):1162.

4. Paul Roberts, The Art of Getting Things Done," *Fast Company* (June 2000): 162–164; Alan M. Webber, "Why Can't We Get Anything Done?" *Fast Company* (June 2000): 168–180.

5. Peter F. Drucker, "The Discipline of Innovation," *Harvard Business Review* (May–June 1985): 67.

6. Stephanie Wu, "Creating an Environment That Produces Exceptional Creativity and Innovation." (Paper prepared for the GOAL/QPC Knowledge Development Workshop, Boston, November 1997).

7. Teresa Amabile and Regina Conti, "Changes in the Work Environment for Creativity During Downsizing," *Academy of Management Journal* 42, no. 6 (1999): 630–40.

8. Peter Drucker, *The Effective Executive* (New York: HarperBusiness, 1993): 71.

9. Teresa Amabile, "How to Kill Creativity," *Harvard Business Review* (September–October 1998): 85.

10. Ibid., 83.

11. James L. Farr and Cameron Ford, "Individual Innovation," in *Innovation and Creativity at Work,* ed. M. A. West and J. L. Farr (New York: Wiley, 1990): 219.

12. Robert Schuller, *Tough-Minded Faith for Tender-Hearted People* (New York: Bantam Books, 1985): 26.

13. David A. Garvin, "Building a Learning Organization," *Harvard Business Review* (July–August 1993): 78–91.

14. Mary Parker Follett, *The Creative Experience* (New York: Longmans, Green, 1924): 11.

15. Alex Osborn, *Applied Imagination,* 3d ed. (Buffalo, NY: Creative Education Foundation, 1993): 156.

16. See Bob King and Helmut Schlicksupp, *The Idea Edge* (Methuen, MA: GOAL/QPC, 1998); and Michael Brassard, *The Memory Jogger Plus+®* (Methuen, MA: GOAL/QPC, 1989, 1996).

17. Bob King, Ellen Domb, and Karen Tate, *TRIZ: An Approach to Systematic Innovation* (Methuen, MA: GOAL/QPC, 1997): 34.

18. Ronald A. Heifetz and Donald L. Laurie, "The Work of Leadership," *Harvard Business Review* (January–February 1997): 127–28.

19. From data collected during the *Survey on Creativity and Innovation in Family Owned Businesses* (Cambridge, MA: Cambridge Center for Creative Enterprise, 1999). Summary available from the author.

20. Eric H. Kessler and Alok K. Chakrabarti, "Innovation Speed: A Conceptual Model of Context, Antecedents, and Outcomes," *Academy of Management Review* 21, no. 4 (1996): 1143–91.

21. Robert M. Burnside, "Improving Corporate Climates for Creativity," in *Innovation and Creativity at Work,* ed. M. A. West and J. L. Farr (New York: Wiley, 1990): 282; see also John R. Hayes, "Cognitive Processes in Creativity," in *Handbook of Creativity,* ed. J. A. Glover, R. R. Ronning, and C. R. Reynolds (New York: Plenum Press, 1989): 140.

22. Kessler and Chakrabarti, "Innovation Speed," 1171.

23. Ibid., 1175.

24. Jeffrey Pfeffer, *Fast Company* (June, 2000): 168–180.

25. Susanne G. Scott and Reginald Bruce, "Determinants of Innovative Behavior: A Path Model of Individual Innovation in the Workplace," *Academy of Management Journal* 37, no. 3 (1994): 580–607; Amabile, "How to Kill Creativity," 77–87; Teresa M. Amabile, Regina Conti, Heather Coon, Jeffrey Lazenby, and Michael Herron, "Assessing the Work Environment for Creativity," *Academy of Management Journal* 39, no. 5 (1996): 1178; Nigel King, "Innovation at Work: The Research Literature," in *Innovation and Creativity at Work,* ed. M. A. West and J. L. Farr (New York: Wiley, 1990): 19; Nigel King and Neil Anderson, "Innovation in Working Groups," in *Innovation and Creativity at Work,* ed. M. A. West and J. L. Farr (New York: Wiley, 1990): 83.

26. Keynote address at the New England Human Resources Association Conference, Hyannis, MA, October 1999.

27. Scott and Bruce, "Determinants of Innovative Behavior," 585; Farr and Ford, "Individual Innovation," 70.

28. Amabile, "How to Kill Creativity."

29. David M. Schweiger, William R. Sandberg, and Paula L. Rechner, "Experiential Effects of Dialectical Inquiry, Devil's Advocacy, and Consensus Approaches to Strategic Decision Making," *Academy of Management Journal* 32, no. 4 (1989): 745–72; Donald Hambrick, "Top Management Groups: A Conceptual Integration and Reconsideration of the 'Team' Label," in *Research in Organizational Behavior,* vol. 16, ed. B. M. Staw and L. L. Cummings (Greenwich, CT: JAI Press,1994): 171–213; see also articles about decision making by Paul Nutt and Ian Mitroff in the Bibliography.

30. See James L. Heskett, Thomas O. Jones, Gary W. Loveman, W. Earl Sasser, Jr., and Leonard A. Schlesinger, "Putting the Service–Profit Chain to Work," *Harvard Business Review* (March–April 1994):164–74; Jeffrey Pfeffer, *The Human Equation* (Boston: Harvard Business School Press, 1998); and Amabile, "How to Kill Creativity."

31. Amabile and Conti, "Changes in the Work Environment for Creativity," 630–40.

Chapter 12 (Developing Your Personal Action Plan)

1. Carl Jung, *Analytical Psychology: Its Theory and Practice* (The Tavistock Lectures) (New York: Vintage Books, 1968): 22.

2. Robert Friedel, "The Accidental Inventor," *Discover* (October 1996): 69.

3. Charles J. Palus and David M. Horth. "Leading Creatively," *Leadership in Action* 18, no. 2 (1998): 1.

4. Anna Muoio, "Are You Sure You're up for the 24-Hour Economy?" *Fast Company* (October 1999): 72

5. If it's personal or emotional blocks that are getting in your way, you might want to check out Julia Cameron's book *The Artist's Way* (Los Angeles: Tarcher/Perigee, 1992); see also James Adams, *Conceptual Blockbusting* (Reading, MA: Addison-Wesley, 1986); or Eric Maisel, *Fearless Creating* (New York: Tarcher, 1995).

6. Peter Russell and Roger Evans, *The Creative Manager* (San Francisco: Jossey-Bass, 1992): 63.

7. Thomas Kuhn, *The Structure of Scientific Revolutions* (Chicago: University of Chicago Press, 1962): 17.

8. Dee W. Hock, quoted in Anna Muoio, ed., "The Art of the Smart," *Fast Company* (July–August 1999): 90.

9. Susan Trausch, "Have Dream, Will Travel," *Boston Globe* (28 May 2000).

10. Dr. Scott McPheat, sermon, Sydney, Australia, 20 September 1998.

11. Carl G. Jung, "Psychological Factors in Human Behaviour," in vol. 8 of *Collected Works of C. G. Jung*, Bollingen Series XX (Princeton, NJ: Princeton University Press, 1971): 118.

12. Carl G. Jung, "The Development of Personality," in vol. 17 of *Collected Works of C. G. Jung*, Bollingen Series XX (Princeton, NJ: Princeton University Press, 1971): 171.

13. Anthony Storr, "Individuation and the Creative Process," *Journal of Analytical Psychology* 28 (1983): 331.

14. Anna Quindlen, Commencement Address, Mount Holyoke College, South Hadley, MA, May 1999.

RESOURCES

Association for Psychological Type (APT)
4700 West Lake Avenue
Glenview, IL 60025
(847)375-4717
Website: www.aptcentral.org

Australian Association for Psychological Type
P. O. Box 768
Toowong QLD 4066
Australia
Website: www.aapt.org.au

Center for Applications of Psychological Type (CAPT)
2815 NW 13th Street, Suite 401
Gainesville, FL 32609
(800)777-2278 or (352)375-0160
Website: www.capt.org

Center for Creative Leadership
One Leadership Place
Greensboro, NC 27438
(336)288-7210
Website: www.ccl.org

Consulting Psychologists Press, Inc. (CPP)
3803 East Bayshore Road
Palo Alto, CA 94303
(800)624-1765
Website: www.cpp-db.com

Creative Problem Solving Institute
Creative Education Foundation (Publisher of *Journal of Creative Behavior*)
1050 Union Road, #4
Buffalo, NY 14224
(716)675-3181
Website: www.cef-cpsi.org

Fast Company Magazine
Atlantic Monthly Company
77 North Washington Street
Boston, MA 02114
(617)973-0300
Website: www.fastcompany.com

GOAL/QPC (Memory Joggers and publisher of *Journal of Innovative Management*)
2 Manor Parkway
Salem, NH 03079
(800)207-5813 or (603)893-1944
Website: www.goalqpc.com

IdeaScope Associates, Inc.
One Design Center Place
Boston, MA 02210
(617)723-4555
Website: www.ideascope.com

Institute for Type Development (Australia)
Website: www.itd.net.au
61 2 97491369

C. G. Jung Institutes

Chicago
1567 Maple Avenue
Evanston, IL 60201
(847)475-4848 or (800)697-7679
Website: www.jungchicago.org.

New York
28 East 39th Street
New York, NY 10016
(212)986-5458

San Francisco
2040 Gough Street
San Francisco, CA 94109
(415)771-8055

Zurich, Switzerland
Website: www.jung-institut.ch

New Zealand Association for Psychological Type
P.O. Box 9842
Wellington, NZ
(0800)756-675

Otto Kroeger Associates
3605 Chain Bridge Road
Fairfax, VA 22030
(703)591-6284
Website: www.typetalk.com

Oxford Psychologists Press Ltd.
Elsfield Hall
15-17 Elsfield Way
Oxford OX2 8EP
United Kingdom
(44) 1865 404500
Website: www.opp.co.uk

Strategic Leadership Forum
435 North Michigan Avenue, Suite 1700
Chicago, IL 60611
(312)644-0829
Website: www.slf.org

Temperament Research Institute (TRI)
16152 Beach Boulevard, Suite 117
Huntington Beach, CA 92647
(800) 700-4874
Website: www.tri-network.com

TRIZ Consulting, Inc.
12013 C 12 Avenue NW
Seattle, WA 98177
Voice: (206)364-3116
Fax: (206)364-8932
E-mail: ZRoyzen@aol.com
Website: www.members.aol.com/zroyzen/triz.html

TRIZ Journal
Website: www.triz-journal.com

Type Resources, Inc.
4050 Westport Road, Suite 207
Louisville, KY 40287
(800)456-6284
Website: www.type-resources.com

World Futures Society
7910 Woodmont Avenue, Suite 450
Bethesda MD 20814
(800)989-8274 or (301)656-8274
Website: www.wfs.org

Adams, James. *Conceptual Blockbusting.* Reading, MA: Addison-Wesley, 1986.

Altshuller, G. S. *Creativity as an Exact Science.* Luxembourg: Gordon and Breach, 1995.

Amabile, Teresa M. *Social Psychology of Creativity.* New York: Springer-Verlag, 1983.

Amabile, Teresa M. "From Individual Creativity to Organizational Innovation." In *Innovation: A Cross-Disciplinary Perspective,* edited by K. Gronhaug and G. Kaufmann, 139–66. Oslo: Norwegian University Press, 1988.

Amabile, Teresa M. "A Model of Creativity and Innovation in Organizations." In *Research in Organizational Behavior,* edited by B. M. Staw and L. L. Cummings, vol. 10, 123–67. Greenwich, CT: JAI Press, 1988.

Amabile, Teresa M. "Within You, Without You: The Social Psychology of Creativity, and Beyond." In *Theories of Creativity,* edited by M. A. Runco and R. S. Albert, 61–91. Newbury Park, CA: Sage, 1990.

Amabile, Teresa M. *Creativity in Context.* Boulder, CO: Westview Press, 1996.

Amabile, Teresa. "How to Kill Creativity." *Harvard Business Review* (September–October 1998): 77–87.

Amabile, Teresa, and Regina Conti. "Changes in the Work Environment for Creativity During Downsizing." *Academy of Management Journal* 42, no. 6 (1999): 630–40.

Amabile, Teresa M., Regina Conti, Heather Coon, Jeffrey Lazenby, and Michael Herron. "Assessing Work Environment for Creativity." *Academy of Management Journal* 39, no. 5 (1996): 1154–84.

Amabile, Teresa M., Beth A. Hennessey, and Barbara S. Grossman. "Social Influences on Creativity: The Effects of Contracted-for Reward." *Journal of Personality and Social Psychology* 50 (1986): 14–53.

Amabile, Teresa. M., K. G. Hill, Beth A. Hennessey, and Elizabeth M. Tighe. "The Work Preference Inventory: Assessing Intrinsic and Extrinsic Motivational Orientations." *Journal of Personality and Social Psychology* 66, no. 5 (1994): 950–67.

Amabile, Teresa M., and Elizabeth Tighe. "Questions of Creativity." In *Creativity*, edited by J. Brockman, 7–27. New York: Simon & Schuster, 1993.

Ancona, Deborah G., and David Nadler. "Top Hats and Executive Tales: Designing the Senior Team." *Sloan Management Review* 31, no.1 (1989): 19–28.

Arieti, Silvano. *Creativity, The Magic Synthesis.* New York: Basic Books, 1976.

Bandrowski, James F. "Orchestrating Planning Creativity." *Planning Review* (September 1984): 18–23, 44.

Barger, Nancy J., and Linda K. Kirby. *The Challenge of Change in Organizations.* Palo Alto, CA: Davies-Black, 1995.

Barnes, Carolyn. "Rooms of My Mind: Introverted Thinking." *Bulletin of Psychological Type* 22, no. 1 (1999): 1, 3.

Barr, Lee, and Norma Barr. *The Leadership Equation.* Austin, TX: Eakin Press, 1989.

Barr, Lee, and Norma Barr. *Leadership Development.* Austin, TX: Eakin Press, 1994.

Bartos, Peter, and Theodora Noble. *Positioning Yourself for Career Success.* Sydney: Forge Connexions Pty Ltd, 1997.

Beebe, John. *Psychological Types in Transference, Countertransference, and the Therapeutic Interaction.* Gaithersburg, MD: Type Resources, 1984.

Beebe, John (speaker). *A New Model of Psychological Types* (5 audiotapes). Evanston, IL: C. G. Jung Institute of Chicago, 1988.

Berens, Linda V. *Understanding Yourself and Others.* Huntington Beach, CA: Telos, 1998.

Blaylock, Bruce K., and Loren P. Rees. "Cognitive Style and the Usefulness of Information." *Decision Sciences* 15 (1984): 74–91.

Bolman, Lee G., and Terrence E. Deal. *Reframing Organizations.* San Francisco: Jossey-Bass, 1991.

Boorstin, Daniel J. *The Discoverers.* New York: Vintage Books, 1985.

Boorstin, Daniel J. *The Creators.* New York: Vintage Books, 1992.

Branden, Nathaniel. *The Six Pillars of Self-Esteem.* New York: Bantam Books, 1994.

Branden, Nathaniel. *Self-Esteem at Work.* San Francisco: Jossey-Bass, 1998.

Brassard, Michael. *The Memory Jogger Plus +®.* Methuen, MA: GOAL/QPC, 1989, 1996.

Bridges, William. *Managing Transitions.* Reading, MA: Addison-Wesley, 1991.

Brown, John Seely, ed. *Seeing Differently.* Boston: Harvard Business School Press, 1997.

Brownsword, Alan. *It Takes All Types!* San Anselmo, CA: HRM Press, 1987.

Brownsword, Alan. *The Type Descriptions.* San Anselmo, CA: HRM Press, 1990.

Bryan, Mark, with Julia Cameron and Catherine Allen. *The Artist's Way at Work.* New York: Morrow, 1998.

Buckingham, Marcus, and Curt Coffman. *First, Break All the Rules.* New York: Simon & Schuster, 1999.

Burns, Tom, and G. M. Stalker. *The Management of Innovation.* London: Tavistock, 1961.

Burnside, Robert M. "Improving Corporate Climates for Creativity." In *Innovation and Creativity at Work,* edited by M. A. West and J. L. Farr, 265–84. New York: Wiley, 1990.

Carlson, Rae. "Studies of Jungian Typology: II. Representations of the Personal World." *Journal of Personality and Social Psychology* 38, no. 5, (1980): 801–10.

Cambridge Center for Creative Enterprise. "Survey on Creativity and Innovation in Family Owned Businesses." Cambridge, MA: Self-published, 1999.

Cameron, Julia. *The Artist's Way.* Los Angeles: Tarcher/Perigee, 1992.

Catford, Lorna. "Creative Problem Solving in Business: Synergy of Thinking, Intuiting, Sensing and Feeling Strategies." Unpublished doctoral dissertation, Stanford University, 1987.

Clancy, Sue G. "STJs and Change." In *Developing Leaders,* ed. C. Fitzgerald and L. K. Kirby, 415–438. Palo Alto, CA: Davies-Black, 1997.

Collier, A. T. "The Business of Creativity." A classic *Harvard Business Review* article, 1953.

Collins, James C., and Jerry I. Porras. *Built to Last: Successful Habits of Visionary Companies.* New York: HarperBusiness, 1994.

Conner, Daryl. *Managing at the Speed of Change.* New York: Random House, 1993.

Cornelius, Helena, and Shoshana Faire. *Everyone Can Win.* Bookvale NSW, Australia: Simon & Schuster, 1993.

Csikszentmihalyi, Mihaly. *Creativity.* New York: HarperCollins, 1996.

Daft, Richard L., and Robert H. Lengel. "Information Richness: A New Approach to Managerial Behavior and Organization Design." In *Research in Organizational Behavior,* vol. 6, edited by B. M. Staw and L. L. Cummings, 191–233. Greenwich, CT: JAI Press, 1984.

Dalzell, Heidi. "How Are You Creative?" *Bulletin of Psychological Type* 19, no. 4 (1996): 6, 8.

Damanpour, Fariborz. "Organizational Innovation: A Meta-Analysis of Effects of Determinants and Moderators." *Academy of Management Journal* 34 (1991): 555–90.

Damelio, Robert. *The Basics of Process Mapping.* Portland, OR: Productivity Inc., 1996.

Daudelin, Marilyn Wood. "Learning from Experience Through Reflection." *Organizational Dynamics* (Winter 1996): 36–48.

DeBono, Edward. *Serious Creativity.* New York: HarperCollins, 1993.

DeBono, Edward. *Six Thinking Hats.* Toronto: Key Porter Books, 1995.

DiTiberio, John K., and George H. Jensen. *Writing and Personality.* Palo Alto, CA: Davies-Black, 1995.

Draxin, Robert, Mary Ann Glynn, and Robert K. Kazanjian. "Multilevel Theorizing About Creativity in Organizations: A Sensemaking Perspective." *Academy of Management Review* 24, no. 2 (1999): 286–307.

Drucker, Peter F. "The Discipline of Innovation." *Harvard Business Review* (May–June 1985): 67–72.

Drucker, Peter F. *Effective Executive.* New York: HarperBusiness, 1993.

Drucker, Peter F. *Change Leaders,* an excerpt from the new book. In *Inc. Magazine* (June 1999): 65–72.

Ealy, Diane. *The Woman's Book of Creativity.* Hillsboro, OR: Beyond Words, 1995.

Faraday, Ann. *The Dream Game.* New York: Perennial Library/Harper & Row, 1976.

Farr, James L. "Facilitating Individual Role Innovation." In *Innovation and Creativity at Work,* edited by M. A. West and J. L. Farr, 207–30. New York: Wiley, 1990.

Farr, James L., and Cameron M. Ford. "Individual Innovation." In *Innovation and Creativity at Work,* edited by M. A. West and J. L. Farr, 63–80. New York: Wiley, 1990.

Firestien, Roger L. *Why Didn't I Think of That?* Williamsville, NY: Innovations Systems Group, 1998.

Fitzgerald, Catherine, and Linda K. Kirby. "Applying Type Dynamics to Leadership Development." In *Developing Leaders,* edited by C. Fitzgerald and L. K. Kirby, 269–309. Palo Alto, CA: Davies-Black, 1997.

Follett, Mary Parker. *Creative Experience.* New York: Longmans, Green, 1924.

Follett, Mary Parker. "How Must Business Management Develop in Order to Become a Profession?" as excerpted in *Mary Parker Follett, Prophet of Management,* edited by P. Graham, 267–281. Boston: Harvard Business School Press, 1996.

Fontana, David. *The Secret Language of Dreams.* San Francisco: Chronicle Books, 1994.

Ford, Cameron. "A Theory of Individual Creative Action in Multiple Social Domains." *Academy of Management Review* 21, no. 4 (1996): 1112–42.

Ford, Cameron M., and Dennis A. Gioia, eds. *Creative Actions in Organizations.* Newbury Park, CA: Sage, 1995.

Frame, J. Davidson. *The New Project Management.* San Francisco: Jossey-Bass, 1994.

Friedel, Robert. "The Accidental Inventor." *Discover* (October 1996): 58–69.

Fritz, Robert. *The Path of Least Resistance.* New York: Ballantine Books, 1989.

Gardner, Howard. "Creative Lives and Creative Works: A Synthetic Scientific Approach." In *The Nature of Creativity,* edited by R. Sternberg, 298–321. Cambridge, England: Cambridge University Press, 1988.

Gardner, Howard. *Creating Minds.* New York: Basic Books, 1993.

Gardner, Howard. *Leading Minds.* New York: Basic Books, 1995.

Garvin, David A. "Building a Learning Organization." *Harvard Business Review* (July–August 1993): 78–91.

Gelb, Michael J. *How to Think like Leonardo da Vinci.* New York: Delacorte Press, 1998.

Glover, John A., R. R. Ronning, and C. R. Reynolds, eds. *Handbook of Creativity.* New York: Plenum Press, 1989.

Goleman, Daniel. *Emotional Intelligence.* New York: Bantam Books, 1995.

Goleman, Daniel. *Working with Emotional Intelligence.* New York: Bantam Books, 1998.

Goleman, Daniel, Paul Kaufman, and Michael Ray, eds. *The Creative Spirit.* New York: Penguin Books, 1993.

Graham, Pauline, ed. *Mary Parker Follett, Prophet of Management.* Boston: Harvard Business School Press, 1996.

Gronhaug, K., and Geir Kaufmann, eds. *Innovation: A Cross-Disciplinary Perspective.* Oslo: Norwegian University Press, 1988.

Gryskiewicz, Stanley. *Positive Turbulence.* San Francisco: Jossey-Bass, 1999.

Guilford, J. P. "Creativity: A Quarter Century of Progress." In *Perspectives in Creativity,* edited by I. A. Taylor and J. W. Getzels, 37–59. Chicago: Aldine, 1975.

Haas, Leona. *Using the Eight Jungian Functions Approach with Organizations* (1997). Workbook from preconference workshop, APT XIII, 1999.

Haley, Usha C. V., and Stephen A. Stumpf. "Cognitive Trails in Strategic Decision-Making: Linking Theories of Personalities and Cognitions." *Journal of Management Studies* 26, no. 5 (1989): 477–97.

Hambrick, Donald C. "Top Management Groups. A Conceptual Integration and Reconsideration of the 'Team' Label." In *Research in Organizational Behavior,* vol. 16, edited by B. M. Staw and L. L. Cummings, 171–213. Greenwich, CT: JAI Press, 1994.

Hamel, Gary, and C. K. Prahalad. *Competing for the Future.* Boston: Harvard Business School Press, 1994.

Hammon, John S., Ralph L. Keeney, and Howard Raiffa. *Smart Choices.* Boston: Harvard Business School Press, 1999.

Hargadon, Andrew, and Robert I. Sutton. "Building an Innovation Factory." *Harvard Business Review* (May–June 2000): 157–66.

Harrington, Donald M. "The Ecology of Human Creativity: A Psychological Perspective." In *Theories of Creativity,* edited by M. A. Runco and R. S. Albert, 143–69. Newbury Park, CA: Sage, 1990.

Harris, Anne Singer. *Living with Paradox: An Introduction to Jungian Psychology.* Pacific Grove, CA: Brooks/Cole, 1996.

Hartzler, Gary, and Margaret Hartzler. *Exercises to Develop the Preference Skills.* Gaithersburg, MD: Type Resources, 1985.

Hayes, John R. "Cognitive Processes in Creativity." In *Handbook of Creativity,* edited by J. A. Glover, R. R. Ronning, and C. R. Reynolds, 135–45. New York: Plenum Press, 1989.

Heifetz, Ronald A. *Leadership Without Easy Answers*. Cambridge, MA: Harvard University Press, 1994.

Heifetz, Ronald A., and Donald L. Laurie. "The Work of Leadership." *Harvard Business Review* (January–February 1997): 124–34.

Hellreigel, Donald, and John W. Slocum, Jr. "Managerial Problem-Solving Styles." *Business Horizons* 18, no. 6 (1975): 29–37.

Henderson, John C., and Paul Nutt. "The Influence of Decision Style on Decision-Making Behavior." *Management Science* 26, no. 4 (1980): 371–86.

Henle, Mary. "The Birth and Death of Ideas." In *Contemporary Approaches to Creative Thinking*, edited by H. E. Gruber, G. Terrell, and M. Wertheimer, 31–62. New York: Atherton Press, 1962.

Hermann, Ned. *The Creative Brain*. Lake Lure, NC: Brainbooks, 1990.

Heskett, James L., Thomas O. Jones, Gary W. Loveman, W. Earl Sasser, Jr., and Leonard A. Schlesinger. "Putting the Service-Profit Chain to Work." *Harvard Business Review* (March–April 1994): 164–174.

Hiam, Alexander Watson. *The Portable Conference on Change Management*. Amherst, MA: HRD Press, 1997.

Hiam, Alexander. *The Manager's Pocket Guide to Creativity*. Amherst, MA: HRD Press, 1998.

Hirsh, Sandra Krebs, with Jane A. G. Kise. *Work It Out*. Palo Alto, CA: Davies-Black, 1996.

Hitt, Michael A., Barbara W. Keats, and Samuel M. DeMarie. "Navigating in the New Competitive Landscape: Building Strategic Flexibility and Competitive Advantage in the 21st Century." *Academy of Management Executive* 12, no. 4 (1998): 22–42.

Howley, Kathleen. "Saving House Where Architect Lived, Worked." *Boston Globe* (12 December, 1999).

"Innovator of the Year: Michael Largent" *National Home Center News* 25, no. 7 (1999).

Isaksen, Scott, ed. *Frontiers of Creativity Research: Beyond the Basics*. Buffalo, NY: Bearly Limited, 1987.

Isaksen, Scott G., Mary C. Murdock, Roger Firestien, and Donald J. Treffinger, eds. *Nurturing and Developing Creativity: The Emergence of a Discipline*. Norwood, NJ: Ablex, 1993a.

Isaksen, Scott G., Mary C. Murdock, Roger Firestien, and Donald J. Treffinger, eds. *Understanding and Recognizing Creativity: The Emergence of a Discipline*. Norwood. NJ: Ablex, 1993b.

Isaksen, Scott G., Gerard J. Puccio, and Donald J. Treffinger. "An Ecological Approach to Creativity Research: Profiling for Creative Problem Solving." *Journal of Creative Behavior* 27, no. 3 (1993): 149–70.

Jacobi, John. *The Psychology of C. G. Jung*. New Haven, CT: Yale University Press, 1968.

James, Jennifer. *Thinking in the Future Tense*. New York: Simon & Schuster, 1996.

Janoff, Sandra, and Marvin Ross Weisbord. *Future Search: An Action Guide to Finding Common Ground in Organizations and Communities*. San Francisco: Berrett-Koehler, 2000.

Jung, Carl G. *Analytical Psychology: Its Theory and Practice* (The Tavistock Lectures). New York: Vintage Books, 1968.

Jung, Carl G. "Analytical Psychology and Education" (Lectures Two and Three). In Vol. 17 of *Collected Works of C. G. Jung*, Bollingen Series XX. Princeton, NJ: Princeton University Press, 1971a.

Jung, Carl G. "The Development of Personality." In Vol. 17 of *Collected Works of C. G. Jung*, 167–86. Bollingen Series XX. Princeton, NJ: Princeton University Press, 1971b.

Jung, Carl G. "Psychological Factors Determining Human Behaviour." In Vol. 8 of *Collected Works of C. G. Jung*. Bollingen Series XX. Princeton, NJ: Princeton University Press, 1971c.

Jung, Carl G. *Psychological Types*. Vol. 6 of *Collected Works of C. G. Jung*. Bollingen Series XX. Princeton, NJ: Princeton University Press, 1971d.

Jung, Carl G. "On the Relation of Analytical Psychology to Poetry." In Vol. 15 of *Collected Works of C. G. Jung*, 65–83. Bollingen Series XX. Princeton, NJ: Princeton University Press, 1971e.

Kanter, Rosabeth M. *The Change Masters*. New York: Simon & Schuster/ Touchstone Books, 1983.

Kanter, Rosabeth M. "When a Thousand Flowers Bloom: Structural, Collective, and Social Conditions for Innovation in Organization." In *Research in Organizational Behavior*, edited by B. M. Staw & L. L. Cummings, 10, 169–211. Greenwich, CT: JAI Press, 1988.

Kanter, Rosabeth M. *When Giants Learn to Dance*. New York: Simon & Schuster/Touchstone Books, 1989.

Kao, John. *Jamming: The Art and Discipline of Business Creativity*. New York: HarperCollins, 1996.

Kaufmann, Geir. "Problem Solving and Creativity." In *Innovation: A Cross-Disciplinary Perspective*, edited by K. Gronhaug and G. Kaufmann, 87–137. Oslo: Norwegian University Press, 1988.

Keirsey, David. *Please Understand Me II*. Del Mar, CA: Prometheus Nemesis Books, 1998.

Keirsey, David, and Marilyn Bates. *Please Understand Me*. Del Mar, CA: Prometheus Nemesis Books, 1978.

Keller, Helen. *The Story of My Life*. Garden City, NJ: Doubleday, 1954.

Kessler, Eric H., and Alok K. Chakrabarti. "Innovation Speed: A Conceptual Model of Context, Antecedents, and Outcomes." *Academy of Management Review* 21, no. 4 (1996): 1143–91.

Kilmann, Ralph H., and Richard P. Herden. "Toward a Systemic Methodology for Evaluating the Impact of Interventions on Organizational Effectiveness." *Academy of Management Review* 1, no. 3 (1976): 87–98.

Kilmann, Ralph H., and K. W. Thomas. "Interpersonal Conflict-Handling Behavior as Reflections of Jungian Personality Dimensions." *Psychological Reports* 37 (1975): 971–80.

King, Bob, Ellen Domb, and Karen Tate. *TRIZ: An Approach to Systematic Innovation.* Methuen, MA: GOAL/QPC, 1997.

King, Bob, and Helmut Schlicksupp. *The Idea Edge.* Methuen, MA: GOAL/QPC, 1998.

King, Nigel. "Innovation at Work: The Research Literature." In *Innovation and Creativity at Work,* edited by M. A. West and J. L. Farr, 15–59. New York: Wiley, 1990.

King, Nigel, and Neil Anderson. "Innovation in Working Groups." In *Innovation and Creativity at Work,* edited by M. A. West and J. L. Farr, 81–100. New York: Wiley, 1990.

Kirton, Michael J. "Adaptors and Innovators: Cognitive Style and Personality." In *Frontiers of Creativity Research: Beyond the Basics,* edited by S. G.. Isaksen, 246–303. Buffalo, NY: Bearly Limited, 1987.

Kosko, Bart. *Fuzzy Thinking.* New York: Hyperion, 1993.

Kuczmarski, Thomas D. *Innovation.* Chicago: NTC Business Books, 1996.

Kuhn, Thomas. *The Structure of Scientific Revolutions.* Chicago: University of Chicago Press, 1962.

LaBarre, Polly. "The New Face of Office Politics." *Fast Company* (October 1999): 80–82.

Land, George, and Beth Jarman. *Breakpoint and Beyond.* New York: HarperCollins, 1992.

Lang, Reginald. "Type Flexibility in Processes of Strategic Planning and Change." In *Developing Leaders,* edited by C. Fitzgerald and L. K. Kirby, 487–511. Palo Alto, CA: Davies-Black, 1997.

Lawrence, Gordon. *People Types and Tiger Stripes.* 3d ed. Gainesville: FL: CAPT, 1993.

Leonard, Dorothy, and Jeffrey F. Rayport. "Spark Innovation Through Empathic Design." *Harvard Business Review* (November–December 1997): 102–13.

Leonard, Dorothy, and Susan Strauss. "Putting Your Company's Whole Brain to Work." *Harvard Business Review* (July–August 1997): 113–21.

Leonard, Dorothy, and Walter Swap. "How Managers Can Spark Creativity." *Leader to Leader* (Fall 1999a): 43–48.

Leonard, Dorothy, and Walter Swap. *When Sparks Fly.* Boston: Harvard Business School Press, 1999b.

Leonard-Barton, Dorothy. *Wellsprings of Knowledge.* Boston: Harvard Business School Press, 1995.

Levesque, Lynne C. "Factors Influencing Creativity in Top Executives." Unpublished doctoral dissertation, University of Massachusetts at Amherst, 1996.

Lyles, Marjorie A., and Ian I. Mitroff. "Organizational Problem Formulation: An Empirical Study." *Administrative Science Quarterly* 25 (1980): 102–19.

MacKinnon, Donald W. "Some Critical Issues for Future Research in Creativity." In *Frontiers of Creativity Research: Beyond the Basics,* edited by S. G. Isaksen, 120–30. Buffalo, NY: Bearly Limited, 1987.

Mahoney, Maria F. *The Meaning in Dreams and Dreaming*. Secaucus, NJ: Citadel Press, 1966.

Maisel, Eric. *Fearless Creating*. New York: Tarcher, 1995.

Martin, Paula, and Karen Tate. *Project Management Memory Jogger*™. Methuen, MA: GOAL/QPC, 1997.

Maslow, Abraham H. "Emotional Blocks to Creativity." In *A Source Book for Creative Thinking,* edited by S. J. Parnes and H. F. Harding, 93–103. New York: Scribner, 1962.

Maslow, Abraham H. *Toward a Psychology of Being*. 2d ed. New York: Van Nostrand, 1968.

Mattimore, Bryan. *99% Inspiration*. New York: American Management Association, 1994.

May, Rollo. *The Courage to Create*. New York: Norton, 1994.

McCaulley, Mary H. "The Myers-Briggs Type Indicator®." Paper presented at Understanding and Nurturing Creativity in People: A Focus on Cognitive Styles, Learning Styles, and Psychological Type, an International Conference hosted by the Center for Studies in Creativity, Buffalo State College, Buffalo, NY, April 28–30, 1997.

Mellick, Jill. *The Natural Artistry of Dreams*. Berkeley, CA: Conari Press, 1996.

Michalko, Michael. *Thinkertoys: A Handbook of Business Creativity for the '90's*. Berkeley, CA: Ten Speed Press, 1991.

Michalko, Michael. *Cracking Creativity*. Berkeley, CA: Ten Speed Press, 1998.

Miller, William C. *The Creative Edge*. Reading, MA: Addison-Wesley, 1987.

Miller, William C. *Flash of Brilliance*. Reading, MA: Perseus Books, 1999.

Mintzberg, Henry. *The Rise and Fall of Strategic Planning*. New York: Free Press, 1994.

Mintzberg, Henry, Duru Raisinghani, and Andre Theoret. "The Structure of 'Unstructured' Decision Processes." *Administrative Science Quarterly* 21 (1976): 246–75.

Mitroff, Ian. *The Unbounded Mind*. Oxford, England: Oxford University Press, 1993.

Mitroff, Ian. *Smart Thinking for Crazy Times*. San Francisco: Berrett-Koehler, 1998.

Mitroff, Ian I., and Ralph H. Kilmann. "Stories Managers Tell: A New Tool for Organizational Problem Solving." *Management Review* (July 1993): 18–28.

Moorman, Christine, and Anne Miner. "Organizational Improvisation and Organizational Memory." *Academy of Management Review* 23, no. 4 (1998): 698–723.

Morgan, Gareth. *Creative Organization Theory*. Newbury Park, CA: Sage, 1989.

Morgan, Gareth. *Images of Organization*. 2d ed. Newbury Park, CA: Sage, 1997a.

Morgan, Gareth. *Imaginization: The Art of Creative Management*. Newbury Park, CA: Sage, 1997b.

Mumford, Michael D., and Sigrid B. Gustafson. "Creativity Syndrome: Integration, Application, and Innovation." *Psychological Bulletin* 103, no. 1 (1988): 27–43.

Muoio, Anna, ed. "The Art of the Smart." *Fast Company* (July–August 1999a): 85–102.

Muoio, Anna. "Are You Sure You're Up for the 24-Hour Economy?" *Fast Company* (October 1999b): 72–74.

Myers, Isabel Briggs, Mary H. McCaulley, Naomi L. Quenk, and Allen L. Hammer. *Manual: A Guide to the Development and Use of the Myers-Briggs Type Indicator®*. 3d ed. Palo Alto, CA: Consulting Psychologists Press, 1998.

Myers, Isabel Briggs, with Peter B. Myers. *Gifts Differing*. Palo Alto, CA: Davies-Black, 1980.

Myers, Katharine D., and Linda K. Kirby. *Introduction to Type® Dynamics and Development*. Palo Alto, CA: Consulting Psychologists Press, 1994.

Nadler, Gerald, and Shigeru Hibino. *Breakthrough Thinking*. 2d ed. Rocklin, CA: Prima, 1994.

Newman, James. "Conundrum No. 1: What Is Introverted Sensation?" *Bulletin of Psychological Type* 17, no. 2 (1994): 17–18, 20.

Norton, Susan. "On Being an Introvert." *Bulletin of Psychological Type* 194, no. 4 (1996): 8, 10.

Nutt, Paul C. "Influence of Decision Styles on Use of Decision Models." *Journal of Technological Forecasting and Social Change* 14 (1979): 77–93.

Nutt, Paul C. "Decision Style and Its Impact on Managers and Management." *Journal of Technological Forecasting and Social Change* 29 (1986a): 341–66.

Nutt, Paul C. "Decision Style and Strategic Decisions of Top Executives." *Journal of Technological Forecasting and Social Change* 30 (1986b): 39–62.

Nutt, Paul C. "The Effects of Culture on Decision Making." *Omega, International Journal of Management Science* 16, no. 6 (1988): 553–67.

Nutt, Paul C. "Flexible Decision Styles and the Choices of Top Executives." *Journal of Management Studies* 30, no. 5 (1993): 695–721.

Nutt, Paul C. "Surprising but True: Half the Decisions in Organizations Fail." *Academy of Management Executive* 13, no. 4 (1999): 75–90.

Oldham, Greg R., and Anne Cummings. "Employee Creativity: Personal and Contextual Factors at Work." *Academy of Management Journal* 39, no. 3 (1996): 607–34.

Osborn, Alex F. *Applied Imagination*. 3d ed. Buffalo, NY: Creative Education Foundation, 1993.

Owen, Harrison. *Open Space Technology: A User's Guide*. San Francisco: Berrett-Koehler, 1997.

Palus, Charles J., and David M. Horth. "Leading Creatively." *Leadership in Action* 18, no. 2 (1998): 1–8.

Parnes, Sidney. *The Magic of Your Mind*. Buffalo, NY: Creative Education Foundation, 1981.

Parnes, Sidney J., ed. *A Source Book for Creative Problem Solving*. Buffalo, NY: Creative Education Foundation, 1992.

Parnes, Sidney J., and Harold F. Harding, eds. *A Source Book for Creative Thinking*. New York: Scribner, 1962.

Pearman, Roger R. *Hardwired Leadership*. Palo Alto, CA: Davies-Black, 1998.

Pearman, Roger R., and Sarah C. Albritton. *I'm Not Crazy, I'm Just Not You*. Palo Alto, CA: Davies-Black, 1997.

Penderghast, Thomas. "Creativity in Organizations." *Bulletin of Psychological Type* 16, no. 2 (1993): 17.

Peters, Tom. *The Circle of Innovation*. New York: Knopf, 1997.

Pfeffer, Jeffrey. *The Human Equation*. Boston: Harvard Business School Press, 1998.

Pfeffer, Jeffrey, and Robert L. Sutton. "The Smart-Talk Trap." *Harvard Business Review* (May–June 1999): 134–42.

Pringle, Charles D., and Mark J. Kroll. "Why Trafalgar Was Won Before It Was Fought: Lessons from Resource-Based Theory." *Academy of Management Executive* 11, no. 4 (1997): 73–89.

Puccio, Gerard J. "An Overview of Creativity Assessment." *The Assessment of Creativity*: An occasional paper from the creativity based information resources project (1994): 5–20.

Quenk, Naomi L. *Beside Ourselves*. Palo Alto, CA: Davies-Black, 1993.

Quenk, Naomi L. *In the Grip*. 2d ed. Palo Alto, CA: Consulting Psychologists Press, 2000.

Quinn, James B. "Managing Innovation: Controlled Chaos." *Harvard Business Review* (May–June 1985). 73–85.

Ray, Michael, and Rochelle Myers. *Creativity in Business*. New York: Doubleday, 1986.

Reich, Robert. "The Company of the Future." *Fast Company* (November 1998): 124–50.

Roberts, Paul. "The Art of Getting Things Done." *Fast Company* (June 2000): 162–164.

Robinson, Alan G., and Sam Stern. *Corporate Creativity*. San Francisco: Berrett-Koehler, 1997.

Rogers, Carl. "Towards a Theory of Creativity." In *A Source Book for Creative Thinking*, edited by S. J. Parnes and H. F. Harding, 63–72. New York: Scribner, 1962. .

Russell, Peter, and Roger Evans. *The Creative Manager*. San Francisco: Jossey-Bass, 1992.

Sandner, Donald, and John Beebe. "Psychopathology and Analysis." In *Jungian Analysis*, edited by M. Stein, 294–304. LaSalle, IL: Open Court, 1982.

Savary, Louis M., Patricia H. Berne, and Strephon Kaplan Williams. *Dreams and Spiritual Growth*. New York and Ramsey, NJ: Paulist Press, 1984.

Schuller, Robert. *Tough-Minded Faith for Tender-Hearted People*. New York: Bantam Books, 1985.

Schweiger, David M., William R. Sandberg, and Paula L. Rechner. "Experiential Effects of Dialectical Inquiry, Devil's Advocacy, and Consensus Approaches to Strategic Decision Making." *Academy of Management Journal* 32, no. 4 (1989): 745–72.

Scott, Susanne G., and Reginald Bruce. "Determinants of Innovative Behavior: A Path Model of Individual Innovation in the Workplace." *Academy of Management Journal* 37, no. 3 (1994): 580–607.

Secrest, Meryle. *Frank Lloyd Wright.* New York: Knopf, 1992.

Segal, Marci. "How Type Helps People Achieve Breakthroughs." *Bulletin of Psychological Type* 22, no. 8 (1999): 41–43.

Senge, Peter M., Charlotte Roberts, Robert B. Ross, Bryan J. Smith, and Art Kleiner. *The Fifth Discipline Fieldbook.* New York: Doubleday, 1994.

Shallcross, Doris J., and Dorothy A. Sisk. *Intuition: An Inner Way of Knowing.* Buffalo, NY: Bearly Limited, 1989.

Shapiro, Kenneth, and Irving Alexander. *The Experience of Introversion.* Durham, NC: Duke University Press, 1975.

Sharp, Darryl. *Personality Types: Jung's Model of Typology.* Toronto: Inner City Books, 1987.

Sinetar, Marsha. *Twenty-First Century Mind.* New York: Ballantine Books, 1991.

Sittenfeld, Curtis. "Be Your Own Futurist." *Fast Company* (October 1998): 42.

Spoto, Angelo. *Jung's Typology in Perspective.* Wilmette, IL: Chiron, 1995.

Staw, Barry M. "An Evolutionary Approach to Innovation." In *Innovation and Creativity at Work,* edited by M. A. West and J. L. Farr, 287–308. New York: Wiley, 1990.

Stein, Morris I. *Stimulating Creativity. Vol. 1: Individual Procedures.* New York: Academic Press, 1974.

Stein, Morris I. *Stimulating Creativity. Vol. 2: Group Procedures.* New York: Academic Press, 1975.

Sternberg, Robert J., ed. *The Nature of Creativity.* Cambridge, England: Cambridge University Press, 1988.

Storr, Anthony, "Individuation and the Creative Process." *Journal of Analytical Psychology* 28 (1983): 329–43.

Stratas, Deb. "A Thinker's Guide to Feeling Types in Meetings." *Bulletin of Psychological Type* 22, no. 8 (1999): 33–36.

"Survey: Innovation in Industry." *Economist* (20 February, 1999): 5–28.

Thompson, Henry. *Jung's Function-Attitudes Explained.* Watkinsville, GA: Wormhole, 1996.

Thompson, Henry. "The Ying and Yang of Sensing." *Bulletin of Psychological Type* 22, no. 3 (1999): 14, 16, 18.

Thomson, Lenore. *Personality Type.* Boston: Shambhala, 1998.

Tieger, Paul D., and Barbara Barron-Tieger. *Do What You Are.* Boston: Little, Brown, 1992.

Tobias, Randall. "Good for Workers, Good for Business." *Boston Globe* (21 December, 1998).

Trausch, Susan. "Have Dream, Will Travel." *Boston Globe* (28 May, 2000).

Tushman, Michael, and David Nadler. "Organizing for Innovation." *California Management Review* 28 (1986): 74–92.

Tushman, Michael L., and Charles A. O'Reilly III. *Winning Through Innovation.* Boston: Harvard Business School Press, 1997.

Vance, Mike, and Diane Deacon. *Think Out of the Box.* Franklin Lakes, NJ: Career Press, 1995.

Van der Hoop, J. H. *Conscious Orientation.* London: Kegan Paul, Trench, Trubner, 1939.

Van De Ven, Andrew. H. "Central Problems in the Management of Innovation." *Management Science* 32, no. 5 (1986): 590–607.

Von Franz, Maria, and James Hillman. *Jung's Typology.* New York: Spring Publications, 1971.

Webber, Alan M. "Danger: Toxic Company." *Fast Company* (November 1998): 152–61.

Webber, Alan M. "Why Can't We Get Anything Done?" *Fast Company* (June 2000): 168–180.

Weisberg, Robert W. "Problem Solving and Creativity." In *The Nature of Creativity,* edited by R. Sternberg, 148–76. Cambridge, England: Cambridge University Press, 1988.

West, Michael A. "The Social Psychology of Innovation in Groups." In *Innovation and Creativity at Work,* edited by M. A. West and J. L. Farr, 309–33. New York: Wiley, 1990.

West, Michael A., and James L. Farr. "Innovation at Work." In *Innovation and Creativity at Work,* edited by M. A. West and J. L. Farr, 3–13. New York: Wiley, 1990.

Wheatley, Walter, William P. Anthony, and Nick Maddox. "Selecting and Training Strategic Planners with Imagination and Creativity." *Journal of Creative Behavior* 25, no. 1 (1991): 52–60.

Woodman, Richard W. "Creativity as a Construct in Personality Theory." *Journal of Creative Behavior* 15, no. 1 (1981): 43–66.

Woodman, Richard W., John E. Sawyer, and Ricky W. Griffin. "Toward a Theory of Organizational Creativity." *Academy of Management Review* 18, no. 2 (1993): 293–321.

Wu, Stephanie. "Creating an Environment that Produces Exceptional Creativity and Innovation." (Paper prepared for the GOAL/QPC Knowledge Development Workshop, Boston, November 1997).

Wycoff, Joyce. *Mind Mapping: Your Personal Guide to Exploring Creativity and Problem Solving.* New York: Berkley, 1991.

Wysocki, Robert, Robert Beck, Jr., and David B. Crane. *Effective Project Management.* New York: Wiley, 1995.

INDEX